D.E. POHREN

The Art of Flamenco

SOCIETY OF SPANISH STUDIES
Apartado de Correos 83
28230 Las Rozas
(Madrid)   Spain

Publisher, and Worldwide Distributor
(except as indicated below):
Society of Spanish Studies
Apartado de Correos 83
28230 Las Rozas
(Madrid) Spain
Tel. 6370079

U.S.A. Distributor:
The Bold Strummer Ltd.
1 Webb Road
Westport, CT 06880 USA
Tel. 203-2268230
ISBN 0-933334-38-9

UK Distributor:
Juan Teijeiro Music Co. Ltd.
Alhamba House
5 The Campsbourne
London N8 7PN, England
Tel. 01-348-9191

CONTENTS

	Page
PREFACE ...	9
PREFACE TO THE REVISED EDITIONS ...	11
PART I: THE PHILOSOPHY OF FLAMENCO ...	13
Introduction ...	15
Donkey Back ...	17
Juerga ...	27
Flamenco and the Bullfight ...	30
Gypsies ...	33
Progress ...	36
PART II: THE ART OF FLAMENCO ...	37
Origin and Background ...	39
What is Flamenco? ...	43
The Song ...	48
The Dance ...	59
The Guitar ...	69
The *Jaleo* ...	80
Reciting ...	81
Comedy ...	81
Flamenco and the Non-Spaniard ...	82
The *Cante* and the Non-Spaniard ...	83
The *Baile* and the Non-Spaniard ...	84
The *Toque* and the Non-Spaniard ...	86
Hard Times and Present Trends ...	90
PART III: ENCYCLOPEDIA OF FLAMENCO ...	97
Discussion of the Verses of the *Cante* ...	99
Genealogy of *Cante* Flamenco ...	99
Genealogy of *Cante* Flamenco ...	101
Encyclopedia Index ...	103
Encyclopedia proper ...	104

PART IV: APPENDICES 163

    1. Breakdown of the Cante, Baile and Toque 165
    2. Flamenco Records of Special Interest 169
    3. The *Juerga* 172
    4. Commercial Flamenco Establishments 175
    5. Flamenco Festivals and Contests 177
    6. Learning Flamenco 181
        Flamenco Instruction in Spain 181
        Flamenco Instruction Outside Spain 187
        Flamenco Methods, Sheet Music, Periodicals 188
        Bibliography 189
    7. The Guitar 194
        Differences between the classical, concert
           and traditional flamenco guitars 194
        Old Versus New Guitars 198
        Care of the Guitar 199
        A Thumbnail History of Modern Flamenco
           Guitar Construction 200
        Flamenco Guitar Constructors Today 204
        Experimentation 206

Glossary 209

Photographs, graphs, and maps:

    Photographs follow pages 32, 96, 176 and 208.

    Maps of Andalusia and Spain, showing the principal
     centers of flamenco's development, P. 54.

    Graph of the Dynasty of the Ortegas, P. 55.

    Graph of the Genealogy of Cante Flamenco, P. 102.

To the true flamencos,
a rare breed in danger of extinction

PREFACE

I have written this book in an attempt to cast a little light on the little-understood (and, more frequently, badly misunderstood) art of flamenco.

To date flamenco has been the only internationally acclaimed art without so much as a basic English-language guide for its many enthusiasts. Until recently, little more has been available in Spanish. This dearth of information has led to the general acceptance, both in and out of Spain, of a cheap, commercial brand of flamenco only remotely similar to the authentic article. I have hopes that this book will help correct the situation.

THE ART OF FLAMENCO arranged itself into four sections. The first, entitled «The Philosophy of Flamenco», consists of experiences and brief essays intended to help the reader to some sort of understanding of the creators and perpetuators of flamenco — the flamencos themselves.

The next three sections get into the meat of the subject, and cover all but the most advanced or specialized facets of flamenco, upon which I intend to elaborate in future works.

Parts of the second section will seem painfully basic to the initiated aficionado, *particularly portions of the section entitled «What is flamenco?» Bear in mind that the book is designed for readers ranging from the neophyte, who still vaguely knows flamenco as «flamingo», to the most advanced* aficionado.

Throughout this book the reader will find constant reference to two basic poles of flamenco, the authentic-traditional and the popular-commercial. The main difference between these opposite poles lies in the types of innovations and creations that make them up; those of the authentic-traditional school always fall within certain well-defined bounds of good flamenco; those of the popular-commercial school are nearly always catchy and worthless, eagerly accepted by the popular public, and then quickly forgotten. In other words, the authentic-traditional flamenco has lasting value, the popular-commercial little to no value.

Flamenco is often compared with jazz. This is logical and reasonable. Both served as emotional outlets for oppressed and underprivileged people; and both are losing their significance as these conditions are

9

alleviated by progress. And in both, this lost significance is being re-placed by meaningless virtuosity and sophistication.

*We can go one step further and speculate on the types of fla-menco that would closely approximate various trends in jazz. The prim-itive, traditional flamenco, for instance, matches up with the authentic blues; concert (progressive) flamenco runs parallel to progressive jazz; and such forms as be-bop and rock n' roll go hand-in-hand with the many impurities prevalent in today's commercial-*tablao *flamenco.*

I express my gratitude to my wife, and to good friends John and Ann Leibold, who have given me valuable aid in the preparation of this book.

The Author
Sevilla, July 1962.

PREFACE TO THE REVISED EDITIONS

When it became necessary to begin revision of this book for its second edition (1967), I was stricken with misgivings. Since it was published, just four years before, I had only occasionally glanced through the book, and in truth could not readily recall just what I had written. Had four years of maturing within the art of flamenco changed my basic ideas? Would I find it necessary to discard much of what I had written and start anew?

You can imagine my relief when, upon going over the book, I found myself agreeing with nearly everything I had written. There were technical mistakes to be corrected, to be sure, as well as additions of new material, some deletions, and bringing up-to-date. In all, quite a substantial revision, but, I was delighted to perceive, my basic ideas not only had not changed, they had become even more strongly ingrained with time and experience. Thus, «Part I: The Philosophy of Flamenco», was hardly touched; «Part II», quite a bit more, particularly the sections «Song», «Dance», «Reciting», «Comedy» (new in that edition), and «Hard Times and Present Trends»; «Part III» was thoroughly gone over and enlarged, with many changes, corrections, and additions, as well as the enriching inclusion of numerous new song verses and their translations; «Part IV», the appendices, also underwent a rather drastic revision, having been enlarged and completely rewritten, with the addition of a great deal of new, up-to-date information. In addition, a bibliography, and bibliographical information, lacking in the first edition, was included.

This revision (1971) has also been quite far-reaching, including again bringing the book up-to-date, as well as other important changes and additions throughout (above all in Parts II and IV). Two of the appendices were completely rewritten; «The Juerga» was enlarged and improved upon, while «Flamenco Records of Special Interest» was expanded to encompass a condensed history of modern flamenco as told through discussions of the lives of some of the artists represented on the records.

A few of the less important photos included in preceding editions have been deleted in order to partially make place for various that have been added. The new additions illustrate the topics «the juerga», «fa-

mous artists of the past», and «flamenco activities at Finca Espartero». In all, this edition contains eight more pages of photos than the last.

Each revised edition is, therefore, more accurate and complete and, I feel, better able to accomplish its mission of providing the reader with ;a solid flamenco foundation and direction.

The Author
Marón de la Frontero (Sevilla)

November, 1971

And now we have a fourth revision. More than eleven years have raced by since the 1972 edition of this book, during which period flamenco has undergone new trends and fads, and suffered to an unprecedented extent the inevitable and ever-increasing encroachment of universal sophistication. These considerations have been discussed in the appendices of this revision. From page 169 on the book has had to be completely updated and rewritten; in so doing the appendices have taken on historical, sociological and economic hues formerly lacking.

There has also been a shuffling of photos, some removed, some new ones added, with the dual purposes of updating, and of stressing certain points more strongly.

Thus, the objective stated in the last paragraph of the 1971 revision has again, hopefully, been fulfilled.

The Author
Madrid
January, 1984

PART I
THE PHILOSOPHY OF FLAMENCO

INTRODUCTION

Flamenco is not just a music of southern Spain, as is generally believed. More than that, it is a way of life that influences the daily activities of many southern Spaniards. One does not have to be a performer of flamenco to be a flamenco: a flamenco is anyone who is emotionally and actively involved in this unique philosophy. For this reason, no book is complete in dealing with the art of flamenco alone, for the art of flamenco is merely the outward expression of the flamenco way of life. The reader must also be made to understand something of its creators and perpetuators, and their philosophies, attitudes, customs, beliefs, likes and dislikes. It is necessary to understand not only what flamenco is, but why it is what it is.

With this objective in mind, I present the following experiences and essays as an introduction to a study of this fascinating but little understood art

DONKEY BACK

We were riding donkey back along the ridge of the *sierra,* often rounding into views of a deep-blue Mediterranean, other times descending into gray-green valleys or winding our way through scented pine forests. It was slow going, but delicious and invigorating, making us glad to have broken away from the contained life of Sevilla.

The morning of the third day we cut inland into the sparsely-populated mountain country between Ronda and the sea, an area famous for its rugged beauty and its bandit and smuggler bands of the past. As the day waned, we came upon a small ranch, from the doorway of which a white-haired old man stood observing us.

«Buenas tardes.»

«Buenas tardes.»

«Can I serve you in some way?» he questioned, looking us over critically, his eyes softening a little as they took note of our two spare donkeys loaded down with provisions and belongings.

«We seek nothing but the honor of having you join us in a cup of good Valdepeñas *tinto,*» my friend answered with Spanish formality, patting one of the large leather wineskins carried by one of the donkeys.

«*Con mucho gusto.* With much pleasure,» he replied. «Do one of you play the guitar?» he asked, nodding at the donkey that was carrying the guitar.

«I do,» I said, «and my partner is an illustrious gypsy *cantaor,* famed in all of Andalucía.»

The old man's interest quickened, although he asked doubtfully. «And you, being a foreigner, know well the flamenco?»

«Of course, my friend. My mother is Spanish, and I have lived in Spain many years.»

This was my time-tested answer which puts all wrongs right. The wine flowed, and soon the old man's family returned from tending the sheep and goats and joined us. They sent for the one neighboring family, and amid singing, playing, animated conversation, and a dinner of *garbanzos* and lamb meat, we became good friends. During the

17

course of the evening the old man told us of a small livestock fair that was to take place in a mountain village two days distant by donkey. He was leaving for it the following day with his sheep and goats, and he invited us to join him, explaining that it was customary for the fair to be highlighted by a gypsy wedding, or weddings, depending on this year's crop of young lovers, followed by days of celebration. Gypsies traveled to this fair from considerable distance and, the old man explained, the festivities would certainly be worth the trip. He thought that we should have no trouble there, my friend being gypsy, and both of us flamencos, an unbeatable combination of door-openers for such an occasion. It sounded like a fine idea, and with a click of earthenware mugs we toasted the trip.

At dawn we rounded up the old man's flock and headed north. We passed through untamed mountain country spotted with cave openings, swooping hawks, and an occasional wild boar. It felt good to ride alongside the tinkling animals, feeling the hot sun on our backs and listening to the talk of the garrulous old man.

«*Bien,* apprentice shepherds. I hope you'll forgive me if I talk too much. We rarely have visitors in these parts, and I get lonesome for someone new to exchange impressions with.»

«How many years have you lived in these mountains?» I asked.

«I was born in the village where we are headed around 1890 — I'm not sure what year — and except for a few trips to Ronda, I've never been away from here.»

«*Ozú,*» exclaimed the gypsy, «many years! Then you must have seen a few bandits in your time?»

Sí, many of these caves hereabouts were hideaways for them. The bandits were like everyone else, some good and some bad. It was always necessary to watch one's women, and to carry a gun when tending the animals, but generally they would leave us poor people alone. They used to make raids on the rich folks in some of the bigger towns, or on the stages on the Ronda road, and then come down here to hide. Fortunately they usually had money and women with them. It became more dangerous when the *Guardia* started to clamp down as they could not raid successfully and they had to come to us for food and wine. I remember when they got drunk they would sometimes have knife fights to the death over a woman, or an insult, or merely for the desire to fight. They were dangerous people, put basically like everyone; some good and some bad. And *coño!, qué flamencos.*»

When conversation fell off, the gypsy would improvise *cantes,* usually humorous, about the animals, making the old man glow with warmth. He was truly an animal lover, treating the animals as humans, recognizing their needs and moods through long years of looking after them.

Ay qué burro, qué bueno es;
A ese burro de punta, tanto le gustan las borriquíllas...

Ay what a donkey, how good he is;
That one leading the line, who is so crazy about girl donkeys...

«I've never heard that one before,» said the old man, laughing.

«Of course not. I just made it up. At least part of it,» the gypsy replied, pleased with his creative success.

«*Oye*, Tumba,» I said, calling the gypsy by his nickname. «tell me, what is so extraordinary about a gypsy wedding? Does it differ so much from a *payo* (non-gypsy) one?»

«*Caray*, is it different! A gypsy wedding is the most exciting thing you'll ever see. And what a celebration afterwards! We're the only people in the world who know how to marry properly. It begins with the *novio* (fiancé) and his friends 'kidnapping' the *novia,* usually with her consent, and carrying her off to the house of his parents. Then emissaries are sent to contact the girl's parents, to obtain their consent. If it is given, the date is set, and all of the relatives and friends of both families converge on the chosen spot, abandoning all of their pursuits for at least three days, the minimum length of a respectable celebration. Often several marriages are arranged for the same time and place, with the resultant celebration being something barbarous.» The gypsy's eyes shown with enthusiasm, obviously remembering distant pleasures. «The test of the girl's virtue is in effect the marriage ceremony; the white silk handkerchief is inserted, and if it becomes stained with the blood of the girl, the ritual of celebration begins. The girl is covered with a deluge of flowers from all directions, and then the ceremony of the adoration of the bride is effected by the parents of the couple falling on their knees around the girl and dancing a dance of the upper torso and arms. The bride and bridegroom are then taken into the bedroom and the *alboreás* (1) are sung. They are truly fine and gay. This is later followed by the bride performing a marriage dance in the middle of a circle of gypsies, who heap upon her showers of almond blossoms. This is usually the last of the rituals, and from then on it is every man for himself until he is too exhausted to continue celebrating.»

We were climbing continually into a green splendor of cascading streams and snow white clouds. There had been a heavy rainfall that spring, which had caused the slopes to blossom with a rash of wild flowers and small animal life. Far below us to the west a little white village nestled in a valley, its houses like mushrooms against the green valley floor. The air felt fresh and clean.

---

(1) See Alboreás in the Part III Encyclopedia for a more complete description of this ceremony.

«*Dios, qué bonito!*» breathed the old man. «I've lived here 70 years and have never gotten over the beauty of spring in this *sierra*. Wait until you see the village where we go. It is out of a fairy tale. It has no roads, and is only accessible to donkey caravans and with great difficulty donkey carts. There are only cobblestones and flowers and wild grass for streets, the houses have red-tile roofs and are newly white-washed every year, there are plants and flowers in every window and balcony, and there is a man dedicated solely to picking up the litter in the village. And there is a beautiful clear stream that runs along the eastern edge, lined with willows and poplars.»

That night we camped on a level spot on the side of a steep, pine-sprinkled slope. A nearby stream swirled downhill, mixing its persistent gurgling with the crackling of our fire. We were content and above worldly preoccupations. The old man made us a steaming-hot mountain drink, a real *quitapenas,* consisting of red wine, cognac, lemon, and a little sugar. Two other donkey caravans had joined us, spotting us from across the narrow valley, and an interesting discussion was launched concerning the gypsies and their niche in life. Some (arguing in the Spanish way, not necessarily out of conviction but out of the desire to prolong the discussion) argued that the gypsies are a «blot» on society, while others maintained that the gypsies led the only plausible way of life (referring to the true gypsies as yet untainted by modern civilization).

«That they have no ambition, that they refuse to work?!! And you consider these failings? *Hombre,* don't you realize that this «ambition» that you praise is the greatest motivating evil the world has known. One must have principles *or* ambition, as these two forces are instinctive enemies and are constantly at each others throats. Woe on the man who has both, for he will have a raging turmoil inside his person. For ambition, in the modern sense of the word, is the desire to 'get ahead', and it is a rare man who can 'get ahead' without sacrificing his integrity and his principles. And this other thing that you consider a fault: the refusal to work in some hated job that the *payo* takes merely to make money, or gain prestige, or 'get ahead,' or what have you. This rejection of work is the greatest of gypsy virtues! We refuse to prostitute our integrity in this way. We prefer to obey our natural instincts, although we may suffer more and work harder in obeying them than we would taking a soft *payo* job and wasting away our lives. Besides, who has the superior intelligence; he who works unhappily within the System, or he who pursues his own interests and remains above the System?» This speaker was a dark-skinned young gypsy with considerable reputation as a poet.

«*Claro está,*» spoke up an obviously respected old man, the leader of one of the newly-arrived caravans who gave the impression of being some sort of tribal wise man or witch doctor, «it is clear that the

20

gypsies have outlived their age. God meant for us to live off the fat of the land, moving from place to place feeding on wild fruits and fowl and abundant animal life, never abusing as the *payo* does, never depleting our sources like fools, never causing the extinction of entire species of animals, never exploiting, but merely taking what we needed. But now, through a complex puzzle of cause and effect not even understood by the *payo* himself, all the lands have fences, the fruits and domestic animals owners, and the wild life is disappearing because of its exploitation by the so-called 'civilized' people. The gypsies should have been cut up for steaks along with the rest of the wild life, because we no longer belong. If we wish to follow our natural instincts, to pursue our way of life, to retain our integrity, we have no other recourse but to steal our daily food and to camp on the property of others. The fool *payo* does not understand that we are the last of God's children, and they are merely slaves to a system which reduces their lives to insignificance. Their instincts are moved when we come into sight, they momentarily realize the purposelessness of their existence, and they are beset by envy and longing. But instead of joining us, they chose to hate us. We have always been a threat to their serenity, we have always made them see the absurdity of their lives, and they have chosen to drive us away, to banish us from their lands and their minds as one will banish a wrong from his conscience.» The snow-white hair and nearly black face of the speaker gave him a primitive appearance in the firelight sharply belied by his words. «We are the symbol of everything that they lack; integrity, individualism, freedom. They cannot permit the gypsy to be the constant reminder of the ball-less void of their lives, so they have humiliated us, attempted to break our spirit, banished us to city slums... they have truly sinned by denying God's children their intended existence.»

«One has but to think of the impertinence of the *payo*,» said our old man, himself a *payo*. «They 'discover' lands that have been inhabited for thousands of years by several civilizations, and they proudly plant their flag and claim the land for their country. Not a thought is given to its present inhabitants, unless the 'discoverers' try to soothe their consciences during their plundering, murdering, and exploitation by deceiving themselves and the world into believing that they are committing their crimes in the names of Religion, the State, and Progress.»

«You are right,» the poet replied vengefully. «It is that mankind is consumed with greed, lust, and a doltish possesiveness. Why can they not leave the lands free, as God intended? How do they have the impudence to place a price on God's real estate? To me, all of civilization paints a bile-retching picture of the strong abusing the weak. Ambition, egoism, and violent stupidity invariably are triumphant over integrity, principles, and goodness!»

Christ, I thought, can these be the ignorant, immoral gypsies that my Spanish friends and acquaintances are constantly belittling? Gypsy reasoning may be innocent and impractically honest, but next to these people my cunning friends have little to feel superior about.

The gysies talked on, of the trials of their lives, their difficulties and disappointments, and as they talked, they became more and more depressed. Their depression became profound and directionless and morbid, almost like an orgy of despondency. They sank into the black and bottomless, but one could sense that, like all depressives, they were spurred on by a certain unconscious pleasure in their very suffering.

Talking was no longer enough. Their expression, as always at such times, turned to poetry and song. I began playing a slow, melancholy *siguiriyas,* and the poet stood up by the fire and dramatically recited one of Lorca's *cante jondo* poems, describing a *cantaora* singing to a dancer robed in long, black trains of silk, symbol of death.

Lámparas de cristal
y espejos verdes.
Sobre el tablado oscuro
la Parrala sostiene
una conversación
con la muerte.
La llama,
no viene,
y la vuelve a llamar.
Las gentes
aspiran los sollozos.
Y en los espejos verdes
largas colas de seda
se mueven.

Crystal lamps
and green mirrors.
Upon a dark platform
la Parrala sustains
a conversation
with death.
She calls,
death does not come,
and she calls again.
The people
are enveloped by her sobs.
In the green mirrors
long trains of silk
move.

Desolate *cantes* followed, each further fomenting the .dejection of the impressionable gypsies. Moments such as these incite the *jondo* in men, and the miracle of the *duende* occurs; for the *duende* is the exposure of one's soul, its misery and suffering, love and hate, offered without embarrassment or resentment. Is is a cry of depair, a release of tortured emotions, to be found in its true profundity only in real life situations, not in the make-believe world of theatres and night clubs and commercial caves as a product that can be bought and sold and produced at will.

A moving *soleá* by a wild-eyed gypsy from Jerez:

> Por ti abandoné a mis niñas,
> mi mare de penita murió;
> ahora te vas y me abandonas,
> ¡no tienes perdón de Dió!

> For you I abandoned my little girls,
> my mother died of sorrow;
> and now you abandon me...
> may you be eternally damned!

A chilling *fandangos de Triana* by Tumba:

> Una mujer se moría
> sus hijos la rodeaban
> y el más chico la decía
> Mamá, mírame a la cara
> no te mueras todavía...

> A woman was dying
> her children surrounded her
> and the smallest said to her
> Mama look at muy face
> don't die yet...

A forlon *playera* of a loved one lost:

> Detrás del carrito
> lloraba mi madre:
> no lloraba agüita,
> que lloraba sangre.

> Behind the funeral cart
> sobbed my mother:
> she didn't weep tears,
> she wept blood.

As the gypsies sang, the campfire caused fleeting visions, now flickering on a rock, now on a tree, of the black-robed, dancing figure of death reigning over her terrible domain: the tragedies of unfortunate love; a dying mother surrounded by her horrified children; the cart of the dead rumbling its burden to the grave, a stricken mother stumbling blindly behind... The singing carried long into the night on the side of that lonely mountain, far from civilization, and finally an indescribable feeling surged to the surface; the moment arrived when mature men could weep cold, grim tears, lamenting the twisted fate of their lives, their race, and all mankind.

* * *

The village was as the old man had described. It smelled of grass and flowers and animals, and it exuded an enchanted feeling of the past, before there were machines or fallout, when the stars were still a mystery and the moon romantic, and when each region of the world had its own personality. People were arriving by horse, mule, and donkey back, many with their flocks of animals to be sold or bartered, others solely to participate in the wedding celebrations.

The old man, Tumba, and myself, together with our new friends of the previous evening, set up camp in a select grove bordering the rushing stream. We noticed that it was ideal for flamenco, having a level clearing in the middle of the grove. We hung the still brimming wineskins on trees, dug a barbeque pit and set up a spit, put the animals to graze, and settled back to watch the activity. Everyone was in the state of fine spirits always caused by the anticipation of a good time. The few gypsies with horses were prancing about with their women balancing effortlessly on the rumps of the horses. Others were in groups talking animatedly, and still others, like ourselves, were resting up for the big blast. There were going to be no less than three weddings, and the competition between the celebrants was expected to be fierce. Who could have a better time longer, drink more, sleep less!?

Our camp was unexcelled for popularity. We had much to offer: two skins full of good *tinto,* an outstanding singer, renowned gypsy intellectuals, and phenomenon of phenomenons, a «*guitarrista americano*». The old man, as was his yearly custom, had singled out two of his best sheep for roasting, and everyone was invited to partake of the sizzling, smoke-flavoured meat. This was, as he explained, his once-a-year fling, and there wouldn't be many more. He was having an absolutely delightful time, half-tight at all hours, and rollickingly gay. Most of the celebrants were old friends of his, and with each he insisted on sharing remembrance cups of wine and of showing off his flamenco friends.

«*Anda, primos,* the *bulerías,*» he would urge, and when we started off he would jump into the clearing and begin dancing. When tight the old man was a natural comedian, and he would have all of us roaring with laughter. Hearing the *jaleo*, other people would run up, and the old man always managed to select as his dancing partner the prettiest *gitana* in the crowd, whom he would set about «winning» with more antics. Then Tumba, with a wink, would dance in and sing to the *gitana*, pretending to woo her away from the old man, who would respond with sham indignation and stage a mock battle with Tumba; all in perfect time to this difficult rhythm. The gypsy girl, entering into the spirit of the dance, would flirt unabashedly with them both, and then, with a flip of her head and a saucy turn of her body, leave them and dance back to her boyfriend. Other gypsies would soon be dancing and singing and playing their guitars, competing, outdoing each other, and the mountain seemed to vibrate with joy. The *bulerías*, the *alboreás*, the *rumba*, the *tangos*, the *chuflas*, all of the merry *cantes* and *bailes* were sung and danced. The weddings took place in the manner that Tumba had described, and for four days the celebrating continued; four days of laughing, loving, love-making, the gypsies driving themselves to a wild frenzy, tearing at their clothes, but always good-humored and staying within certain gypsy limits and laws regardless of their delirious drunkenness.

The whole village took part in the celebrations. Small children and old women danced gaily in the streets, old men sang with cracked voices, and gnarled working hands played antique guitars. Wine could not be purchased. It was everywhere, and it was free. The simple village houses were open to all. Romance was natural and without complications, and strangely innocent and clean. Pacts were made, promises were whispered, only to be forgotten with the next day's adventures. For four days and nights our campsite played host to the composite caprices of wine, love, flamenco, and gaiety.

On the fifth day it happened. No one knows quite how or why. A flash of knives in the village bar, and a gypsy, unknown to us, fell with his heart punctured. The celebration died with him; the craziness filtered away and left the bedraggled remains of four tumultuous days and nights. The knifed man was buried further down the mountain, and the wailing of a gypsy song of mourning carried eerily to our campsite. A weariness and depression settled over the village like a dense fog as the voice from downstream, raucous and miserable, sang of death, hopelessness, the futility of life:

> Con las fatiguitas de la muerte
> a un laíto yo me arrimo;
> con mi arma destrozá
> sufro mi sino...

With the weariness of death
I creep to one side;
with a soul void of hope
I suffer my destiny...

After a time the voice stopped, and the oppression began melting away before an overpowering fatigue that could no longer be ignored. Senses were numb and minds blank with tiredness as the tempestuous gypsies fell to the ground, exhausted. The celebrations and the mourning had finally ended.

Across the clearing village lamps blinked out one by one, and an occasional dog challenged the infringing darkness. Small night sounds crept stealthily about as the campfires flickered low, and the gypsies succumbed to a deep, unmoving sleep.

JUERGA

The *juerga* (flamenco session) began at my place at about 10 p.m. I had an ideal set-up in the Barrio Santa Cruz, the picturesque old Jewish quarter in Sevilla where summertime flamenco can be heard issuing from surrounding plazas. Of course, outdoor *juergas* are against the law now, but they go on just the same, reminding the old-timers nostalgically of the gay, wide-open Sevilla of thirty years ago.

«*Leche,*» they confide, «how you would have enjoyed Sevilla in those days. Down by the *Siete Puertas* (1) every building had a bar, and every bar flamencos. Sevilla had the reputation of being the gaiest town in Spain. It was a kind of tonic; people came from all over Spain to escape their lives and problems in the activity of Sevilla. Now they prohibit singing, dancing, and even the guitar in the bars. It is truly a changed, sad city.»

But this particular *juerga* was anything but sad. It was one of the many that we had at my place, which were the scandals of the neighborhood. Inappropriately, that romantic tangle of old crooked passages and hidden gardens is inhabited by traditional families with their noses to the social grindstone. They greatly disapprove of gypsies and flamencos in the neighhorhood, and more so of people who entertain them.

The *juerga* was one of the good, serious ones. The artists and the audience were few, and carefully chosen for their ability, knowledge, and compatibility. There were two *cantaores,* a *bailaora,* and a guitarist, four of Spain's non-commercial best, and five listeners, all devout *aficionados.*

We started out with good Jerez wine, olives, fried fish, *chorizo,* and conversation, encouraging the old-timers to reminisce about legendary flamencos, and the merits of contemporary ones. They would illustrate their points by singing, or playing, passages of former greats, often comparing them with present styles. ·

A discussion of two of flamenco's legendary *cantaores* arose, and one of the singers, Juan Talega, expounded an interesting comparison:

«Antonio Chacón, of course, was a far superior singer, but Manuel Torre, when in the mood, *era único* (was in a class by himself). His

---

(1) The *Siete Puertas* (Seven Doors), formerly also called La Europa, is a bar which still exists in Sevilla, and which used to be the center of Sevilla's flamenco life.

cante struck straight at the heart in a manner that was unbelievable. Chacón, also, was capable of evoking great emotion, but Torre had a *duende* that only one in a million possesses. The trouble with Torre was that unless he was moved he could not sing at all, while Chacón always sang beautifully.»

Then Juan, who had been a personal friend of both, demonstrated the differences in their styles and approaches to the *cante* in a manner that would be invaluable in a good anthology.

As the wine took effect faces became illuminated and gaiety paramount, and *cantes por bulerías* irrepressibly bubbled forth, intermixed with a maze of gypsy guitar *falsetas* (passages) and an occasional dance. The *juerga* was soon in full swing, and the music and dance flowed, seriously or lightly as moods changed, into the early hours of the morning. How dawn arrived so quickly no one could explain, except that in a good *juerga* hours seem to pass as minutes.

Finally we became restless, and the *juerga* began developing into good-natured hell-raising. We decided to go out to a neighboring village, a famous outpost of flamenco, for coffee and *aguardiente* and whatever adventures might arise.

Upon arriving we installed ourselves in a local *taberna*, and before long were joined by the cement factory workers who began dropping in for their early-morning *copitas* (eye-openers). (By the time they had both eyes open more than one decided that work could wait, and joined in).

And the juerga carried on, and grew, and grew; we soon outgrew the little *taberna*, and spilled up the street to a larger, more central *café* where we were joined by still more of the local flamencos.

The town was up and about by now, which added color to the festivities. Groups of *chiquillas* hazarded by to the accompaniment of devastating flattery (so we thought) and irresistible flamenco. We were the shameless recipients of dagger-like stares thrown by indignant, Mass-bound women in black. The old fellow from the hardware store down the block closed shop and joined us. A few bankers, lawyers, and doctors embarrassedly skittered in, supposedly out on business calls. The festivities became such that even the eternal domino game broke up when an apprentice bartender leaped on the table and danced until he went tumbling, table and all.

The proceedings were becoming a bit scandalous, a local *guardia* pointed out, in view of which one of the more enthusiastic *aficionados,* a local bull breeder, prudently suggested we move out to his *finca* (ranch); we did, en másse.

By this time the *juerga* was developing into a town *fiesta,* and we were joined by many of the village adventurous. In the corral of the *finca* the breeder broke out one of his *utreros* (young fighting bulls), which proceeded to inflict minor injuries on wine-reckless *afi-*

cionados. After a few such one-sided encounters, the town hopeful finally jumped in and showed us how to fight, passing the bull time and again with serious *naturales* and *manoletinas* to thunderous shouts of «*olé*»!

«Another Manolete,» his admirers claimed.

«*Veremos.* We'll see,» replied tough old-timers, who had too often seen young flashes wither away.

Finally the boy turned his back on the bull and stalked to the corral wall, displaying by his coolness his complete domination of the bull. His followers could contain themselves no longer; up on their shoulders he went, to be paraded about the *finca* in heroic confusion.

By now countless local *aficionados* were dancing and singing in large groups about the patio, and the din of boisterous singing, laughing, and shouting began to make our heads throb. During the proceedings some gypsy girls chanced along, and one of the singers proposed that a group of us escape to the tranquility of his place in Alcalá. He is a very fine singer, but one of the non-commercial, non-prosperous breed, and his «place» is a cave cut into a hillside overlooking the river Guadaira, just below the ruins of an old Roman castle. Who could resist the idea.

On arriving we lounged about at the entrance to the cave, sipping *fino* and feeling mellow and somehow exalted after our night of *juerga.* Below us women washed clothes in the river, and nude children played blissfully in the high grass along the edge. A donkey stood picketed nearby, watching us with ancient eyes as God must watch fools in their folly. I began stroking the guitar softly, lazily, and the girls sang romantic verses in low, caressing, gypsy voices...

> *La luna es un pozo chico,*
> *las flores no valen nada,*
> *lo que valen son tus brazos*
> *cuando de noche me abrazan...*

> *The moon is a little well,*
> *flowers are worth nothing;*
> *what is of value are your arms*
> *when at night they embrace me....*

As the music blended with faraway sounds, an overwhelming sense of peace pervaded the group. For the moment we were all brothers, differences forgotten, prejudices dissolved...

Across the river distant olive groves simmered in the afternoon sun, and time, and the *juerga,* droned contentedly on...

FLAMENCO AND THE BULLFIGHT

Flamenco and the *Fiesta* (spectacle of bullfighting) are deeply related. This connection is undeniable, and vital for an understanding of either. Both stem basically from the common people, and they stir the same basic emotions and passions. Both are given flashes of erratic genius by gypsies, and a sense of indomitable steadiness and responsibility by the Andalusians. And they have in common another important factor: they are the two most probable ways that the commoner can break out of his social and economic level.

This relationship has been dealt with often, but is still little understood. The guitarist Sabicas has tried to capture it on his record «Day of the Bullfight». The poet García Lorca wrote inseparably of flamenco and the bulls. González Climent dedicated an entire book to the psychological and physical ties between the flamenco dance and song, and the *Fiesta*. My brief contribution follows, spiced with the fabulous poetry of García Lorca:

Late in the afternoon on bullfight days the sun slants menacingly against the irregular geometry of Andalusian villages, illuminating the stark-whiteness of humble houses crowding haphazardly about churches, Moorish ruins, and, symbols of Andalucía, bull rings.

On these days the air is charged with excitement, anxiety, fear... and a source-less undercurrent of a flamenco guitar, sounding at first slowly, clearly, profoundly, and then growing louder and raspier and cruel as the blood of man or beast spills to the sand...

A las cinco de la tarde.
Eran las cinco en punto de la tarde.
Un niño trajo la blanca sábana
a las cinco de la tarde.
Una espuerta de cal ya prevenida
a las cinco de la tarde.
Lo demás era muerte y sólo muerte
a las cinco de la tarde

¡Que no quiero verla!
Dile a la luna que venga
que no quiero ver la sangre
de Ignacio sobre la arena (1).

At five in the afternoon.
It was five sharp in the afternoon.
A small boy brought the white sheet
at five in the afternoon.
A basket of lime was already prepared
at five in the afternoon.
Everything else was death, and only death,
at five in the afternoon.
I can't stand to see it!
Tell night to fall;
I don't want to see the blood
of Ignacio on the sand.

The eternal guitar plays on, and its *duende* seeps into *aficionados,* the walls, the wine, everywhere, and makes the village vibrant and explosive. It does not subside until long after the bullfight and the inevitable *juergas,* and even then never completely disappears.

For this guitar is the soul of flamenco, the soul of bullfighting... the timeless essence of Andalucía.

Empieza el llanto
de la guitarra.
Se rompen las copas
de la madrugada.
Empieza el llanto
de la guitarra.
Es inútil callarla.
Es imposible
callarla.
Llora monótona
como llora el agua,
como llora el viento
sobre la nevada.
Es imposible
callarla.
Llora por cosas
lejanas.
Arena del Sur caliente
que pide camelias blancas.

---

(1) From «*Llanto por Ignacio Sánchez Mejías*», by Federico García Lorca.

Llora flecha sin blanco,
la tarde sin mañana (1).

The cry
of the guitar begins.
The crystals of dawn
shatter.
The wail
of the guitar begins.
It is useless to silence it.
It is impossible
to silence it.
It cries monotonously
like water cries,
like wind cries
over frozen peaks.
It is impossible
to silence it.
It bemoans
distant things.
It is the hot Southern sand
craving white camellias.
It is an arrow without destination,
the afternoon without tomorrow.

---

(1) *«La Guitarra»*, by Federico García Lorca.

Photo: D.E. Pohren

Breeding places of flamenco. Many flamencos lived in Andalusia's caves, such as the one above, hollowed out from the base of the Roman castle in Alcalá de Guadaira, near Sevilla.

Breeding places of flamenco: the stark white towns of Andalusia, such as Arcos de la Frontera, pictured above.

Breeding places of flamenco. Triana, as viewed from the Sevilla bank of the Guadalquivir river. Triana has for centuries been a mecca for gypsies, as well as a principal center of development for their art.

Photo: Ira Gavrin
Breeding places of flamenco. Flamenco thrived in the back rooms of Andalusia's poorer bars.

Breeding places of flamenco. In the cities, flamenco roared unchecked in tile-studded bars that never closed their doors. In Madrid, *Los Grabieles,* shown above, shared flamenco honors with another colmado, the *Villa Rosa,* during the last half of the past century and the first half of the present. Los Grabieles, located on the Calle Echegaray, still functions as a bar.

Photo: Ira Gavrin
Breeding places of flamenco. Many of flamenco's forms grew up in the country, such as the *trilleras*, the cante of Andalusia's wheat farmers.

Photo: D.E. Pohren

Workers had ample time for song during the cutting of the wheat (left), but even more so during the seemingly endless hours of going round and round over the spread-out wheat on mule-drawn cutting sleds that chopped it into ever smaller pieces (above).

Photo: Ira Gavrin

Breeding places of flamenco. Nearly everyone sang in Andalusia before the noise of mechanization and the haste of progress took their toll. The muleteers, for instance, invariably sang away the boredom of their long treks.

GYPSIES

That which is Gypsy
is found in the surge of blood
and in the grooves of hands...

SOLEARIYAS

The gypsies in Spain have various class distinctions and ways of life There are those who have entered wholeheartedly into the «civilized» *payo* (non-gypsy) way of life. Others have accepted some *payo* customs, but remain on the fringe. And others, a small minority, have remained true to their traditional way of life, and have thus far rejected *payo* society.

Those who have accepted the *payo* way of life wholeheartedly have done so to the extent of actually working steadily, and even opening their own businesses. These people are a relatively respected element in their communities, and in the process have had to sacrifice many of their gypsy instincts and drives.

More interesting are the fringe gypsies, by far the largest group. These are the people who have been lured, or driven, from their natural life on the open road to a life of squalor in urban slums. The exceptions to this are the talented — the bullfighters, flamenco artists, literary people, etc., whom, if they are willing to work commercially, can make enough money for the essentials. But the others, the non-talented who cannot find work (gypsies are not known as good employment risks), or who are convinced that the gypsies are above ordinary work, and should live by their wits alone, usually fare badly on the fringe. Other than work they have only two alternatives: to go hungry, or to become con men. The latter explains the gypsies roaming all large Andalusian towns who approach tourists with offers of women, contraband, and what have you. Fast fingers and basic begging are also common.

The gypsies who most excite the imagination are Spain's nomads. They are the aristocracy of the gypsies, and feel an unconcerned scorn for their «contaminated» brothers and their *payo* ways.

In modern times these nomad gypsies band together in families

33

or clans, rarely consisting of more than fifteen or twenty members. These people live basically the same life that they have lived for centuries. They are still constantly on the move. They still talk a form of Romaní, the gypsy language that was derived from the Indian Sanskrit. And they are still one of the few races that can honestly claim a degree of true liberty.

These nomad gypsies travel from natural campsite to natural campsite, doing what they can to provide for their basic essentials. They have an admirable lack of respect for material things, and all they really need is enough food, drink, and clothing to survive. To obtain these essentials they perform, tell fortunes, sharpen knives, trade in horses and antiques (buying useless looking objects from house to house and reselling to antique dealers), and so forth. (Some nomad families even consider these part-time activities «undignified»). Their performances are generally of flamenco, acrobatics, sundry musical instruments, and trained animal pets, and are given in the streets or in taverns for tossed coins. During hard times they are not above raiding chicken coops, orchards, and clothes lines, and they have fame of sometimes stealing for pleasure. They are usually dirty, ignorant of *payo* ways (as we are ignorant of theirs), superstitious, violent, clannish... and at the same time clever, funloving, faithful, tender, proud, individualistic, and (virtue of virtues) free.

I recently talked to one such nomad family that was overflowing a wooden cart drawn by two donkeys. They were twelve and multi-talented. The parents are *cantaores,* and most of the ten children perform flamenco and acrobatics. Before coming to Spain some fifteen years ago, the parents had roamed Italy, France, and the Slavic countries, and seemed to speak six or seven languages more or less fluently (including *Romaní, Serbio,* Spanish, French, Italian, and Yugoslavian). The father claims to come from an aristocratic Yugoslavian gypsy family that lost its wealth during Warld War II. He is obviously educated, and talked intelligently and clearly of their life and philosophy. After chatting awhile, I asked him why he preferred his rootless existence (typical *payo* phraseology) to a normal *payo* life.

He replied with a dissertation.

«*Hombre,* do you realize what it is to live with nature, to amble alongside this old cart in the sun and sleep under the stars, to have no ties and do exactly as I damn well please? When we desire entertainment we travel to gypsy reunions and *fiestas,* where there is always plenty of food, drink, and good times. When we need money we perform in town plazas and taverns — what we earn in a week of performing carries us over for a month or two. You see, I have no need for *payo* necessities or luxuries. I have no desire to own a house, or a car, or to go to work everyday like a halfbrain. It seems to me that the *payo* works all of his life for things that he does not really want or need. He sits in a closed office dreaming of open fields and mountains and beaches, and when he finally is allowed a vacation he travels to a resort area milling with people and pushes his way around for two weeks and spends his savings. He lives in fear and anxiety of his employer, a possible depression or war, old age, and a thousand other things either completely beyond his control or not worth the effort. But we, in our simple existence, have everything that we need to be happy. I have a wonderful, talented family. If we feel like spending the summer on a beach, or in a mountain forest, we do so. We have friends and relatives in all parts of Spain. Of course, there are hardships — the rain and cold, occasional hunger — but the life of no one is perfect. *En fin,* as long as we are left alone, we can't ask for anything more. You look like you understand what I am trying to say. *Verdad?*»

«Yes, I'm afraid I do, only too clearly,» I replied, adding in a soft undertone, more for myself than for the old gypsy, «that's the problem.»

PROGRESS

Apart from their music, the traditional flamencos are natural actors. Their preferred life is in the streets and *cafés,* where they can see and be seen, admire and feel admired. They enjoy being nattily dressed, and they have an indestructible attitude of being somebody unique. Armed with these assets, and a glass of two of *aguardiente,* they strut like cocks, being at once expansive, authoritative, friendly, condescending, formal, dignified, and, above all, individualistic. They are not ambitious, and are capable of living happily with only the basic necessities. The concepts and developments of progress are incomprehensible to them. They scorn the rat race and its participants, together with such obnoxious modern phenomena as demanding traffic lights, motor-cluttered streets, shining stainless-steel *cafeterías,* and grim, unseeing civilization bustling to no destination.

Inevitably traditional flamenco philosophy will give ground to progress. Materialism, life insurance, grave sites on installments, and pressing demands will take their toll, and self-confident flamenco faces will cloud with doubt and insecurity.

This is progress as it affects flamenco.

PART II

THE ART OF FLAMENCO

ORIGIN AND BACKGROUND

Contrary to a widespread belief, the Spanish gypsies were not the sole creators of the mysterious art called flamenco. Rather, it is generally agreed that flamenco is a mixture of the music of the many cultures that have played important roles, directly or indirectly, throughout the centuries in Andalusia, the most important of these being the Muslim, Jewish, Indo-Pakistani and Byzantine.

When did flamenco begin? No one knows. It seems reasonable to suspect, however, that folklore similar to flamenco existed in Andalusia long before it became known as flamenco. The Arabs (centuries VIII-XV) and the Sefardic Jews, particularly, both had advanced musical cultures, as did some of Andalusia's earlier rulers, particularly the Greeks and Romans. It would be ridiculous to believe that the common people of those epochs did not air their sentiments through song, dance and musical instruments.

When did the gypsies enter the scene? One wave of gypsies came to Spain in the XV century, after having been persecuted and expelled from India by Tamerlane around the year 1400 A.D. Apparently, after their expulsion many tribes wandered west, spreading throughout the Middle East and along both sides of the Mediterranean. Other tribes traveled north through Russia, the Balkans, Germany and France, finally arriving to Spain in 1447. This migration, and its eventual arrival to Barcelona, is confirmed by various documents and manuscripts of that period.

Other theoreticians insist that there was another migration of gypsies to Spain long before the XV century. This migration, they say, took place in the VIII century, when many tribes of gypsies entered Andalusia as campfollowers of the invading Muslim forces. This theory is reinforced somewhat by the notable differences found between the gypsies of northern and southern Spain. The language, customs, temperament and even general aspect of the two vary considerably. The gypsies of the north are, generally speaking, far more determinedly aloof from Society and typically «gypsy» in appearance, while those in the south, whose families have theoretically been in Spain seven centuries longer, have mixed to a considerable degree with the inhabitants of Andalusia, losing much of their gypsy appearance and many of their customs in the process.

Be that as it may, most theorists agree that flamenco as we know it today did not begin its development until the XVI century, which is when the Kingdom of Castilla decided to rid Spain of minority groups in an effort to propagate pureness of race and religion (a lamentable policy that so depopulated Spain of its professional, mercantile and laboring classes that Spain was plunged into a decline from which it is recovering only today). All Jews and Muslims that refused to convert to Christianity were expelled from the country, and all gypsies who would not leave the open road and settle down to useful sedentary occupations were also encouraged to leave (the decree against the constantly-moving gypsies was much harder to enforce, needless to say, and many of them escaped expulsion). These laws were enforced by the Inquisition, which took serious steps against those of the forbidden cultures who refused to obey, or who were considered insincere in their newly adopted Christian religion.

As a consequence, these three persecuted cultures, the Jewish, the Muslim and the Gypsy, with outwardly little in common, found themselves united against a common foe — the hated Inquisition. Many of the rebellious elements of these cultures grouped into bands in uninhabited mountain regions, hiding in the wilderness and making forays against Christian communities and caravans for food and provisions. They were soon joined by many Christian fugitives and dissenters, who added a fourth distinct culture.

It is thought probable that from the common life of these persecuted peoples appeared the first semblances of flamenco, as we know it. Muslim, Jewish, Indian and Christian religious and folk music blended, developing over the years into a musical form clearly sophisticated in many ways, yet developed at a primitive level by an outcast society. (In my opinion, the flamenco forms created and developed in this underground atmosphere make up much of flamenco's repetoire. There are others, however, the folk forms of the «straight» Andalusian, that developed apart and quite normally, and have only recently been included under the common heading of Flamenco) (1).

The reader might wonder why I suggest that the East has had such a strong influence in the development of flamenco. Mainly, this this is the contribution of the gypsies, who arrived, as we have seen, from India and Pakistan (2). In my opinion, it is mistaken to suppose,

---

(1) The *trilleras, bamberas, temporeras, caleseras, nanas, campanilleros, marianas, sevillanas, verdiales, zorongo, guajiras, milongas, vito, columbianas* and *garrotin*, to name the most likely.

(2) It has been demonstrated, to the satisfaction of the most meticulous historians and researchers, that the gypsies came from these countries. Their language derives from Sanskrit, many of their traditions and legends are similar or identical to those of the nomadic gypsy tribes living in India and Pakistan even today, and (a lesser proof) many moments of flamenco singing and guitar closely resemble instrumentation in ragas and the *cante jondo* of those countries. There is also considerable resemblance between the flamenco dance and certain forms of Indian dance.

40

as a surprising number of flamencologists do, that the gypsies arrived to Spain with no music of their own, having come from countries so well-developed musically (1). Many of these same theoreticians also deny even the possibility of Arabic and Jewish influence in flamenco when they insist that flamenco developed solely among the Andalusians, free from outside influences. This argument if full of naive patriotism, but a patriotism in favor of whom, or what? What is an Andalusian if not a mixture of various cultures, predominent among them precisely those the theoreticians choose to deny: the Arabic, Jewish and Gypsy.

Let us study another riddle. Where did the term flamenco come from? Again, no one knows, but theories abound. The word «flamenco» originally meant (according to Spanish dictionaries) «Flemish» and «flamingo», today also means «coarse and flippant». Naturally, these formal meanings have given rise to theories. One of them, embraced by several English-language encyclopedias, is that the term was applied to the art form because certain positions of the dancer are reminiscent of the flamingo bird (a bit ridiculous, but colorful). The «Flemish» theory is more feasible. It claims that the Spanish Jews who migrated to Flanders were allowed to sing their religious chants unmolested. These songs were referred to as «flamenco» songs by their kin who remained in Spain, who were forbidden them by the Inquisition. The other theory derived from the dictionary meanings of the word «flamenco» says that as the flamencos were «coarse and flippant», the already-existent word «flamenco» was applied to them. However, in my opinion the flamencos have been around longer than this meaning of the word, which just dates back to the last century. In other words, I would say the word «flamenco» acquired the new meaning «coarse and flippant» in the last century precisely because the flamencos, already so-called, were coarse and flippant.

Possibly the most likely theory states that the word «flamenco»

---

(1) These flamencologists argue that if the gypsies brought flamenco to Spain with them, the many tribes that stayed in countries along the way (Russia, Germany, France, the Balkans, Turkey, Greece, Italy, to name a few) would also play, sing and dance flamenco. I respond to this by repeating that the gypsies did not bring flamenco as such, but only had a share in its development, once in Andalusia, by their Indo-Pakistani contribution. Why then, ask the doubters, have not gypsy tribes in other countries developed some sort of musical tradition, even if it is not flamenco? The answer is, many have. What of the gypsy violins of the Balkans? The gypsy guitars of Germany-France (in this century playing jazz; i.e. Django Reinhart)? The more primitive song-dance of the Russian gypsies? And so forth. Nevertheless, they say, many other tribes do not seem to .have any musical tradition whatsoever. Why? The answer to this is that some gypsy tribes were (and are) much more musically inclined than others. Like the Hindus, whose profession is designated them from birth by the caste system, each gypsy tribe traditionally practiced a trade. Some tribes (not many) were basically music minded, others worked metal, others weaved baskets, others bred horses and beasts of burden, others made pottery. Thus, it is not strange that all gypsies scattered around the world today are not musically inclined. In addition, another factor is involved. It seems reasonable to suppose that the social and musical atmosphere of the adopted countries would strongly affect the progress and even survival of the gypsies' music. In other words, in countries, or regions of countries (such as Andalusia) where music flourished, the gypsies' contribution was absorbed and a new musical form developed. In musically poor countries and regions that showed little interest or economic support for the gypsies' music, the music merely died out.

is a mispronunciation of the Arabic words «*felag*» and «*mengu*» (*felagmengu*), which means «fugitive peasant». It is likely that this term was borrowed from the Arabs (Arabic was a common language in Andalusia at that time) and applied to all the persecuted people who fled to the mountains. Through usage in Spanish «*felagmengu*» was transformed into «flamenco», until eventually the term flamenco was adopted by the fugitives themselves and in turn applied to their music.

The main form of flamenco at that time, the *cante jondo,* expressed the suffering of these outlawed people, who through the years were condemned to serve in the galleys, in chain gangs, and in the Spanish army in America, were prohibited to talk their own language, and who, during one prolonged period, suffered the death penalty for just belonging to a wandering or outlawed band. Somehow their spirit remained unbroken, and their mode of expression — their flamenco — developed to magnificent heights through the centuries, culminating in the *Café Cantante* period of the last century. From this «Golden Age» flamenco declined sharply, passing through a period of decadence and abuse in the first half of this century which nearly caused its extinction. The reasons for this decline, as well as for the present trend of renewed purity and hope, will be discussed later in the book (in the section «Hard Times and Present Trends» and the appendix «Flamenco Records of Special Interest»).

WHAT IS FLAMENCO?

Present day flamenco consists of

singing *(cante)*
dancing *(baile)*
guitar playing *(toque)*
jaleo (rhythm accentuation) and reciting,

each of which I shall deal with separately in succeeding chapters. They are all distinctive arts in their own right, and can stand alone, although the complete visual, musical, and emotional image of flamenco can only be grasped through the participation of all of these fundamental components. This is not to say that during a *juerga* particular solo numbers featuring a soloist or any combination of performers cannot be a rewarding experience. It merely suggests that to achieve the perfect moment in flamenco, the singing, dancing, and the guitar all have to blend together in complete harmony.

A past experience of mine can serve as an example. I attended, as the only non-Spaniard and one of the few non-gypsies, a homage for the singer Antonio Mairena. The guests of honor, other than Mairena, were Juan Talega, the old master of the traditional school of *cante jondo,* la Fernanda and la Bernarda de Utrera, the guitarist Diego del Gastor, and others.

The *juerga* began in the traditional manner, with dinner and quantities of wine, erupting around midnight into gay dancing, singing, and *jaleo,* totally carefree and uninhibited. We carried on in this state during the emptying of many more cases of wine, amid the excellence of the gay *cantes* of Mairena, la Fernanda, la Bernarda, and others, until a quiet expectancy slowly settled over the gathering. The time had arrived when moods were mellow, and bodies and throats wine-warmed and flexible. Diego began drumming a slow, melancholy *siguiriyas.* Mairena, infected with the *duende* of Diego's playing, started singing this despairing rhythm amid absolute stillness. He sang beautifully and with great emotion, finishing on a note of tragedy, pervading the room with a quieting depression. La Fernanda was shamelessly weeping. The guitar sounded again, this time the sluggish, persistent call of the *soleares* (loneliness). Juan Talega began singing, and despondency deepened. He sang interminably, in ancient ways that are nearly forgotten, slowly, methodically. Suddenly a barefoot girl was dancing. No one saw her begin; they only saw her somehow appear in the middle of the dirt floor, surrounded by the mahogany faces of spell-bound gypsies. She moved in a tortuous way, dancing in the superb manner that the moment demanded, moving only her hands and arms, completely lost in the trance of the charged flamenco atmosphere. The singer sang to her, the guitarist played for her, and she moved toward them, responding with a pureness of dance and movement that had the effect of somehow exalting the crowd, while at the same time intensifying their desolation. They had reached the culmination, fla-menco's perfect moment, when all of flamenco's components were com-bined in a rare purity of expression. The monotonous, beating rhythm continued, slower and slower, until, without warning, the guitar seemed to die at the perfect time. We were all quiet a moment, completely entranced, a little ashamed of our raw emotions, and yet savouring the impact of the experience that we knew would rarely be repeated.

That was the climax of the evening, and not long after, the *juerga* broke up. Further performing was meaningless. *Ya estaba todo dicho.* Everything had been said.

* * *

The major scope of flamenco (singing, dancing, guitar) can be divid-ed into four categories:

profound or deep flamenco (*jondo* or *grande*)
intermediate flamenco (*intermedio*)
light flamenco (*chico*)
popular flamenco.

The *jondo* flamenco is the means by which a manic-depressive society expresses its black moods. Serious and melancholy, it is com-parable, emotionally, with the authentic blues of the Negroes of the southern United States. Of all flamenco, it is the most difficult to understand and the most difficult to interpret properly. Those who master this deep-rooted base of flamenco (and its masters are few) are the true *maestros*, deeply respected within the world of artists and *aficionados* of integrity and real understanding. These *maestros* appeal to a small, select following, and rarely achieve the monetary success of the popular flamencos, or even that of the good intermediate or light flamencos. Nevertheless, the *jondo* artists are *the* nobility in the world of flamenco.

The fact of being a virtuoso in his field, be it song, dance or the guitar, does by no means qualify an artist for this category. The true flamenco *grande* artist may, or may not, have an outstanding tech-nique, but it is imperative that he possess the abilities of identifying himself with the *duende* that he is unfolding, and, of equal importance, of being able to transmit this emotion, or series of emotions, to his audience. It cannot be overemphasized that flamenco, above all, the *jondo* flamenco, is basically an emotional art, and that the artist needs only enough technique to enable him to transmit his emotions to himself and to his public. The improving of technique to the point of virtuosity is not usually synonymous with the improvement of the artist's ability to communicate. Conversely, the opposite is more often true. The virtuoso often becomes a cold machine, too concerned with his technique, too complicated, too entangled in his own virtuosity, too conscious of the fact that the majority of public is awaiting this virtuosity more than any *duende* he may impart.

Many exponents of flamenco insist that only the Spanish gypsies and the Andalusians possess the inherent temperamental qualities necessary in the true flamenco. This argument is close to the truth, but there have been exceptions. It is inevitable that the aspirant have an extremely sensitive and receptive nature. Armed with these qualities, he must sally forth, firstly to attain a reasonable technical proficiency, and secondly in search of the elusive *duende,* for without the *duende* flamenco is often vulgar and dull, and always disappointing. The quest for the *duende* is particularly difficult for those living outside of Spain, as it can only be attained through long and constant association with true flamenco in Spain itself, almost necessarily in Andalusia. This statement is sustained by the many inconsolable examples that I have witnessed of recent arrivals to Spain who attempt to dazzle the local flamencos with a sharp technique gained through years of arduous lessons, practice, material pilfering from records and tapes, etc., and who are almost invariably dismissed with a shrug and a «*no dice ná*» «he says nothing». What these students have to realize is that they have taken only the first step. The second, the search for the *duende,* is more difficult, and yet a delightful and adventurous undertaking, for the search will bring one into contact with emotional, vibrant people who are living an alluring philosophy; a philosophy difficult to understand by those outside of it, and impossible to absorb if not in constant contact .with it.

Flamenco *intermedio* consists of a set of forms that tend towards the flamenco *grande*. The main difference is that the *grande* is the true foundation of flamenco, the root from which all the rest of flamenco stems, while the intermediate is a less pure offspring, not as difficult to perform properly, and not as profoundly moving.

Flamenco *chico,* in comparison with the *jondo,* will usually have the opposite impact on the spectator. It is a multitude of things; gay, vivacious, frivolous, sensuous, tender, amorous, poetic, fleetingly sad; and very charming when done well. Regrettably it is not usually done well, due to a mistaken belief by artists and onlookers alike that great quantities of noise, shouting, stamping, and frenzied move-

45

ments are the framework of Gaiety. Obviously (or perhaps not so obviously), it is not necessary to sacrifice dignity in order to be gay. Of course, the artists and the non-*aficionado* public (even in Andalusia the large majority of people cannot distinguish good flamenco from bad) have become ensnared in a vicious circle. The artists give the public what they believe the public wants, and the public wants what they are accustomed to. Nevertheless, of the three categories that we have discussed, you are much more likely to see good *chico* than good *jondo* or intermediate flamenco.

Popular flamenco is that conglomeration of colorful garbage that has managed, in the brief span since the *Café Cantante* period, to gnaw at the platform of pure flamenco, causing its decadence and near collapse. It is a base commercialization of all forms of flamenco. It knows no taboos or untouchable gods. In the course of one theatrical «flamenco» show you may squirm through the debasement of all types of pure flamenco *(grande, intermedio, chico),* as well as the flamenco-ization of Spanish and Spanish-American regional music, North American and French popular and folk songs, and so forth. This popular malady is the «rock and roll» of Spain, aimed at the immature, uneducated public, rocking them away from any music of worth or beauty.

It can safely be said that a large portion of the organized flamenco that is offered in and out of Spain will belong, sadly enough, in this category. This includes the major part of the flamenco offered in theatres, tablaos, night clubs, caves, and other commercial establishments.

Improvisation and Compás

As in American jazz, improvisation plays an important role in flamenco. An experienced artist, mature and imaginative, will improvise at will. Many imaginative guitar instructors will not remember the improvisations taught in a preceding class, much to the annoyance of their pupils.

Each of the *cantes* and *toques* of flamenco has become adapted to a certain basic set of guitar chord structures. Within these structures, and the *compás* (if the *cante* or *toque* is rhythmical) improvisation is encouraged. Occasionally an artist will innovate new elements or a new style within a traditional *cante, baile* or *toque,* which innovation, if deserving, may be informally associated with its creator (*soleares* de Joaquín de la Paula), or with his home town (*soleares* de Alcalá/town near Sevilla), or both.

The beginner should become extremely well-versed in all aspects of flamenco before attempting to improvise, or the chances are that he will come up with non-flamenco improvisations that are meaningless. Many artists never reach the degree of excellence which permits them to improvise freely and well within the bounds of flamenco, even after a lifetime as a flamenco.

Of equal importance and difficulty in the art of flamenco is the keeping of the *compás*. Rhythmically, flamenco is divided into those *cantes* and *toques* (1) having a set *compás* (rhythm), all of which are danceable, and (2) those of a free, undetermined *compás*, which are rarely danced due, of course, to the lack of a danceable *compás*. There is very little abstract dancing in flamenco, although it is becoming increasingly fashionable in theatrical circles.

The beginner will notice that many of the *cantes, bailes,* and *toques* seem to have the same, or a very similar, *compás*. In reality this is true; the basic *compás* of several *cantes,* for example, may be identical, but the accentuations, inflections, and moods of the *compás* vary considerably. The artist of many years experience will often not recall that the *compás* is the same in two *cantes* (*bailes, toques*), as he has such a well-defined notion of the above-mentioned differences between the two that to him they are entirely dissimilar. In time all *aficionados* arrive to this desired state. Until then, the *compás* is a confusing business.

Commercial and Juerga Flamenco

It is necessary to emphasize throughout this book the wide gulf that separates commercial from *juerga* flamenco. Although the basic forms performed are the same in each (when they are done seriously), their impact is quite distinct. An obvious and very significant difference is that of the atmosphere in which the flamenco takes place. The small *juerga* is all intimacy, wine, friendship, while the commercial is cold and indifferent. Artistically speaking, the difference is just as great. A good *juerga* artist will not usually go over on stage, where his all-important personality is largely nullified, nor will a good commercial performer generally fit into the more roughhewn, spontaneous atmosphere of a *juerga*. The contrast might be summed up as primitivism versus polish, warmth versus anonymity, creation versus rigidity, emotion versus intellect, instinct versus schooling, fun versus formality.

When one considers that flamenco, like the blues, must remain a primitive, intimate art if it wishes to retain its whole foundation of being, there is little doubt which of these forms is preferred by the sensitive and well-versed *aficionado*. Readers who, after having experienced both forms, find themselves disagreeing with this point are very likely those that hyper-civilization has left with an appreciation for only the polished. Is that case, I respectfully suggest they turn to the more refined classical fields.

THE SONG

The *Cante* (Song) holds the select position in flamenco. It is the preferred mode of expression (as opposed to the dance and the guitar) of nearly all Spanish *aficionados*. I emphasize «Spanish» *aficionados* as this is not true of non-Spaniards, who will generally prefer the guitar and dance to the singing due to the unfamiliar, oriental style which characterizes the *Cante*, and to their lack of understanding of the verses. It is too drastic a change for the Western foreigner steeped in the vocal styles of his country, and he has to become accumtomed to the *Cante* by degrees. To achieve a complete appreciation of the *Cante* flamenco, one must develop a taste for it, slowly learning to savour its flavor and grandeur like the novice introduced to good wines and brandies. More important than the understanding of what is being sung is the appreciation of how it is being sung; in good or bad taste, with a well or badly-guarded *compás*, with authenticity, with *duende*...

The basic breakdown for the *Cante* is as follows:

   cante grande or *jondo (hondo)*

   cante intermedio

   cante chico.

The *cante grande (jondo)* is the original expression of flamenco. It is the pure *cante*, the trunk from which all other *cantes* branch. In its oldest form it was derived from ancient religious chants and songs, which later developed into a more generalized lament of life.

This category, consisting basically of *cantes* originally gypsy-inspired, includes by far the most difficult group of *cantes* to interpret. It has to be dominated by the full use of the lungs and throat, and it demands great emotion and effort. When sung properly, it has the power to sweep the *aficionado* on its melancholy course. When sung badly, it is pitiful and often grotesque. Realizing this, the singer of integrity who is not of the *grande* caliber will wisely refuse to sing *cantes* of this category.

Not many decades ago it was commonly believed that only a gypsy, or a person of Oriental descent, had the special something in his throat to enable him to emit the proper sounds for the *jondo*; that is, the possession of a voice «*afillá*» (1). Such a voice is still considered most desirable, as it can greatly assist the singer to express the wild, primitive cry that is the *cante jondo.* However, the «*voz afillá*» by no means predominates in the *cante jondo* today. As more and more non-gypsies take up the *jondo,* and as the gypsies continue losing racial purity due to widespread intermixing with non-gypsies, this vocal quality is virtually becoming a rarity. But those gypsies who do possess a «*voz afillá*» today are still highly esteemed, perhaps more so than ever, to the point that they are considered by purists the singers whose *cante grande* most profoundly reaches the heart.

The cante intermedio is less intense and more ornamental than the *cante grande,* although still very moving and difficult to interpret. Many of the *cantes* categorized as *intermedio* are characterized by certain strange discords and rare oriental melodies, obviously the influence of the Moorish rule in Spain, such as can be observed in the *tarantas, taranto,* and *cartageneras.* Its *cantes* are mostly without *compás,* which is to say that they are sung with a freedom unimpeded by a set rhythm (and are therefore not danceable). It is believed that this group of *cantes* were basically Andalusian-developed (non-gypsy), which seems to be borne out by the fact that a clear, melodious, rather high-pitched voice is more in keeping with them than a gypsy «*voz afillá*».

Nearly all of the *cantes intermedios* were conveived from the *fandangos grandes.* Some have been created by toiling miners, others by mountaineers, farmers, fishermen. In the main, due to the lack of the grating raucousness which the gypsies brought to the *cante grande,* the *cantes* of the *intermedio* category are the most sophisticated and vocally beautiful of all flamenco.

The *cantes chicos* are both technically and emotionally the least difficult *cantes* to interpret. Consequently there are many more *chico* singers than singers of the other categories. This does not mean to say that the *cantes chicos* are by any means easy to sing; all well-sung flamenco is difficult.

The *cantes chicos* are characterized by an emphasis on the rhythm, and by their optimistic outlook. Their verses deal poetically with love, women, animals, and Andalusia and its people. There are country *cantes,* mountain *cantes,* inland *cantes* and sea *cantes* from the southern Mediterranean coast, all characterized by one power; the ability to stimulate, exhilarate, and sweep away one's cares.

The *cante* is often referred to in terms of various vocal types, styles, and manners of delivery, into which I go into some detail in

---

(1) The term «*afillá*» was derived from Diego el Fillo, a singer of the early last century, who is said to have had the perfect *jondo* voice, which had a rough, coarse quality and could be cracked, or split, at will. This quality is also referred to as «*eco gitano*» and «rajo» (raucous).

Lives and Legends of Flamenco. Here we shall only touch upon three basic categories:

cante gitano
cante bien
cante bonito.

Any individual *cante* can be delivered by either or all of these ways of singing, although particular singers will have a voice and style that will almost invariably fit into only one of these categories. There are very fine differences between these styles.

The term «*cante gitano*» implies that it must be sung by gypsies. Generally this is true, although there have been non-gypsy singers who have been able to sing with the special gypsy air and manner of delivery (i.e. Silverio Franconetti). In almost all cases the *cante gitano* singer possesses either a voice *afillá* (Manolo Caracol, Fernanda de Utrera, Manolito de María, Terremoto de Jerez, etc.), or is capable of injecting a great deal of *rajo* (raucousness) into his *cante,* although his voice is not actually *afillá* (Manuel Torre, Antonio Mairena, Juan Talega, Niña de los Peines, etc.)

The singers included in the *cante bien* category have smooth voices devoid of *rajo,* and are consequently not able to achieve the roughness so desirable for the *cante gitano.* Their voices are, therefore, better suited for the non-gypsy *cantes.* There are exceptions. There are gypsies born with clear voices, some of whom sing excellent *cante gitano.* Tomás Pavón was one such gypsy singer, and he is considered one of the great gypsy singers of all time. However, it is generally agreed that could he have produced more *rajo,* more courseness, in his *cante,* he would have been a far more emotionally *jondo* singer in addition to his outstanding techniques and vast knowledge of the *Cante.* Among the famous non-gypsy singers in the *cante bien* category we can list Antonio Chacón, Juan Breva, and today, Aurelio Sellé, Pericón de Cádiz, and many others.

The style disparagingly called *cante bonito* (pretty song) is that conglomeration of bad taste that falls under the already-mentioned «popular flamenco» category. This type of *cante* is characterized by the following:

(1)   art succumbing to the desire for money and mass recognition.
(2)   irresponsibility.
(3)   the tendency to mix different styles of a *particular cante,* or different *cantes* themselves, capriciously, in an effort to achieve originality, or to display virtuosity or knowledge.

Since the mixing of different styles of a particular *cante,* or different *cantes,* is so often confused with originality, not only by the public but even by the performers, some clarification of this point seems necessary.

Over the years each *cante* has been subjected to the extremely strong personalities of the truly ingenious and inventive interpreters. These exceptional *cantaores* have left the stamp of their genius on their favorite *cantes,* which is distinguishable to the truly knowledgeable *aficionado.* Also, certain regions within Andalusia may develop a «school», which will sing a particular *cante* with a peculiar flavor. This growth or maturation of a *cante* leads to various styles within that cante. Let us select one *cante,* the *soleares,* as an example. There are many styles within the *soleares,* each with its singular personality and emotional quality. For instance, there are the *soleares* that were perpetuated and further developed by the late Joaquín de la Paula, one of the past geniuses of the *Cante* from the town of Alcalá de Guadaira. These *soleares* are referred to, therefore, in two equally as common ways: the «*soleares de Joaquín de la Paula*» and/or the «*soleares de Alcalá*». By the same token, the *soleares* developed in the town of Utrera are known interchangeably as the «*soleares de Utrera*», or by their most famous developer, Merced la Sarneta (*«soleares de la Sarneta»*). The same is true of the *soleares* developed by the famous Enrique el Mellizo, which are known as the «*soleares del Mellizo*» or by his home town, the «*soleares de Cádiz*». And again with the «*soleares de Jerez*», also known by their creator, Frijones (*«soleares de Frijones»*). And so forth.

Purists consider it inappropriate to intermix these various styles during the interpretation of a particular *cante,* as this entails the clashing of personalities and drives, tending to confuse the continuity and emotional intensity of the *cante.* By this they mean that if one is to interpret the *siguiriyas* of Manuel Torre, for instance, he should limit himself strictly to that style throughout his entire *cante,* a happening that rarely occurs. Mostly, I believe, in an attempt to expose knowledge, nearly all singers jump from style to style during a *cante,* such as singing a verse of Manuel Torre, then one of Marrurro, then one of another singer, etc.

The mixing of more than one *cante* is a much graver sin in the minds of the purists, excepting some endings of *cantes* which we shall discuss later in the chapter. It is felt that a mixture of styles within a *cante* is really not so bad, and could even be done through ignorance, but that a *cantaor* could not mistakenly confuse two *cantes.* A well-known «mixer of *cantes*» is Pepe Marchena. One of his famous mixtures begins with the *soleares,* continues with the *bulerías,* then the *caña,* and ends with the *fandangos.* This is ridiculous to the knowledgeable *aficionado,* a classical example of saying nothing as, of course, he never approaches the essence of any of these *cantes.* This type of misusage is still very common among the vaudeville type of flamenco performer. Understandably enough, I might add, considering that Pepe Marchena has become a rich man through such blatant impurities, a

51

circumstance that does not cast too favorable a light on the general public.

The *cante bonito* is the style that is preferred by a majority of non-*aficionados*, whatever their nationalities. Its interpreters are highly paid singers, some of whom can sing good flamenco but who find the *cante bonito* more lucrative. The most notorious of these singers are:

Angelillo (D)	Manuel Gerena
Antonio Molina	Manzanita
Chiquetete	Pepe Marchena (D)
El Principe Gitano	Niña de Antequera (D)
El Turronero	Pepe de Lucía
Enrique Montoya	Rafael Farina
Juanito Valderrama	Miguel de los Reyes

(D signifies Deceased, I have included these singers because their cante lives on in their recordings)

Another important distinction is made between singers who sing in a natural manner, and those who utilize unnatural vocal tricks, shout, or strain their voices excessively. It is generally felt that the pure *cante* should be sung in a natural way, which is less flashy and more difficult, and the only way to arrive directly to the essence of the *Cante*. This is especially true in the *cante gitano*. There is another school of thought on this point, however. There are those who feel that to really reach the ultimate in a gypsy *cante* the singer must «fight with it» *(pelear),* by which they mean he should struggle through a *cante* beyond his physical capabilities, or, if he can normally sing it with ease, purposely sing it in such a high tone as to have to unnecessarily strain his voice, oftentimes having to actually shout, in order to keep his voice from breaking. To their way of thinking singers «put more into it» in that manner. To my way of thinking it is a senseless practice that tends to grate on one's ears and take years off the singer's career. As for the feeling of the *cante,* I would say that it suffers is the battle.

As we have seen, *cantes* and styles of *cantes* have come to be known by the towns or regions in which they were developed. Let us consider this important point in a little more detail.

The *Cante* was developed throughout Andalusia. Each region contributed one or two or more *cantes,* and even today, although regional boundaries and traditions are fast disappearing, nuture and prefer their original contributions. These overall areas and their basic *cantes* are:

Provinces of Sevilla and Cádiz, including such centers as Triana (Sevilla), Jerez de la Frontera, Puerto de Santa María, Puerto Real, Cádiz, Alcalá de Guadaira, Utrera, Morón de la Frontera, etc. These provinces were the birthplace of the gypsy *cantes,* which include most of those of the *cante grande* category, and many of the *cantes chicos* (see breakdown, Appendix I).

Within this gypsy area quite distinct styles developed of the same *cantes* as they spread from region to region, town to town, and singer to singer, as we have seen previously in this chapter. This is also true of the *cantes* in all of the regions that we discuss in continuation.

Province of Huelva. This province gave birth to the Andalusian *Cante,* including the *cantes fandangos grandes* and *fandanguillos.*

Province of Málaga. The province of Málaga bolstered the Andalusian school, developing several *cantes* based on the *fandangos grandes,* which include the *malagueñas, verdiales, jaberas,* and *rondeñas.*

Region of Levante (southeast Spain). This region contributed several Andalusian *cantes,* also based on the *fandangos grandes,* most of which developed in the mines of the southeastern costal area. They are, basically, the *murcianas* and *cartageneras, cantes* from the province of Murcia, *tarantas* and *taranto,* mining *cantes* from the province of Almería, and the *granadinas* and *media granadina* (often pronounced «*granaína*»), *cantes* from the province of Granada.

All of the breakdowns that we have studied so far may seen extremely confusing. Actually, they are not. For instance: Juan Talega, a *cante gitano* singer, sings, among others, the *siguiriyas,* a gypsy *cante grande,* in the «style of Triana» with a natural voice; la Paquera, a *cante gitano* singer, sings the *bulerías,* a gypsy *cante chico,* in the «style of Jerez de la Frontera» with a natural voice; Antonio Molina, a *cante bonito* singer, sings the *malagueñas,* an Andalusian *cante intermedio,* in a popularized version of the «style of Antonio Chacón» with a voice anything but natural; lastly, Aurelio Sellé, a *cante bien* singer, sings the *alegrías,* a gypsy *cante chico,* with a natural voice in the «style of Cádiz».

To burrow further into the core of the *Cante,* we can break each individual *cante* down into its component parts. As González Climent has written («¡Oído al Cante!», P. 32), each *cante* can contain various sections, called *tercios,* which are listed in continuation. Whether all or some of the *tercios* are included in a particular *cante* depends on the *cante* itself, as well as on the momentary inspiration of the singer (he may feel like singing the *cante* primitively short and direct, or lengthening it to his pleasure by means of singing more *tercios,* repeating one *tercio* more than once, or lengthening considerably one or more of those he chooses to sing). The *tercios* are:

(1) *Temple* — warming up to the ryhthm by modulations of the voice, without the use of words (often repeating «ay»).

(2) *Planteo o tercio de entrada* — the entrance or introduction to the *cante.*

(3) *Tercio grande* — the heart of the *cante.*

(4) *Tercio de alivio* — relieving, or easing up, on the emotional substance of the *tercio grande.*

(5) *Tercio valiente o peleón* — the personal touch of the singer,

IMPORTANT CENTERS IN THE DEVELOPMENT OF FLAMENCO

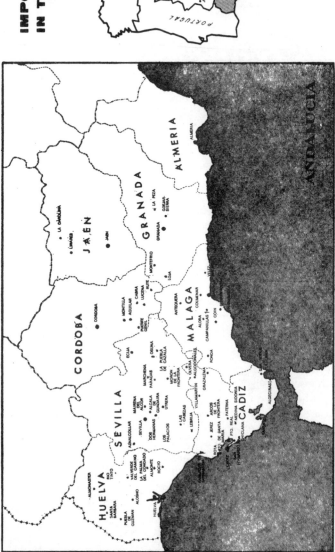

PRINCIPAL SONG FORMS FROM EACH PROVINCE:

Huelva: Fandangos.
Sevilla: Soleares, siguiriyas, bulerías, cantes «a palo seco», fandangos and tangos from Triana, sevillanas, cantes camperos.
Cádiz: Soleares, siguiriyas, bulerías, cantes «a palo seco», alegrías, mirabrás, romeras, caracoles, cantiñas, tangos, tientos, tanguillo, chuflas, cantes camperos.
Málaga: Malagueñas, verdiales, rondeñas, jaberas, serranas, tangos del Piyayo, cantes camperos.
Córdoba: Soleares and alegrías from Córdoba, fandangos de Lucena, cantes camperos.
Jaén: Cantes mineros, cantes camperos.
Granada: Granaína, media granaína, zambra.
Almería: Tarantas, taranto.
Murcia: Cartageneras, from Cartagena and La Unión.
Badajoz: Fandangos and tangos extremeños.

THE ORTEGA MASS

The Ortegas, originally from Cádiz, are a typical example of the flamenco dynasties of the past, when everyone in the family, from grandma to grandchildren, was steeped in flamenco. At family gatherings everyone performed, although in this chart I have singled out as artists only those who became professionals in their specialties.

Until recent times members of flamenco dynasties and their partners in art, bullfight dynasties, stuck pretty close together. Thus in this chart, which encompasses approximately the period 1800 to the present, we see the Ortegas marrying members of other famous flamenco and bullfight dynasties, which included: flamenco — the Ezpeleta (Ignacio), the Jiménez (Enrique el Mellizo) and the Pavón (Arturo, Tomás and the Niña de los Peines); bullfight — the Gómez (Fernando «El Gallo» and his famous sons, Joselito «El Gallo» and Rafael «El Gallo»), Ignacio Sánchez Mejías, Manolo Martín Vázquez, and so forth.

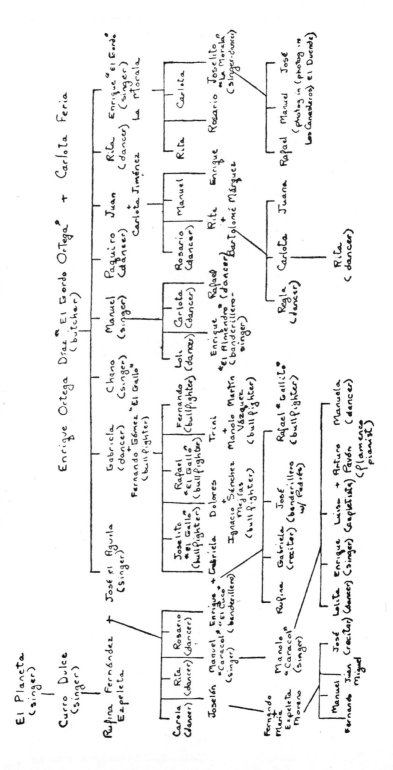

his «flight of fancy», a little creativeness within the main body of the *cante*.

(6) *Cambio o remate* — the *cambio* is the closing of a *cante* by means of a specific variation to the theme, while still utilizing the substance of the same basic *cante*. For instance, utilizing another style of the same *cante*. The *remates* are the closing of a *cante* by switching to another very similar *cante*, frequently changing from a minor to major key. Oftentimes the singer will switch from a slow, melancholy *cante* to a gay, fast one, a kind of combining of the *tercio de alivio* and the *remate*. This practice has the advantage of advising the listeners and guitarist that the singer is about to finish singing, and the disadvantage of spoiling the effect achieved by the melancholy *cante*. On the other hand, the public is not left with their faces down to their knees, and the party surges on. In situations where the festive spirit reigns, I would say that *rematando* with a bit of gaiety is a good practice. On the rare occasions when the singer and the listeners really get into and are living the *cante*, however, it is perhaps too aburpt a change of mood.

To complete this rather technical discussion I shall briefly explain a few other terms and ideas that are an integral part of the *Cante;* namely, the *machos, a palo seco,* and the *compás.*

A *macho* is the singer's individual seal, an original or perhaps traditional passage with which he will usually close a particular *cante.* More simply put, a *macho* consists of a verse tacked on to the normal ending of a *cante*, any *cambio* or *remate,* for instance, that the singer habitually uses.

You will hear reference to a group of *cantes* referred to as *a palo seco.* This group includes the *martinetes, tonás, carceleras, deblas,* and *saetas,* all *cantes grandes* characterized by the lack of guitar accompaniment.

The *compás,* or rhythm, of a *cante* was kept by beating wooden staffs, or canes *(bastones),* on the floor until as recently as forty or fifty years ago. It is said that these staffs date back to the days when they were used as walking sticks, and, as guitars were scarce, they also served as a rhythmical guide for the singer. These staffs became a tradition and were used for many years, even when guitars were widely available, until their disappearance shortly after the decline of flamenco's Golden Age. Such staffs would still be a valuable asset in small towns and villages, where there is a dearth of guitars, and few guitarists who can keep a decent *compás*. In such localities the *compás* often suffers so badly at the hands of the local *aficionados* that it is sometimes difficult to distinguish just what *cante* they are interpreting.

There are *cantaores* who will purposely stray from the *compás* during certain passages of their *cantes* in order to gain the liberty necessary for their self-expression. This is a very tricky practice, and should be avoided unless it is an absolute indispensability in the makeup of the artist, as most singers who vary the *compás* only accomplish the destruction of the mood and the authenticity of their interpretations.

In closing the *Cante* section, we might ask a basic question: is the *Cante* today a creative, spontaneous, breathing art, or has it fallen into the mummified stage, as happens with so many of the folk arts?

Mummification, I am afraid, is the tendency. There have been no new *cantes* introduced for many a moon, nor have any truly original styles of *cantes* made their appearance. At present, the old is being revived, and whatever creative instinct the *cantaores* possess is directed merely towards adapting these *cantes* to a more advanced age; which means to say, oftentimes taking old *cantes,* perfect in their simplicity and understatement, and lengthening them, usually at the expense of the very continuity and *duende* that made the *cante,* or style of *cante,* worthwhile. The possible reasons for this smothering of the creative instinct are discussed in the section «Hard Times and Present Trends».

The following is a list of some of the better flamenco singers, together with a few of their favorite *cantes.* All of these singers are capable of great purity of expression, although this will not always be the case (Manolo Caracol, for example, not infrequently sinks to the lowest depths of commercialism. Even la Fernanda and la Bernarda, until recently institutions of pure *cante,* are not above mixing popular ditties into their *bulerías* these days. The same can be said of la Paquera. And so forth). The list does not attempt to include all of flamenco's good singers, but only intends to serve as a guide for *aficionados* who want to be sure they are searching out the authentic. (A few of the listed singers have died recently, but their *cante* lives on in obtainable records).

In order to avoid an overly lengthy list of favorite *cantes,* I have used five general classifications, in addition to the names of individual *cantes.* The general classifications, and the *cantes* they include, are:

A palo seco — Tonás, deblas, martinetes, carceleras and saetas.

Cantes de Cádiz — Alegrías, tientos, tangos, romeras, mirabrás, cantiñas, and styles of bulerías, malagueñas, soleares and siguiriyas.

Cantes de Málaga — Malagueñas, jaberas, verdiales, serranas and rondeñas.

Cantes de Levante — Tarantas, taranto, cartageneras, granaínas and media granaína.

Cantes camperos — Trilleras, nanas, bamberas, temporeras and marianas.

Singers	Favorite Cantes
Agujetas de Jerez	Siguiriyas, soleares
Antonio Mairena	Siguir., soleares, bulerías, a palo seco
Aurelio Sellé	Cantes de Cádiz
Bernarda de Utrera	Bulerías, tangos
Bernardo de los Lobitos	Cantes de Málaga and Levante
Carmen Linares	Mining songs, general
Camarón de la Isla	Bulerías, siguiriyas, soleares, tangos
Chaquetón	Cantes de Cádiz
Chocolate	Soleares, siguiriyas, a palo seco
Calixto Sánchez	Soleares, siguiriyas, a palo seco
El Cabrero	Fandangos, soleares, siguiriyas
El Lebrijano	Soleares, siguiriyas, bulerías, tangos
Enrique Morente	Cantes de Málaga and Levante
Fernanda de Utrera	Soleares, bulerías, fandangos
Fosforito	Cantes de Cádiz, siguiriyas, a palo seco
Francisco Mairena	Siguiriyas
José de la Tomasa	Siguiriyas, soleares, a palo seco
José Menese	Siguiriyas, soleares, a palo seco, tangos
José Mercé	Soleares, siguiriyas, bulerías, tangos
Juan Talegas	Siguiriyas, soleares, a palo seco
Juan Varea	Cantes de Málaga and Levante
Juanito Villar	Cantes de Cádiz
Joselero de Morón	Siguiriyas, soleares, a palo seco
Manolito de María	Soleares and bulerías de Alcalá
Manolo Caracol	Siguir., soleares, bulerías, a palo seco
Niña de los Peines	Bulerías, siguiriyas, tangos, peteneras
Paquera	Bulerías de Jerez
Piriñaca de Jerez	Siguiriyas, soleares
Pepe el Culata	Siguiriyas, soleares, a palo seco
Pepe de la Matrona	Siguir., soleares, serranas, a palo seco
Pericón de Cádiz	Cantes de Cádiz
Perla de Cádiz	Cantes de Cádiz
Rafael Romero	Soleares, siguiriyas, caña, a palo seco
Rancapino	Cantes de Cádiz
Roque Jarrito Montoya	Cantes de Málaga and Levante
Sordera de Jerez	Bulerías, soleares, siguiriyas
Terremoto de Jerez	Bulerías, soleares, siguiriyas, fandangos

THE DANCE

Introduction

In the section «What is flamenco» I pointed out the wide gulf that exists between commercial and *juerga* flamenco. This difference is most pronunced and obvious in the dance, due to its more extroverted nature.

As most people who read this book will have contact with only the commercial side of the dance (this is not true of the *cante* and *toque* due to records and tapes), I have largely limited this section to a discussion of the finer points of good commercial dancing. I have, however, interspersed this and other parts of the book with enough references to the *juerga* style (country-gypsy, primitive) to give, I hope, the reader an idea of the basic feeling and difference between these two styles of flamenco dance.

The Dance

To the majority of public not well versed in flamenco, the dancer is the show stopper, the scene stealer of flamenco. The popular public considers the dancer *the* attraction, with the rest of the *cuadro* serving as noisemaking satellites. Nearly all theatrical and night club groups feature the dancers. They take the bows, coin the money, swagger to fame, and are often the least flamenco of the group. This is possible because the dance is the only component of flamenco that the popular public can vaguely understand. Even if completely ignorant of the art of flamenco, they can still appreciate the dancer's grace and sensuality, his (her) facial expressions, colorful dress, and polished movements. To the popular public the singer is shouting something or other, the guitarist is doing God-knows-what, and consequently all of their attention is riveted on the dancer.

Ironically, flamenco's greatest deficiency is its lack of good dancers. The number of *bailaores* that are capable of being profundly moving can be counted on both hands, and many of them are nonprofessional unknowns. This is not to say that there are not many dancers who are enjoyable, having many excellent qualities in their dance. It is merely

59

that there are few truly great flamencos (just as there are few great personalities in any of the arts), and of the few that exist the dancers are in a definite minority.

In modern times various misconceptions and trends have diluted the commercial dance, including the over-emphasis on techniques, a lack of instinct in the dancer enabling him to differentiate the good from the vulgar, the introduction of castanets, and others that we shall discuss in the following paragraphs.

Within commercial surroundings there has traditionally been a sharply-defined difference between the dances of the *bailaor* and *bailaora*. The male dancer emphasized the footwork, a symbol of strength and virility, and the female dancer the *baile de brazos* (dance of the upper torso, literally «dance of the arms»), symbol of femininity and passion. In modern times the dance tends towards bi-sexuality, as do many of its interpreters.

The *bailaora* seems to have lost her instinct of natural femininity. Too often her arms and hands are stiff, her movements ungainly, her angles, not her curves, pronounced. The footwork aggravates this un-gainliness, as the *bailaora* will show bony knees in awkward positions. The all-important techniques of moving the arms, hands, and shoulders, and arching the back, in a flamenco way, seem known to only a few. In place of these basic essentials the *bailaora* substitutes back-bending acrobatics, frenzied, shapeless movements, unnatural facial expressions, overly exaggerated body postures, and excessive tossing of her head, hair, and dress.

The male dancer, on the other hand, has a better idea of how to be masculine. He performs well his strong, intricate footwork, his body is rigid and straight, his fingers snap fire, he tosses his head like a stallion, his facial expressions are fierce... and yet, it usually just doesn't come off. Most male Spanish dancers (and dancers in general) are quite unmanly, and generally no amount of high caliber acting can alter the fact. This condition is passable in the Spanish Ballet, but leaves much to be desired in the *Baile* flamenco.

These impressions are aggravated if you see much flamenco dancing in theaters, *tablaos* and night clubs, as many of the dancers who are hired for such places are classical Spanish ballet dancers who also dance a little flamenco. The expression «also dance flamenco» signifies that they have studied the *compás,* footwork and mimicry, and have learned a few flamenco dance arrangements, which they perform night after night with unvarying loyalty. Many of these so-called flamenco dancers have to stumble to a stop if they confuse their arrangement, or if the guitarist happens to vary his accompaniment, of the dance. Certainly a study of, or a familiarization with, the dance techniques, together with arrangements with which to practice these techniques, is necessary in the *Baile* flamenco. But these techniques should become second nature, and the dance arrangements digested and then forgotten; for these methods are only means to the end, not the end itself. The *jondo* dancer, when he feels himself moved during the course of a *juerga*, has to respond with the creation of his own flexible world, with a release of stirred passions and emotions that are far beyond arrangements or practical memories. The techniques help him achieve this end, the arrangements help solidify the techniques, but his inner passion is the motivating force. I have seen completely untrained gypsies and *payos* who can cause the spark, *que dicen algo,* while many highly-trained heroes of the *Baile* simply do not come through. La Chunga, when she started, came out of the gypsy quarter of Barcelona with a dance as natural as her beauty. She was born with all of the meaningful «techniques». She literally did not know that dance arrangements existed, and she was a constant source of *duende.*

In days past, in fact, this type of dance, which we could call «primitive» or «country-gypsy», was *the* flamenco dance, existing long before flamenco stepped upon platforms, and which has managed to survive behind the scenes even today. In this dance neither the men nor the women use footwork or castanets, but rely more on the dance of the upper torso and, even more important, on their personalities, or *gracia.* It is a completely spontaneous dance, and when done well gives one the exhilarating impression of just what flamenco was before it was caught up in the webs of commerce. The *bulerías* is its rhythmical mainstay, and a lively sense of humor indispensable for a proper appreciation of it. The best of its interpreters can «out-flamenco» (in contrast to «outdance») any of their more polished rivals.

These primitive-style dancers rely strongly on the accompanying verses of the *cante,* as their dances often consist of humerous little skits. Whether they rely on a singer, or sing themselves (very frequent), their dance will usually consist of illustrating what is being sung, and wild dance breaks *(desplantes)* between verses.

Some of the better of these dancers are:

Andorrano de Morón	Paco de Valdepeñas
Beni de Cádiz	Pepa de Utrera
Juana la del Revuelo	Lola Flores (not her speci-
La Pipa de Jerez	ality, but she can be very
Miguel Funi	flamenca when she wishes)

It is extremely difficult to explain what does, or does not, make a great flamenco dancer. As in all of flamenco, *duende* and *gracia* are prized possessions, followed by an instinctive *compás* and an underrated «good taste». Other than these essentials, there are not any clearly defined techniques that have to be used. It is strictly up to the dancer to use whatever technique he wishes in whatever manner he wishes, within certain broad limitations, as long as they help him to express what he feels, whatever he is striving to communicate. Of course, only certain types of movements and techniques are accepted as being flamenco in nature. The knowledge of these is inherent, or acquired through constant exposure to good dancing, or both.

Although it is impossible to state that a good flamenco dancer has to do such and such at any given time, I can list the best qualities of, and, inversely, practices avoided by, the outstanding flamenco dancers that I have seen; the unconscious movements and techniques that make their performances exceptional, that give them a certain «something» that sets them apart. I shall divide this grouping into

(1) *baile grande* (and *intermedio*) — female
(2) *baile grande* (and *intermedio*) — male
(3) *baile chico* — male or female
(4) mixed dancing

(1) *Baile grande* (and *intermedio*), *female*. The *baile* of the arms, hands, shoulders, and fingers, the very essence of the feminine dance, is the main attribute that can distinguish a great from a mediocre performer. The arms are raised and moved fluidly and slowly, naturally curved without pointing elbows (with exceptions in certain arm positions), raised and lowered with the palms of the hands facing downwards (the underside of the arm facing downward). Facing the palms downward will, in turn, cause the shoulders to move properly, as the shoulders are moved together with the arms to the extent desired by the dancer. The hands move flexibly from the wrists in a circular motion in either direction, also slowly and fluidly. The fingers are placed together (1). or in exaggerated positions (mostly while posing), keeping in mind that the middle and ring fingers have to be utilized, with the thumb, for playing the *pitos* (finger-snapping). I repeat that in the *baile grande* the arms, hands, and shoulders are moved slowly and with great gravity.

The carriage of the dancer is very important. The back is arched backwards from the waist at an angle which should not exceed 45° and will usually be less, with the head generally inclined a little forward and to one side, eyes downcast. You will often see dancers do deep 90° backbends, which are nothing but acrobatics and are meaningless.

The facial expressions, if the dancer feels her dance, will naturally be *jondo*. You may wonder at the spectacle of a dancer performing a

---

(1) There are two schools of thought in the way the fingers should be moved. The modern Sevillanan school advocates the moving of all of the fingers separately during a wrist-turn. Vicente Escudero is strongly opposed to the modern school. He claims that the fingers should be placed and moved together during a wrist-turn.

serious dance with a fixed smile pasted on her face. This signifies only one thing: she has no idea.

Sex-appeal is certainly a motivating force in the female *baile grande*. The hips are moved in a graceful, natural, sensuous manner, but always bearing in mind that the flamenco dancer is not Rosie la Derriere, bumping and grinding herself to a burlesque climax. This sounds facetious, but in actuality the burlesque routine is coming into vogue in flamenco, a development of such bad taste (performed by *bailaores* and *bailaoras* alike) that it cannot be attacked with enough vehemence. It is done not by «bumping» so much as by «grinding», the circular motion of the hips in a cheap, suggestive manner completely out of keeping with the *Baile* flamenco.

In the *baile grande* the *bailaora* dances as stationarily as possible. This will allow her to concentrate on the *jondo* elements of her dance, and will better hold the public's attention. Rapid turns and sudden stops (minor climaxes), with a corresponding raising of the arms slowly and intensely, can be very effective.

The *zapateado* (footwork), used sparsely and with good taste, can intensify the female dance. If overdone, as it often is, the viewer will become bored and lose the trend of the dance. The *zapateado* (an intricate interplay of heel and toe taps, utilizing both feet) is often over-emphasized with the purpose of showing off technique, or of taking up time in an uninspired dance.

The playing of the *pitos* is a complex and effective practice. By snapping the middle and the ring fingers (rarely the little finger) against the thumb of the right hand, combined with the thumb and the middle finger of the left hand, a fascinating set of intricate rhythms and counter-rhythms can be played. In addition, a «secret» technique that is not often divulged to newcomers (unless they are astute enough to catch it) is used, which is a clacking sound made by the tongue which sounds very similar to finger-snapping. This same vocal technique is also used in conjuntion with the *palmas*, and helps explain why one expert playing the *pitos* or the *palmas* can sound like an entire orchestra. The playing of the *pitos* strongly and well is difficult, and very important in both the female and the male dance.

The use of castanets is an excellent way to destroy the *jondo* effect of a dance. The castanets, if used at all, should be used in such regional-flamenco dances as the *sevillanas* and the *fandangos de Huelva*, and perhaps in a few other light rhythms. They should never be used in the *baile grande,* as they lend a distraction which is incongruous with the *jondo* and, worse, they detract from the hand and arm movements, the very basis of the feminine dance. The most *jondo* of flamenco dances, the *siguiriyas,* is being danced more and more with castanets, a development which causes it to lose much of its potential meaning.

Another time-honored way of cutting down the effectiveness of a dance is to swing into a gay rhythm (usually a fast *bulerías*) at the end of a *baile grande*. This is done, strangely enough, so as not to leave the public with the very effect that the dancer has attempted to build up throughout her entire dance, and also as a proven way to draw more applause from an ignorant audience. There is little sense in crusading against this practice, however, as it is too strongly entrenched in today's flamenco dance. The most that can be asked is that the dancer use a slow «*bulerías a golpe*» at these moments, instead of a thoroughly non-esthetic fast *bulerías*.

(2) *Baile grande* (and *intermedio*), *male*. Only the *bailaores* who are, or can simulate that they are, honest-to-goodness men can effectively dance the *baile grande*. It is a dance of passion, virility and arrogance.

The scarcity of good, manly *bailaores*, I believe, is due to the fact that the *Baile* demands *bailaores* with a certain rare personality; a man who can exhibit his emotions and passions and body unconditionally, and yet remain uneffeminate. Most manly *bailaores* dance coldly, relying on their technique to transmit what they wish to communicate. They are afraid, or unable, to reveal their inner passions, to let themselves go, because it is just not in their physiological makeup. Others, of effeminate nature, have the ability to appear completely masculine when they dance. It can be said that the outstanding male dancers of the *baile grande* are of two types; those who are truly masculine and who are able to «let themselves go», and those who are definitely effeminate, but who possess the ability to tranform themselves into *machos* (real men) when they dance. Both types are rare, with a resultant lack of truly moving male dancers.

The *bailaor* carries his body straight, perhaps bending back slightly at the waist. There is no pattern of movement, except that he moves around as little as possible within the possibilities of the effect desired. He is fluid, slightly exaggerated, developing his movements from slow and intense to perhaps suddenly rapid, with an unexpected stop. His footwork is strong, clear, pronounced, his arms and hands slightly curved, without the flexibility of the female arms. He does not move his hands circularly as the *bailaora,* but rather guards the strong line of the arm, his fingers straight except when playing the *pitos.* His *pitos* are forceful, as they are a strong asset for the *bailaor.* Showy acrobatics are avoided (sliding along the floor on the kness, throwing himself down on his hip and thigh, spinning around on the floor on one knee, jumping onto, and off of, tables etc.), as should the even less flamenco acrobatics of doing the splits, revolving on the legs and one arm, and such, which can be seen all too frequently. In short, we can say that the *jondo* dance of the great *bailaor* will contain passion, dignity, force, and manliness, as well as the essentials *duende,* tastefulness, and a superior *compás.*

(3) *Baile chico,* male or female. Here the same basic techniques are used, as described in (1) and (2), but the stoppes are lifted. Gaiety takes the place of melancholy, faces are illuminated, movements become faster, festive *palmas* and *pitos* and the rhythms and counter-rhythms of a driving guitar lead the dancers to a carefree exuberance. Increased footwork, flashing colours, whirling stops, slow, sadness-tinged beginnings again led by the song, guitar and *jaleo* into uncontained gaiety. The dances become lighter, more suggestive, humorous. Flowers fly from whirling heads, dresses rise above blurred hips. Merriment is the mood, Gaiety king, but... care has to be taken. Many *chico* dances are spoiled by the dancer completely abandoning restraint and frenziedly stomping about the floor in an ungraceful loss of dignity. Dignity is basic. If lost, the dance is no longer flamenco.

(4) *Mixed dancing.* The themes of mixed dances are love, jealousy, passion, difficulties interrupting or denying love, trio complications, and such. The dancers will communicate their love or anger by their *zapateados,* looks, and *pitos,* or by their castanets, if they use them. You will notice that one dancer will tap out a *zapateado,* and the other will answer. If they are «talking» and «answering» frequently and loudly, the chances are they are arguing. In nearly all mixed dances one of the dancers will make the other jealous by chasing after a third dancer, or an imaginary partner. The usual ways of ending the mixed dances are the man dominating the woman and dragging her off stage by the hair, the woman doing the same to the man, the couple exiting in a «happy-ever-after» embrace, or each dancer stomping furiously off of opposite ends of the stage.

To be effective, the dancers have to throw themselves into mixed dancing wholeheartedly. If they are portraying love or hate, they should momentarily love or hate, as it is obvious when one of the dancers is off in a day-dream, or intensely dislikes his partner, or is vainly dancing for himself. Mixed dancing is usually entertaining, interesting, and, during the rare times when both dancers can escape themselves and momentarily live their dance, very moving.

Many people are under the impression that each of the various movements of flamenco has a specific meaning, and that in turn each dance is conveying a particular story. For instance, one misconception is that a dancer raising his arms (towards heaven) symbolizes praying, and that this fits into a particular story that is supposedly being unfolded. The truth is that the techniques and movements in flamenco are not symbolic in themselves, and that in a solo dance no actual story is being told. The dancer utilizes the techniques and movements of his dance to help him to express his inner self, and whatever passions or moods are affecting his inner self at the time he is dancing. For this reason the guitarist and the singer are so necessary for the dancer, as

65

they set the mood, and incite the inner fire of the dancer so that he must release these passions through his dance. Consequently, the same movement or technique can denote tragedy or gaiety, love or hate, depending on the manner in which it is done, and the mood of the dance and dancer. Dancing is much like abstract painting; two viewers will be moved differently by the same dance, and the same viewer will be moved differently by the same dance seen on separate occasions, (depending also on the mood of the viewer).

A story of sorts may be unfolded in a mixed dance, as we have seen, but more than a story, the dancers are interpreting a variety of moods and feelings that will be understood by the public. The story itself will rarely become more complicated than boy meets girl, they fall in love, girl flirts with another boy, original boy jealously beats on second boy and triumphantly carries off the admiring Miss. The story is secondary; primarily important are the emotions on which the story is based.

All who have seen commercial dancing will have marveled at, and perhaps wondered about, the picturesque costumes worn by the *bailaoras*. These are the result of many years of evolution. We can readily see, in photos, paintings, and sketches of the last century, that the flamenco wear of that period was nearly identical to the street wear. Details included a tight-fitting waist and upper body of the dress; skirts to the ankles, full, voluminous sleeves, fringed shawls (*mantones*), large combs worn in the hair (*peinetas*), *mantillas*, full petticoats and, for special occasions, a special dress with a short train (*bata de cola*). The main difference between street and dance wear was that the dance dress had a much more ample skirt, which billowed and rose nicely on turns, and a ruffle at the bottom, which facilitated movement. With time the dance dresses became more and more exaggerated, until arriving at the two styles we know today. 1) The *bata de cola* developed a longer and longer train, until it became a rather senseless art just to be able to move it around esthetically and gracefully. 2) The more common-type dress kept inching up from the ankles, while adding more and more ruffles, until reaching the modern extreme (not in wide practice, thank goodness) of mini. In the process the full sleeves were gradually lost, and plunging necklines swept into the scene. These changes were, of course, introduced so as to give the casual spectator in commercial establishments a bigger thrill. The shows became all legs and cleavage, while the emphasis on good dancing dropped alarmingly. What we might call «girlie flamenco». Happily, there are those few female dancers who have successfully resisted this trend, and who today are leading a return to the less flashy dance fashions of old.

As regards the gypsies, they adopted this Andalusian style of dress, and proceeded to make their inevitable innovations by adding polka dots to the dresses, and by developing a flairing skirt and an accompanying full-sleeved blouse, sometimes tied at the waist. With a tenacity peculiar to the gypsies, they were the last to succumb to the modern «universal» way of dressing, and even now it is possible to encounter gypsies dressed in the traditional manner. This way of dressing is now associated more with gypsy than with Andalusian women, and the dresses are consequently referred to as «*trajes de gitana*».

The ranch men in Andalusia, above all the bull ranch foremen (*mayorales*), have better managed to authentically maintain their traditional *trajes cortos,* boots, and broad-brimmed hats. The regal capes and broad-brimmed hats of the city man nearly disappeared entirely. The capes are now somewhat fashionable among students and artistic groups in the larger cities.

However, in commercial flamenco establishments this style of dress has been preserved intact by the male dancers. Their more formal *trajes cortos* are usually set off by white shirts ruffled on the chest and cuffs, while less formal gypsy wear might include a polka dot shirt tied at the waist, and a polka dot neckerchief. Capes and broad-brimmed hats are also frequently used, and boots, much like those used on the ranch, of varying height.

There are a few highly paid dress makers and tailors who dedicate themselves to this art, and the best of them have become nearly as renowned as the artists they fit. Those in Spain are excellent and relatively low-priced (in comparison with other countries). In Mexico City there are several good, medium-priced craftsmen. In the United States there are also a few such craftsmen, notably in New York, but the quantities of money asked are usually as spectacular as the costumes.

As a fitting finish to this chapter I had the intention of listing some of the better flamenco dancers of today, as I have done with the singers and guitarists (and have done with the dancers in other editions), but find that a list of authentically good dancers is much harder to come by. Nearly all the acclaimed flamenco dancers today dance commercially, which signifies that they are necessarily carriers of the mannerisms, affectations and habits most liked by their unknowing public. This, combined with the deadly night-after-night routine, can only lead to dancers who prostitute and vulgarize themselves until they lose their sometimes great potential.

What are some of the bad habits they acquire? Let us start with the fact that they all use routines, danced identically night after night. No *duende* can survive this. Their boredom is insufferable, which they attempt to relieve with their constant joking with, and often malicious ribbing of, the other components of the group. Then there is the excessive use of castanets at all the wrong moments; the *bailaoras* dressing up like *bailaores,* a la Carmen Amaya, and offering long routines of thoroughly unfeminine footwork; false passions and faces, like bad theatre; the groping choreography of dance troupes in search of originality; impossibly long and boring dances (the ultimate in this trend, in my experience, was a 27 minute routine of *siguiriyas por martinetes,* about four times the length of a dance that might hold the public's attention and be meaningful); and so forth. Equally disheartening is the spectacle of the public eating it all up, thereby encouraging the artists on to even worse taste.

Do these commercially-orientated dancers let their hair down at *juergas* and dance in an authentic manner? Rarely. The crowds, the applause, the stage, the money, the fame quickly drive all desire for authenticity from them. They actually come to belittle good natural dancing as oversimplified and primitive, forgetting (if they ever knew) that such dancing, in flamenco at least, is the only that arrives to the heart, that a fluid, non-theatrical play of arms and upper torso and a release of *duende* slowly and at close quarters, are the only factors that matter. Factors that are almost never created in a commercial atmosphere.

Thus, from a purely flamenco point of view (not theatrical), a list of good dancers is not relevant. It would be pitifully small.

THE GUITAR

Introduction

In order to talk of the flamenco guitar, certain preliminary explanations of guitar terms and playing techniques are necessary. Included in this list are the terms *toque, falsetas,* and *compás,* the right-hand playing techniques *rasgueado (rasgueo), pulgar, picado, arpegio,* and *trémolo,* and the left-hand playing techniques *ligados* and chording.

The term *toque* is usually thought of as «a guitar piece or composition.» Actually it is neither — there are no guitar «pieces» in flamenco, and the word «composition» falls far short of the true meaning of the word. The all-inclusive meaning of the word *Toque* is «all flamenco played on the guitar». The word *toque,* with a small «t», refers to a particular segment of the all-inclusive *Toque.* Examples: (a) the *toque jondo* is a sub-division of the overall *Toque;* (b) the *toque* of the *soleares* (all of which is played within the traditional framework and basic *compás* of the *soleares)* is a particular segment of the all-inclusive *Toque,* and is included within the sub-division of the *toque jondo.* These definitions also apply to the *Cante (cante)* and the *Baile (baile).*

Falsetas are the melodic variations inserted into a *toque* that depart from the basic techniques of *rasgueados* and strumming.

The most important element of playing good flamenco (other than the *duende),* and the most basic, is the mastery of the *compás.* Without the *compás* the guitarist is playing his own type of music, perhaps flamenco in nature, but not true flamenco. Regardless of the proficiency of his technique, a guitarist will be mentally dismissed from the minds of *aficionados* if he loses the *compás.* Those who have a natural sense of rhythm have no great problem; the *compás* will come with time and experience, working its way into the sub-conscious so that it is perfectly kept without effort or thought. Others, more unfortunate, have to memorize the *compás* of each *toque,* and with great concentration attempt to stay with it. Obviously the performance of these luckless guitarists suffers with their inability to move freely within their *toque.*

As occurs in the *Cante,* the flamenco guitarist may sometimes purposely stray from the *compás* in order to achieve an effect. This practice is less justifiable in the *Toque* as there is no need for such devices. It does not usually enhance the self-expression of the guitarist; to the contrary, it loses the thread of the *toque,* damaging whatever *duende* the

69

guitarist may be conveying. The great guitarist Sabicas will often deter considerably from the *compás* in his solo interpretations of the *siguiriyas*. He does this for the sake of virtuosity, not in the cause of emotional and artistic improvement.

The most important right-hand flamenco guitar-playing techniques are the *rasgueado* and the *pulgar* (thumb). The *rasgueado* consists of running the fingers over the strings individually, but in a continuous motion, producing a thunderous, rolling effect. The meaning of the term is also generally extended to include the strumming (stroking) of the strings by the fingers as a group, propelled by crisp wrist movements. There are various types of *rasgueados*, too intricate to explain individually, each of which produces a distinct effect. The *rasgueado* is the basic playing technique of flamenco, and one of the most difficult to perfect.

The thumb *(pulgar)* is the fastest finger of the hand, and when developed properly, can achieve astonishing effects. It is used to strike strings in sequence, achieving a series of individually struck notes which can be interweaved with any number of *ligados*. It is often used in combination with the index finger. I have known guitarists who employ only the right-hand techniques of the *pulgar* and *rasgueados*, and who play outstanding *jondo* flamenco.

The other techniques of the right hand, the *picado, arpegio* and *trémolo*, play an extremely important part in modern concert flamenco. The *picado* is the alternate striking of a string by the index and middle fingers, or, less commonly, by the middle and ring fingers, the index and ring fingers, or, rarest of all, the index and little fingers. When developed well the *picado* can be lightening fast. *Arpegios* consist of the thumb striking a bass string, with two, or three, fingers alternately striking different treble strings. There are various types of two and three finger *arpegios* which can be classed as forward, reverse, circular, and combinations. The last and least important playing technique is the *trémolo*. There are three, four, and five-sound *trémolos*, all of which entail the striking of a bass string by the thumb, and a particular treble string, usually the first, by two, three, or four fingers, alternately. The three-sound *trémolo* is usually played in this order: thumb, index, and middle fingers; the four-sound: thumb, ring, middle, and index fingers; and the five-sound: thumb, index, ring, middle, and index again. The five-sound *trémolo* is the most commonly used in flamenco, while the four and the three-sound *trémolos* are more widely used in classical playing.

Left hand techniques consist of *ligados* and chording. A *ligado* is the tecnique of pulling a finger down and off of a string, causing it to sound. This technique can be employed by all of the fingers of the left hand, except the thumb, causing a rapid, slurring effect. When well-developed, entire sections of a *toque* can be played by *ligados* without so much as touching the guitar with the right hand. Of course, utilizing *ligados* to such an extent is merely showmanship. The *ligado* is an important, basic technique, and should be well-developed by all flamenco guitarists.

«Chording» means the assuming of different chord and single string postures by the left hand, and is one of the four *(rasgueados,* thumb, *ligados)* most important playing techniques of the flamenco guitar.

The Guitarist

The guitarist is the unsung hero of flamenco. With a few notable exceptions, the guitarist is the least paid and the least acclaimed of flamenco's interpreters; an unjust condition, as the guitarist is flamenco's hardest worker. He works much harder to learn his art than the dancer or singer, as he not only has to master his instrument, but as an accompanist he has to throughly familiarize himself with all elements of the *Cante* and the *Baile.* The development of the classical style of flamenco guitar playing obligates the guitarist to spend hours every day for uninterrupted years in mastery of present day techniques. As a flamenco concert guitarist of high caliber he has to devote himself to his art as much as a Segovia or a Paderewski, with an additional task; the great flamenco guitarist is not merely an interpreter of compositions, but is himself a spontaneous composer. His material comes from within. If he does not possess an inventive genius and a sense of spontaneity, combined with deeprooted senses of *compás* and the omnipresent *duende,* he is not top flight. On top of this he lives with a constant fear of injuring his hands, arms, or fingers. Merely straining a finger tendon will interrupt and possibly end his career as a concert guitarist.

In the not distant past the flamenco guitar was basically an accompanying instrument. The guitarist that accompanied well was not expected to be a technician; in fact, the concept of modern day techniques was not even dreamed of. The guitarist of the past concentrated on the rhythm and the accompaniment, utilizing almost exclusively the basic right-hand techniques of *rasgueado,* thumb, and simple *picado.* The left hand assumed only the basic chords of the particular *toque,* combined with many *ligados.*

Then a young boy, who began his guitar career as an accompanist during the *café cantante* period of the last century, revolutionized to the core the techniques of the flamenco guitar. This boy, Ramón Montoya, was endowed with a creative genius which is unexcelled in the known history of flamenco. He greatly admired the classical guitar style, and was strongly influenced by the famous composers and classical guitarists

71

Tarrega and Llobet. He consequently adapted certain techniques of the classical guitar to the flamenco guitar, namely the *trémolo,* the *arpegio,* an increased emphasis on the *picado,* and a stronger and more difficult left hand (1). He also contributed, during his 60-odd-years as a professional guitarist, a wealth of material, styles and *toques* that have become integrated into flamenco. Every living flamenco guitarist has been strongly influenced, directly or indirectly, by the genius of Ramón Montoya. He died in 1949, the undisputed *maestro* of the flamenco guitar.

Now to pose the inevitable question. Did the integration of classical techniques into flamenco actually improve the art of the flamenco guitar?

·If the «art of the flamenco guitar» is construed to mean the complementing of the singing and·dancing by the guitar, with the objective of molding all of flamenco into one emotional entity, the answer is that the integration of these classical techniques probably did more harm than good. The decorative *trémolos* actually detract from the *toque jondo.* The *toques* of this group are of down-to-earth, emotional stuff, and are not suited for flowery nothings. The *arpegios* and *picados,* although more flamenco. should also be used sparingly and with good taste in this category. The danger lies not in the existence of these techniques, but in the fact that few guitarists have the integrity and/or the instinct to use these devices properly. Contrastingly, a good *picado* and *arpegio* fit extremely well into the makeup of the *toque chico,* adding an element of diversity and excitement previously lacking, and a little *trémolo* in the intermediate forms can enhance their characteristically flowing tranquility.

On the other hand, if we consider the «art of the flamenco guitar» to mean concert flamenco that can stand alone on a concert stage or on a long play record, the classical techniques were a definite necessity. Concert flamenco needs all of the sundry tricks and techniques that have been, and may be, developed, since what it lacks in *duende* and authenticity has to be made up for in virtuosity. It is progressive jazz as opposed to the authentic blues; virtuosity and effects on one side, emotion and depth on the other.

One danger in this virtuoso trend lies in the fact that the present day concert flamenco guitar has not only borrowed classical techniques, but is becoming increasingly classical in nature. A major reason for this is that the virtuoso, in order to develop the classical techniques, will utilize classical guitar exercises and most probably learn several classical compositions, which have a way of creeping into his flamenco. Close scrutiny of various long-play flamenco guitar records will reveal

---

(1) Before Montoya, a guitarist called Paco Lucena is credited with certain innovations of classical techniques. These were absorbed and expanded by Montoya.

many passages taken from Spanish and European classical-composers, as well as from the folklore of various countries. The interpretations of these classical flamencos are consequently becoming more and more abstract, the *compás* increasingly blurry. (A similar trend is taking place in jazz, as the progressive school grazes further and further into classical pastures).

This classical tendency may be arrested somewhat by the renewed interest in the pure, traditional flamenco, which will cause a re-realization of the importance of the unadorned *jondo* guitar.

History. The guitar was originally an accompanying instrument. It is of oriental derivation, thought to be a descendent of the *kithara* (Greek for zither), an ancient stringed instrument. It is fairly certain that it was introduced into Europe, by way of Spain, by the famous Arabian singer and musician Ziryab in the IX century A. D. Ziryab was called to Córdoba by the reigning *Califa* (Arabian ruler) to teach the court musicians songs and their accompaniments on a four stringed guitar-type instrument. In time one string, and then another, were added to Ziryab's guitar, and the present day guitar came into being. Through the compositions and virtuosity of the classicists Tarrega and Andrés Segovia, and the flamencos Ramón Montoya, Sabicas, and others, the guitar has only recently merited consideration as an art form.

The Guitar. The guitar plays an extraordinary role in the life of a dedicated guitarist. An outstanding guitar can immeasurably improve a guitarist's playing, his outlook on life and flamenco, and, to say the least, will give him great pleasure. A guitarist has only to open his case and smell the sweet dry-wood odor of an old guitar to feel a certain luxurious enjoyment. As he strokes the deep strings of a quarter-of-a-century old guitar, the sonorus, age-mellowed sound will give a thrill, a *jondo* sensation, a desire to play and to play well.

A superior guitar becomes the guitarist's passion, to be protected at all costs. It becomes a part of him, something that he can part with only with great effort and sorrow. In many cases, such a guitar will even become a status symbol, elevating just another guitarist to the level of a celebrity. There is just such a celebrated guitar in Málaga, owned by a wonderful old man called Pepe el Calderero. As a guitarist he is moving, and an excellent accompanist, but technically *(the* modern basis for judgement) mediocre. Nevertheless, among *aficionados* all over Spain he is the famous owner «*de esa Santos tan magnífica*», «of that *Santos* (name of the guitarmaker) so magnificent». He is continually tempted by fat purchase offers for his *Santos*. When I asked Pepe if he would ever sell, he replied:

«¿Hombre, pa qué?» What for? Without my guitar I'd be just another old broken-down guitarist. I would spend the money, and then what? *Ni mi Santos, ni el dinero, ni ná.* No *Santos*, no money, nothing.» (1).

Accompaniment. Sound accompaniment is of basic importance to the flamenco guitarist, and constitutes an art in itself. The outstanding accompanist has to know all of the *cantes* and *bailes* almost well enough to sing or dance them himself, and he must also be blessed with an instinct which permits him to anticipate the next move of the singer or dancer. He has to be able to follow the caprices of these performers, know when to stop, when to insert *falsetas*, how to blend himself with their moods, how to carry the singer or dancer to his climax... for the good accompanist definitely improves the performance of the other performers.

For instance, the performance of a *cantaor* can be greatly improved if the guitarist is aware of, and observes, the following unwritten rules: if the singer is particularly inspired, the accompanist should play short *falsetas* so as not to break the singer's mood. On the other hand, if the singer seems listless or undecided, the guitarist should launch into a long *falseta*, or series of *falsetas*, in order to give the singer time to regroup. The accompanist has to also take note of the condition of the singer's voice. If it seems weak or unusually hoarse, the low or high notes of the *cante* may be difficult for the singer to execute, in which case the guitarist comes on strong in an attempt to partially drown out the voice. If the voice is strong and healthy, the guitarist should stay well in the background except when playing solo *falsetas.*

Diego del Gastor, an outstanding guitarist to whom you have been introduced in an earlier *juerga*, contributed immeasurably to the excellence of the singers and dancers of that *juerga*, although only the performers and a few others recognized this. When he accompanies he is a joy to watch. He loses all track of his whereabouts and all semblance of self-consciousness as he seemingly becomes one with the singer. He instinctively knows how long the singer will hold a note, when he will suddenly pause, and exactly the type and length of *falseta* to insert to capture, and enhance, the mood. When the singer accomplishes a particularly difficult *tercio* well, Diego beams with pleasure, as if he had sung it himself, and is inspired to more intensified playing.

Many modern flamenco guitarists dislike accompanying, as they feel that it is an unrecognized art. On the surface this seems true, but among informed *aficionados* the outstanding accompanist is the recognized (if hungry) *maestro.*

---

(1) Since this was written, in 1962, Pepe sold his guitar in a moment of need. The result is just as Pepe predicted; he quickly went through the money, and now has «no Santos, no money, nothing.»

74

Peculiarities of Flamenco Guitar Playing. There are two practices that immediately distinguish a flamenco from a classical guitarist; the way of holding the guitar, and the use of the capo *(cejilla)*.

The flamenco guitarist rests the guitar, rather awkwardly, on his right thigh. This is a very proud, but impractical, posture, as it necessitates his holding his wrist at a sharp angle to the right in order to assume the classical right-hand position which is necessary if the guitarist wishes to play the modern classical techniques properly. This disadvantage is particularly pronounced in the long-armed guitarist, as it causes undue wrist and arm tension and could possibly cause tendon injury. This way of holding the guitar also makes it very difficult to see the fingerboard, and the beginning guitarist will have ample cause for cursing before he is able to play without looking.

The flamenco way of holding the guitar was perfectly acceptable in the old days, before the classical techniques were introduced to the flamenco guitar. Present day guitarists, unwilling to give up this flamenco tradition (but only too willing to give up others), will grudgingly admit that the mentioned difficulties exist, but they will often claim that they are justifiable because of the improved sound of the guitar when held in the flamenco position. To the contrary, holding the guitar in the flamenco position causes the back of the guitar to rest against, or very near, the chest of the guitarist, which has a tendency to deaden the sound. To arrest this muffling of the sound many flamenco guitarists will rest their guitars well out toward the knee, which causes them to arch over the guitar and leaves considerable distance between the guitarist's chest and the guitar. This corrects the muffling tendency, but in turn causes an even more unnatural position. The flamenco position also causes certain balancing difficulties, as the guitar has to be held solely between the right thigh and the right upper arm, with no support from the left hand, which has to be left completely free to roam the fingerboard. The flamenco guitarist will undergo long months and years of a slipping, sliding guitar and an impeded right arm circulation before this technique is mastered. Of course, the guitarist who has held the guitar in this way for many years eventually considers it a perfectly comfortable position. It is the beginner who suffers.

The classical way of holding the guitar, on the other hand, is both practical and comfortable. The left foot is rested on a foot stand, and the guitar rests snugly between the legs, the elevated left leg against the indented part of the ·guitar, the right leg supporting the bottom. The guitar is completely secure in this position, and both hands are left free for playing. This also facilitates a view of the fingerboard, natural positions for the arms and hands, and no sound-muffling problem, as the guitar is held away from the body.

Regardless of the impracticality of the flamenco guitar-holding position, it is the first test a guitarist must pass in order to be considered a true flamenco. The flamencos are proud of the very difficulty of this posture; if it is impractical, it cannot be helped — it is flamenco!

The capo *(cejilla)* is used to raise or lower the tuning of the guitar without having to actually re-tune each string By placing the capo across the neck by the second fret, for instance, the neck is in effect shortened by these two frets, and the tuning of all of the strings is raised correspondingly. This was originally practiced to facilitate the accompaniment of singers, as the guitar has to be repitched for each *cante* that is sung, in compliance with the singer's vocal range. Now it has become widely practiced to use the capo even when playing solos, due to the increased brilliance of sound achieved by raising the pitch. It is thought to sound more *«flamenco»* when the capo is used, which to a certain extent may be true. But beyond the second or third fret is exaggeration. A rule of thumb could be: the less *jondo* the *toque,* the higher the guitar can be effectively capoed.

Physical Precautions of the Guitarist. The care of the arms, hands, fingers, and even the fingernails is of utmost importance to the flamenco guitarist. The injuring of the tendon which affects the ring and the middle fingers of the right hand is a common, and often incurable, misfortune. It may be injured, while playing the guitar, by holding the right hand in a tense, or bad, position, or by playing too many violent *rasgueados.* Apart from the guitar, this tendon could be damaged by excessive lifting, pulling, or a strong blow. Such an injury will make it impossible to utilize the *trémolo* and most *arpegios,* as I can disclose from my own experience. Some years ago I injured this particular tendon while playing in a *cuadro flamenco* in a San Francisco night club, due, I believe, to playing excessively strong *rasgueados* while accompanying. I have tried several cures, including the whirlpool and sound waves, to no avail. It has hampered my use of the ring and middle fingers and I have consequently had to give up all *trémolos* and most *arpegios.* This has caused me little consternation, however, as the «earthy» flamenco can be played without these techniques. The well-known guitarist Perico el del Lunar suffered the same fate, and he continued playing in a magnificent *jondo* style. Nevertheless, this would be disasterous to the concert flamenco guitarist.

Flamenco guitarists with easily breakable fingernails suffer countless minor misfortunes, as the fingernails of the right hand are instrumental in all of the playing techniques. The nails are worn at varying lengths according to the preference of the guitarist, and they are employed in different manners. Some guitarists insist that the string must bounce off of the tip of the finger (or thumb) onto the nail in order to attain the proper sound. Others use the nail alone to strike the string, which produces a sharper, twangier sound. In either case, if a particular fingernail is broken, the corresponding finger will miss its intended string, or at least nullify the sound, infuriating the guitarist and causing him to scrounge through women's cosmetics departments in search of nail strengtheners. Desperate guitarists try clear Geletin (orally), Revalon's Nail Fix with tissue paper, types of hard glue, applying raw garlic to the nails, vitamins expressly marketed for strengthening finger nails, hand baths, and so forth. Such practices can be most embarrasing, and at times socially unacceptable. Fortunately, this weak nail condition seems to disappear with time in most cases, although there are guitarists who are plagued by this seemingly unimportant inconvenience for life.

The flamenco guitar today.—As is fitting in modern life, the flamenco guitar has become industrialized. Assembly line guitarists and interpretations, fast, nervous, duende-less playing, fierce competition, and, inevitable in the process of industrialization, the annulation of personality as all flamenco guitarists sound more alike each day.

Few guitarists are able to resist, or even attempt to resist, this destruction of their individuality. Fortunately, however, a few do remain islands apart, and these individualists stand out more each day as industrialization leaves them further and further behind. The resultant wide separation of styles and emotional direction can be readily demonstrated on records by listening to any of the moderns (Sabicas, or Paco de Lucia, on any of their records), and Perico el del Lunar on the Hispavox Antología del Cante Flamenco.

First, let us listen to, for instance, Sabicas. We are immediately struck by his phenomenal technique; thundering *rasgueados,* lightening *picados* and thumb work, crystal clear *arpegios* and *trémolos,* astounding chording effects and *ligados,* a deluge of notes and more notes. We are left breathless, awe-struck. How can he play so perfectly, have such inventive genius to create most of his complex material, weave in and around the *compás* with such natural ease? Sabicas, great virtuoso of the flamenco guitar!

Then we put on one of the Anthology records featuring Perico el del Lunar, until his death in 1964 one of the few masters of the art of accompanying the *Cante*. Perico could accompany anything that was sung, and a few *cantes* that had been forgotten. He knew the *Cante* better than most *cantaores,* and probably better than any other guitarist with the illustrious exception of Manolo de Huelva. The record spins, and Perico plays an introduction, subdued, quiet, preparing the way for the singer. His style is simple and unassuming, effortless, and somehow ingenious. He has the talent of capturing the mood of each *cante,* and of influencing the singer to greater emotional depth. He remains in the background, and yet is unpretentiously in the foreground, inserting always the appropriate *falseta* to enhance the feeling of the *cante*. His *falsetas* are in excellent taste, simple and *jondo*. We are not left in awe, nor are we breathless. But we are left with a feeling that we have heard something important; the combination of a guitar and a singer creating an unforgettable *jondo* flamenco, steeped in *duende*.

Are there many left of the old school? I am afraid not. In today's «mod» world such guitarists are not fashionable, and they scrape by playing in fewer and fewer *juergas* for a diminishing group of sensitive *aficionados* who have somehow also escaped industrialization. The best and most individualistic of these guitarists, to my mind, is Diego del Gastor, a gypsy who describes himself a «good *aficionado*», who has passed his 60-some years in or near Morón de la Frontera creating and playing his own material, always indifferent to the commercial temptations surrounding him. Diego can justly be described as the «essence of the flamenco guitar»; to hear him at his best is to hear the flamenco guitar at its most expressive.

Another guitarist capable of much majesty and emotion in his playing is the legendary Manolo de Huelva, now in his seventies, living in Sevilla nearly completely retired from all guitar activity.

Antonio Sanlúcar, Vargas Araceli and a few others are also well worth listening to. Among those who participate in the commercial flamenco world but are still capable of subtlety and emotion in their playing we can cite two outstanding examples, Melchor de Marchena and Pedro del Valle, son of the late Perico el del Lunar. Melchor, accompanying the *cante* (above all *por siguiriyas*), can play magnificently, and Pedro, when not virtuositizing, knows well the very flamenco, beautiful old-time style of his father.

What can we say of the «industrialized» guitarists of today? Nearly all of them are knowledgeable accompanists of both the song and the dance, as before achieving their goal of recital guitarists, they pass through an extended apprenticeship accompanying commercial flamenco groups. The authentic virtuoso, however, is never content merely accompanying, but ever aspires to the position where he can strictly play solo. Among the virtuosos, Sabicas has long reigned king of them all, a claim strongly disputed today by the 23-year-old marvel, Paco de Lucia. Not lagging far behind them are a bevy of excellent modern-style guitarists, including Alberto Vélez, Andrés Bautista, Benito Palacio, Carlos Ramos, Esteban Sanlúcar, Juan Carmona «Habichuela», Juan Maya «Marote», Juan Serrano, Justo de Badajoz, Luis Maravilla, Manuel Moreno «Morao», Mario Escudero, Niño Ricardo, Paco de Antequera, Paco del Gastor, Pepe Martínez, Víctor Monge «Serranito»... and others, a surprising number of others, who play the modern style of flamenco guitar extremely well, a fact that again demonstrates that the principal factor in this style of playing is neither genius nor flamenco instinct, but long hours and years of hard work in the form of constant practice. If nothing else, the modern style is democratic, for any reasonably talented guitarist can arrive if he works hard enough at it and has a bit of contact with flamenco.

You have left a few guitarists out, the reader might say. What of Carlos Montoya, for example? A likeable showman who used to play passable flamenco. And Manuel Cano? More classical than flamenco, he lurks about the outer fringes of flamenco doing more harm than good with his campaign to «sophisticate the flamenco guitar». And the famous Manitas de Plata? A farce among flamenco guitarists, alarmingly deficient in his knowledge of flamenco, generally off even in his *compás,* of mediocre technique, but good, if nothing else, for a laugh.

THE JALEO

The *jaleo* is a necessary and intricate component of flamenco. It usually serves as an accompaniment and encouragement for flamenco's other components, but I have also heard *cuadros* perform the *jaleo* very effectively as a solo number.

The *jaleo* is basically made up of hand-clapping and shouts of encouragement, and can also be supplemented by finger-snapping and rhythmical punctuations with the feet (from a sitting position).

The hand-clapping is composed of two techniques: (1) the middle three fingers of the right hand striking the extended palm of the left, producing sharp, penetrating sounds. This technique can be .developed to a machine-gun rapidity, and is used mainly in the faster rhythms; (2) the cupped palms of both hands coming together, producing a hollow, more *jondo* sound, which is used mainly in the slower rhythms. Technique (1) can also be supplemented by a clacking movement of the tongue, which, done strongly and well, will sound like another handclap.

Three good *jaleadores* (performers of *jaleo*) can sound like ten. One will carry the rhythm, another the counter-rhythm, and the third will weave in and about the *jaleo* of the other two. If there are more *jaleadores*, they will select one of these three courses, adding an exciting impetus and strength.

Among the shouts of encouragement will be heard *olé* (approval), *así se canta* or *así se baila* (that's the way to sing, or dance), and an infinite number of others, usually spontaneous, often humorous.

The *pitos* are a lesser used *jaleo* technique, not being loud enough to compete with the *palmas* and the shouts.

Uninitiated spectators will often attempt to join in on the *jaleo*, not realizing that it is a science in itself. Sadly enough for the non-performer, none of flamenco's components, including the *jaleo*, can be attempted successfully without extensive training.

RECITING

Singing is by no means the only way of expressing poetry in flamenco. Reciting also plays an important role, and it is the rare *juerga* at which someone does not break forth with a poem by García Lorca or another of the «flamenco» poets. These moments can be surprisingly stirring, especially when well accompanied by the guitar.

COMEDY

There is a branch of flamenco, and group of artists, that has been largely ignored by all writers on the subject, including, to date, myself. Strangely enough, I should add, for these artists are among the most entertaining and spontaneous in flamenco. Who, or what, are they? We have talked about singers, dancers, guitarists, *jaleadores,* and reciters. What can be left?

The artists in question are hard to categorize. They sing a little, but are not considered singers. They dance, recite, and may even play the guitar, but are not specialists in any of these fields. They do all of these things, but their main role is still another: they are flamenco's comedians.

And they are funny, so funny (if you understand Spanish) that, when in good form, they can keep any group in stitches. They fit perfectly into *juergas,* when their humor mixes delightfully with the *bulerías* and other light flamenco of the first sparkling hours.

Some of the better-known of these artists are:

El Gasolina	El Gran Simona
El Brillantina	Emilio «El Moro»
El Gringo	La Coriana

81

FLAMENCO AND THE NON-SPANIARD

Introduction

The non-Spanish *aficionado* should be warned of one thing — regardless of his proficiency in performing flamenco, or his accumulation of knowledge about flamenco, he will always be thought of, and referred to, as that fellow who performs well, or knows a lot, *considering* he is a foreigner. Rarely will he be accepted on the level of the *andaluz.* This is due to a rooted belief that only the *andaluces* can perform, or even understand, flamenco properly. This belief is so strongly imbedded in the nature of the *andaluz* that even if disproven through discussion or performance, it remains intact. Like the Japanese in judo and the Americans in jazz, the southern Spaniard hates to admit that other races are capable of performing, of even fully grasping, his art.

Hemingway and other non-Spanish bullfight critics have had to contend with the same attitude. On the surface, Hemingway was accepted by Spanish *aficionados* as a true critic. But in event of any serious discussion or argument about the bulls, his viewpoint could always be discounted if only because he was a foreigner. This same reasoning is prevalent in flamenco.

Roughly, the hierarchy of flamenco is as follows:

Andaluces, performers and then *aficionados,* the older the wiser.
Other Spaniards.
Latin Americans.
All others.

This manner of thinking is changing gradually as more and more non-Spaniards become interested in flamenco. In the meantime, expect and accept this attitude and your flamenco days will be a lot happier.

82

THE CANTE AND THE NON-SPANIARD

The *Cante* is the least likely flamenco form to be mastered by a non-Spaniard. The language alone takes years to dominate to a sufficient degree and is, of course, the principal reason why few non-Spaniards take up the *Cante* seriously.

There are exceptions. A few non-Spaniards have thrown themselves very seriously into the subject, and have emerged with impressive knowledge about the various forms and how they should be sung. One woman, Elaine Dames, competed in the 1959 Córdoba *Concurso de Cante Jondo*. Another, Moreen Carnes (María la Marrurra), recently cut a Spanish LP, accompanied by Melchor de Marchena.

But perhaps the most interesting example of a non-Spanish singer that I know of is the Pakistanian Aziz Balouch, a singer of both Pakistanian folk songs and flamenco. In his book dealing principally with himself, and secondarily with the evolution and origin of *cante jondo*, Mr. Balouch claims that flamenco is a direct descendant of Indo-Pakistanian religious and folk songs. Based on this premise (very likely correct, at least in part), and upon his ability to sing both flamenco and Pakistanian folklore, Mr. Balouch sets about to purify the flamenco «way of life» by applying Yoga and operatic training techniques to the flamenco singer. He suggests the following:

(1) Abstention from all alcoholic beverages, especially during and before singing. He suggests that the singer drink weak tea or tepid water.

(2) Special dietary practices. For best results it would be wise to go all out and become a vegetarian.

(3) Limiting sexual activities to a bare minimum, with complete abstention on singing days. He has offered no solution for those who sing every night.

(4) 15 minutes of lung development a day by vigorously inhaling and exhaling fresh air.

(5) Cleaning of the nasal passages daily by sucking water up one nostril and releasing it through the other, and vice versa. Repeat as desired.

It must be recognized that these practices may give the singer a

83

clear, bell-like tone, and perhaps an operatic resonance. What Mr. Balouch apparently does not realize is that these are the very vocal qualities that the flamenco singer avoids. He also seems unaware that flamenco is not just singing, but a unique philosophy, a way of life. These people are born flamencos, with everything the word implies: quantities of booze, women whenever and wherever possible, long lasting blasts. Their art is vital, but flamenco is their life. If they are blessed with artistic talent, well and good. But they do not see things as other cultures do, and will not behave like other cultures; they won't give up life's pleasures (and the flamenco way of life is definitely a pleasurable one) and their inherent philosophy merely to delicate themselves to an art form.

Perhaps one of my memorable flamenco experiences will state more clearly what I am trying to say. It occurred in the lonely Andalusian countryside, far from civilization. As I tramped up a winding road, I found myself encompassed by a haunting voice drifting down from the surrounding hills. The voice was untrained, cracked with age, and yet carried an impact of intensity and emotion that I have never heard excelled... an old man with his plow, expressing his loneliness through song. This is the essence of flamenco, summed up in a single, simple paragraph.

I shall hazard a recommendation. Unless the beginner is possessed by a fanatical urge to become a *cantaor de flamenco,* and with an exceptional singing talent, he should not venture into this difficult territory as a performer. For, sadly enough, in not a single case have I heard a non-Spaniard that could be taken for a good Spanish flamenco singer sight unseen. Happily, the same cannot be said for the guitar or the dance, far more receptive fields for the non-Spanish *aficionado.*

THE BAILE AND THE NON-SPANIARD

The dance is the easiest and the quickest way for talented non-Spaniards to break into the commercial flamenco world as performers. Even in Spain ballet and night club choruses, and a few star spots, are sprinkled with foreigners.

The theatrical chorus is the least difficult to qualify for, requiring from the dancer, be he male or female, the following attributes; a desire to dance flamenco for art's sake, under rugged conditions and for near-starvation wages; a minimun sense of grace; an eagerness to learn (and a basic knowledge of) flamenco and regional dances, as well as an infinite amount of patience with routine, dull work; and an unquestioning obedience to the heads of the company. Let us discuss these individually.

Dancing flamenco in a traveling company chorus is no bed of roses. Within Spain it means traveling thousands of kilometers in far from comfortable conditions. It means playing all of the one-horse towns to a public that is there strictly for the kicks. It means going along for the experience, as the salary is only sufficient to maintain; nothing is put away. It means staying in second-rate pensions and hotels, eating cheap food, and sacrificing all privacy. Outside Spain, on European or American tours, conditions and pay are better, although not enough to cause prolonged rejoicing.

In the chorus the dancer must be graceful enough to avoid calling attention to himself by his ungainliness, or by stumbling or tripping too often. He has to be able to syncronize his movements with those of the rest of the chorus and to move well, but not well enough to detract attention from the stars of the show.

He needs a basic knowledge of flamenco consisting of a good *compás* and an idea of the various dance movements. Having these assets, he can quickly be taught everything that he will need as a chorus dancer. Whatever dance arragements he may know from previous lessons or experience will probably be forgotten, as he will rarely be a soloist. He will be taught the chorus arrangements that will be danced without variance night after night until he can do them asleep. Ballet companies do not change their routines for one or more seasons, and the routines become crashing bores to the dancer with imagination.

The dancer must have an absolute obedience to the heads of the Company, which consists of one thing: to keep in mind at all times that his sole purpose is to support the lead dancers. He is expected to stay gracefully in the background and to do everything in his artistic power to make the whole group look good, for which the lead dancers will gracefully take the bows. It is a thankless job, with little self-gratification, but it does give a dancer not-so-valuable experience.

The next step up from theatrical chorus groups are night club choruses. These are harder to break into. Competition is stiff, as such jobs are softer and pay better. Also, the dancer has to be better qualified, as he may have to do a solo number. As a rule, it is wiser for the foreign dancer to perfect his dance until he can break in as a minor night club attraction, especially in those clubs (the majority) in which the choruses are made up of soloists. The qualified non-Spanish dancer will have the advantage of being able to capitalize on his being non-Spanish, a curiosity-invoking phenomenon in flamenco. He will have the disadvantage of being more strongly criticized if he cannot fulfill the public's expectations.

Far better in the long run for those students of the flamenco dance who are happily disposed of time, talent, and money, is to live and study in Spain. In this manner rapid progress can be made, and the exceptional student will be able to break into the professional world further up the ladder, perhaps in first-class night clubs, or as a soloist in a theatrical company. Such dancers can also return to their native countries to perform and teach, which is more lucrative, and eliminates most competition. The drawback to this course of action is that in time the dancer loses touch with flamenco, and his dancing suffers.

The most famous non-Spanish flamenco dancers include four Mexicans, Manolo Vargas, Roberto Jiménez, Luisillo and Roberto Iglesias, and one Italian-American, José Greco. These dancers have worked their way to the top of the professional ladder, each presently having his own successful Spanish Ballet company (these companies are not exclusively flamenco, nor are they intended to be. They combine classical, modern, regional, and flamenco dances, with flamenco perhaps being their strongest component.)

It is very improbable that the non-Spanish flamenco singer and guitarist achieve the monetary success of these dancers (artistic, yes); the dancers, Spanish or non-Spanish, have the voodoo sign on the big money, glittering lights, and international fame, although the situation, through the present popularization of the *Cante* and the *Toque*, could possibly alter in the future.

THE TOQUE AND THE NON-SPANIARD

A few years ago, the guitar was the most assured way for a non-Spaniard to make a decent showing as a flamenco. As very few people understood the intricacies of the guitar, and fewer still of the flamenco guitar, the beginner who learned a few chords and a few *falsetas* of two or three *toques* was an expert guitarist, *mú flamenco* to everyone outside of Spain. Flamenco guitar records are rapidly changing this enviable condition, and the beginner today finds that he is expected to compete with the great recorded guitarists, most of whom have been playing since childhood. The new «snob» *aficionados* will corner the quavering beginner with demands to hear Sabicas' *soleares,* Lucia's *bulerías,* Niño Sinvergüenza's *tangos por media granaína,* etc. The beginner may haltingly (aware that he is in the presence of a well-versed *aficionado*) play a version of the *soleares.* If it doesn't happen to be

86

identical with Sabicas'version, our well-versed snob will tell him, in no uncertain terms, that he is not playing the *soleares* properly.

The above situation is entirely possible because of two popular misconceptions concerning the flamenco guitar; (1) that it is necessary to play like Sabicas to play good flamenco, and (2) that each *toque* is a composition never to be varied, like classical music. Idea (1) has been covered sufficiently in the guitar chapter. Idea (2) could perhaps be rehashed a little. As has been stated, each guitarist is entirely free to create what he wishes within the bounds of the *compás* and good (flamenco) taste. (Carlos Montoya, for example, has gone a little too far with his St. Louis Blues *por bulerías*). If he is a truly creative guitarist, he will never play a particular *toque* the same way twice. Various guitarists encourage the idea of flamenco compositions by publishing versions of *toques*. These pieces of music are strictly individual versions, and are not to be taken as *the* way to play that particular *toque*. Other guitarists will add to the composition impression by playing never-varying versions of a *toque* for years, signifying only that they are extremely limited guitarists without imagination or creative ability.

The non-Spanish flamenco guitar beginner will go through a period, more prolonged outside of Spain, in which he will think only of the guitar. For him, the guitar will be the beginning and the end of flamenco. He will find himself becoming irritated when the singer breaks in on the guitar introduction to begin his *cante,* or when the dancer leads the guitarist away from a beautiful *falseta* in the course of the accompaniment. He would much rather listen to guitar solos than view the entire *cuadro* perform. Gradually he will grow away from this as he begins to understand the other elements of flamenco. He will learn to appreciate the thrill of a well-sung *tercio,* the depth of a truly *jondo* dance, and the vital force contained in the *palmas* and the *jaleo* of a fast *bulerías*. He will remain basically a guitarist, but he will have the quality of being able to appreciate equally all of flamenco's components.

The non-Spaniard can learn flamenco by two methods; taking lessons, the wise and costly method, and taking material from records and tapes, the cheap and unsatisfactory method. For those studying outside of Spain, a combination of both is perhaps the wisest, with by far the strongest emphasis placed on the formal lessons. Those fortunates studying in Spain who have a sociable disposition can learn most satisfactorily by daytime lessons and nighttime *juergas,* spent in looking, listening, participating, and absorbing. This is probably the only way to capture the *duende*. It is also great fun!

Depending on his luck and personality, the non-Spaniard may have difficulties in his studies with many flamenco guitarists who deign to teach him. Regardless of the guitar instructor's economic condition or the sum agreed upon for the lessons, he makes it understood by his attitude that he is doing the student a great favor by cramming him into a tight schedule. A fairly universal rule seems to be that the student is capable of absorbing two *falsetas* per lesson, plus a little *rasgueado* and rhythm. These two *falsetas* may take the student ten minutes, or a half an hour, to learn, and the rest of the hour is supposed to be taken up by practicing what has been learned. During lessons with unsatisfactory instructors, I used to pick up the two *falsetas* in a few minutes, and then during the rest of the hour be advised from a distance whether or not I was playing them well. During those practice periods the instructor might be absorbed in any number of tasks; cooking, dressing, eating, shaving, talking on the phone, or merely being sociable with friends in another room. It is usually necessary to switch instructors until one is found with a reasonable amount of formality.

Another quite understandable trait of many guitar instructors, especially gypsies, is their reluctance to part with their favorite material. This is especially true of the guitarist who creates his own material, as he often becomes obsessed with the idea of keeping it for himself. (It is infuriating for many creative guitarists to hear every Tom, Dick, and Harry playing their creations, usually badly, causing them to lose all originality and become vulgarly popular). There was the well-known case of the gypsy guitarist who would not teach his material to his own son, nor even play the guitar in his presence. Manolo de Huelva is another advanced example of this. His hatred of being plagiarized is basically what prompted him to renounce all playing commitments other than private *juergas*. He not only declined numerous record-making propositions, but he disliked, and usually refused, to play in front of a guitarist whom he considers musician enough to copy his material. The singular Manolo has become a legendary figure as much for his extraordinary playing as for his eccentricities. He frequently used to lock himself in a hotel room with his wife and a bottle, and play up a storm for their private pleasure. As this idiosyncrasy became know, people used to gather outside of his hotel room hoping to hear him during one of these sessions (which have been described to me as «unbelievable») when he could really let himself go. He also seems untouched by the lust for money or fame. On many occasions he refused to play for private *juergas* that offered him 4000 or 5000 pesetas, unheard of sums for a guitarist in Spain (above all, at that time), only later to accept ten times less to play in a *juerga* that was to his liking. He has also been frequently known, during the course of a *juerga*, to wordlessly pack up his guitar and walk out, refusing all payment, when his audience did not pay the proper respect to his art.

Regardless of the difficulties encountered in taking flamenco guitar lessons, they must be taken. Flamenco is too complicated to be learned solely from records, books, and sheet music. The guitarist's *compás* would most certainly be hopeless, and his *falsetas* inaccurate versions of the recorded guitarist's. His technique would be bad, and his *duende* and *«aire»* non-existent.

I have listened to many non-Spanish flamenco guitarists in and out of Spain. With few exceptions they have strived overly hard to achieve technical perfection, to the inevitable detriment of their *duende*. They are not satisfied unless they laboriously play, or rather attempt to play, ridiculously complex *falsetas*. They play too fast, and they don't usually «feel» their *falsetas;* they don't accentuate them properly, and they skip from one to another in unvarying monotony. In an effort to achieve a «well-rounded» *toque,* they try to mix in all of their techniques without a thought as to whether they fit into the pattern which they have set, and into the emotional makeup of the *toque.* These faults are certainly not confined to the non-Spaniards, although they are more pronounced in the foreign guitarist due to his lack of experience and knowledge of flamenco. It has to be recognized that it is certainly difficult not to fall into bad habits when the guitarist draws his inspirations from virtuoso records, as do most non-Spanish guitarists, as many virtuoso guitarists are not-so-subtle carriers of these very failings.

It can be asserted that the foreign guitarists who are capable of meaningful playing, *que dicen algo,* are those who have spent an extended time in Spain, mixing with the true flamencos.

HARD TIMES AND PRESENT TRENDS

Back in the years 1850-1900 flamenco hit a peak which has been tabbed its «Golden Age». Since that time it has gone downhill, reaching at one stage the point of disappearance. During the past 15 years flamenco has regrouped, and is presently on a strong upswing. This section is a study of the bad times and present trends.

Before its Golden Age the music and dance of flamenco existed only as an integral part of a way of life. But little by little it gained popularity, and by the middle of the last century sharp businessmen realized that flamenco could be exploited profitably in commercial enterprises. It was then that *cafés cantantes* came into being, and the groundwork for flamenco's Golden Age was laid. *Cafés cantantes* were typical taverns which attracted customers by the novel presentation of *cuadros flamencos* (groups of flamenco performers). Each tavern had its *cuadro*, usually supplemented by guest artists from other *cafés* (1). During their heyday, the last forty years of the past century, these taverns abounded with *aficionados* who were offered a type of flamenco that decreased in purity as the century wore on.

The *cafés cantantes* have been a double-edged blade in the modern history of flamenco. They were the chief propellent of flamenco's Golden Age while, curiously enough, they were at the same time initiating flamenco's swift decline to near-extintion. Contradictory as this seems, it can be easily explained. The *cafés cantantes* were the first commercial enterprises to actually pay the flamencos for their art, resulting in the birth of the commercial flamenco artist. Things went extremely well for three or four decades. Never had there been so many outstanding flamenco performers or so many knowledgeable *aficionados*. Competition between the *cafés*, and the flamenco artists, was fierce. In time the fanfare became so great that many non-*aficionados* began coming in to see what it was all about, most of whom were interested only in the

---

(1) Some of the more famous *Cafés Cantantes* were: Sevilla —*Café Silverio* (which was owned by the singer Silverio Franconetti, one of the great singers in flamenco history), *El Burrero*, and *La Marina* (which still exists as a bar downstairs, a refuge for wayward young ladies upstairs); Málaga —*Café de Chinitas* (made immortal by García Lorca), and *El Café sin Techo*; Madrid —*El Brillante*; Jerez de la Frontera —*La Primera* (which still exists as a bar).

color of flamenco, not its art. The proprietors of the *cafés*; realizing this, urged their *cuadros* to please these new clients. From that time on, the popularity of flamenco grew as its art declined. It spread to the general public in all parts of Spain, and around the turn of the century it was finally ripe for theatrical production.

If flamenco was a little distorted when it went into the theater, it became badly disfigured there. Pure flamenco does not suit the theater, nor the insensitive masses. Many adaptations had to be made, each diluting further the purity of the flamenco presented. In the meantime, the *cafés cantantes,* the unsuspecting creators of this dilemma, lost their public and ceased to exist. The theatres and night clubs now remained the sole perpetuators of commercial flamenco. Within a period of two generations the public believed theatrical flamenco to be the true flamenco, and by midcentury (1950) pure flamenco had nearly died out, together with many of the pure artists and *aficionados.*

The following excerpt from a poem, dedicated to the untainted singer Aurelio Sellés by the poet José María Pemán, summed (and sums) up the opinion of knowledgeable *aficionados* concerning the state in which flamenco found (and still, to a lesser extent, finds) itself:

¿A dónde va esa mano de Aurelio hacia adelante?
Va a ahogar veinte gargantas de veinte cantaores
para limpiar las tablas de las escenas
del ruidoso tropel de las mentiras,
¡Y que vuelva a ser pena lo que es pena!

Where is Aurelio's hand reaching?
It is reaching out to choke twenty throats of twenty cantaores
in order to purify the platforms
of the noisy jumble of lies;
and then let sorrow again be sorrow!

But things could only get better. During this period, the double edged blade phenomenon again occurred... the theatre, itself the butcher of huge chunks of flamenco, also acted as the wandering minstrel, spreading the grandeur and color of Spanish folklore, which has resulted in a period of renewed hope for true flamenco. By means of the traveling Spanish ballets, theatrical flamenco has been introduced to vast new audiences outside of Spain.

Many of these foreign viewers were captivated by what they saw, and an influx of new *aficionados* came to Spain in search of flamenco in its proper atmosphere. These people ranged deep into the olive grove and vineyard country of Andalusia, seeking out the legendary non-commercial figures of the flamenco world. They found them in white-washed villages and towns, performing for their own pleasure, completely forgotten by all but the remaining *aficionados*. In this way these people learned what true flamenco is, and through their impetus and that of a few Spanish *aficionados*, recordings were made in the 1950's of some of the remaining *jondo* artists in the form of anthologies of flamenco. Most of these recorded singers were older men, and they remembered and revived many *cantes* and styles that were obsolete and nearly forgotten. These records appeared in France, the United States, and in other countries long before there was a market for them in Spain. When they finally did appear, they astonished the Spaniards, many of whom heard true flamenco for the first time. These records are not only re-educating the Spanish *aficionados*, but they are renewing the interest of the Spanish *cantaores* in these rare *cantes* as well, with the result that these *cantes* are being heard much more frequently, re-inserting diversity and a broadened scope to a decadent flamenco; a flamenco that was depending, among the general public, on popular renditions of a few *cantes* for its diversity. There is presently a new, strong trend to sing the *cantes* in the formal, traditional, *jondo* way. The popular idols, the Marchenas, Molinas, Valderramas, so long the Kings of flamenco, are losing ground. The names of the great *cantaores* are more and more on the lips of the people. Completely unknown artists within Spain suddenly find themselves international flamenco figures, sought after by the new *aficionados* much to their own amazement.

This renewed interest has caused flamenco to boom in the past ten years. Many promising *aficionados* are turning seriously to flamenco who would have gone into other professions a few years ago. Flamenco festivals, contests, and study-weeks, almost without exception offering the pure, are springing up everywhere. Serious records and anthologies are exploring each obsolete corner of flamenco, books and articles are praising the worthy, condeming the cheap, and groups and centers dedicated to the perpetuation of the authentic are doing what they can.

However, hand in hand with this progress we see, unraveling before our helpless eyes, the repetition of the very *café cantante* phenomenon that led flamenco to its downfall last century. Today they are called *tablaos*, and the possibility is strong that they will prove as harmful to flamenco as did their granddaddies. As was the case with the first *cafés cantantes*, the first *tablao* to open, La Zambra, in 1948, did so with the sincere intent of making available to the public the pure and traditional in the art of flamenco. The dozens of other *tablaos* that have opened their doors since then, however, have no such idealistic intentions. They are businesses, and are out for only one thing: profits. They are fully prepared, and in a way compelled, if they wish to remain open, to sacrifice everything —authenticity, purity, integrity— to the profit and loss statement. Even La Zambra has had to modify its program a bit in the interests of self-preservation; now only their small *cuadro* offers anything of value.

History, therefore, is repeating itself in a most startling way, but today we have the advantage of being forewarned, of being able to at least attempt to stem the tide. This, needless to say, is hard going. The lure of the nightly take home pay offered by the *tablaos,* night clubs, and theatrical groups is more than many fine flamenco artists are willing, or can afford, to turn down. And once into the System, they begin changing, adapting, modifying, prostituting. This is inevitable if they wish to remain.

An example of the System at work could be the following hypothetical case of Juan Fulano, a young guitarist from a small Andalusian town. Juan wants to play the guitar for a living. He loves flamenco, and he loves his guitar. Motivated by this and his family's needs, Juan approaches an agent in search of a club or theatrical booking. Upon auditioning, Juan plays a beautifully moving, primitive *siguiriyas.* The auditioner, who may or may not comprehend what he has heard, will have the following reaction:

«*Muy bonito, Juan, pero como comprenderás, eso no vende.* Very pretty, Juan, but you have to understand that it won't sell. I would advise you to concentrate on your technique. You know, throw in a lot of *arpegios* and *trémolos* and the other razzle-dazzle, and try to incorporate into your playing *falsetas* based on popular and semi-classical music. You know, give the public something they'll recognize. Also, concentrate on the fast, rhythmical stuff. That's what they eat up. Come back when you've got it worked up.»

This, of course, is the beginning of the end of the pure in Juan. Few artists can prostitute themselves and retain their *duende.* A similar reaction would be experienced by a dancer, who would be advised to (1) utilize numerous fast turns, (2) overwork her hips and bottom and whatever sex appeal she (or he) may have, (3) use much rapid staccato footwork, and (4) make cute gestures and faces. Also, she would be told that to be a modern-day dancer one has to know not only flamenco but regional and some classical dances, and to concentrate on the fast and rhythmical. The singer would have to insert more flourishes, work on attention-calling gestures, and learn how to sing popular songs to flamenco rhythms.

All of this, of course, is contradictory to the very essence of serious flamenco. I have personally viewed a number of artists who have traveled this bitter road. The famous dancer La Chunga is a distressing example. I saw her dance on numerous occasions in Mexico in 1957. She was magnificent. She knew no footwork, and consequently danced barefoot. Her costumes were simple gypsy skirts and blouses. She did not dance by arragements, but improvised as her moods demanded. Her outstanding assets, and those most difficult to find in a dancer, were the beauty and grace of her arms and hands, the suppleness of her movements, the authenticity of her facial expressions, her refreshing naiveté, her complete abandon to her *duende,* and, above all, her naturalness. There were pressures on her and her manager at the time, propagated by envious artists, and businessmen mistakenly attempting to increase her commerciality, to teach her dance arrangements, footwork, a more commercial form of flamenco. Her manager successfully avoided these commitments as long as he could, but he eventually succumbed. La Chunga began taking lessons and preparing a more elaborate wardrobe.

Soon she returned to Spain, and with great clamor was propelled to the first figure in the flamenco dancing world. I did not have an opportunity to see her again until 1960, in a night club on the Andalusian coast. It was a depressing experience. Through contact with commercial flamenco she had lost much of her authenticity, her naiveté, and, worst of all, she was no longer natural. Her movements and facial expressions were studied, with an obvious attempt at timing them to achieve the greatest effect. She did tricks with her dress, hair and body, and exploited her sex appeal, mostly in a cheap, superficial manner (causing the opposite of the desired effect). She did an excessive amount of footwork. She was no longer sure of herself, I believe in great part due to her association, as a student, with flamenco's commercial technicians. She needed someone to shake her by the shoulders and tell her to kick off her shoes and mannerisms and dance in the way in which only a few of the gifted are capable. From one of the most moving dancers I have seen, the System may possibly succeed in making her just another night club attraction.

This «system of artist commercialization», as it might be called, is not the only obstacle in the road. There is another serious one, more subtle, almost more menacing because it is more difficult to combat. It stems, oddly enough, from the very gentlemen, nearly all intellectuals, who are striving to resuscitate and perpetuate the pure in flamenco. They write most of the books, organize many of the contests, study weeks and festivals, and edit most of the records and anthologies, usually on a very scholarly level. Now I realize that this is par for the course. It happens all over the world to folk art forms that are outliving, or have outlived, their significance and urgency due to social and educational progress. It follows that the gentlemen in question, and a large segment of the public in general, must necessarily approach these folk arts from an intellectual point of view, because they are not an integral part of the disappearing art and philosophy. They have no choice but to act in the only way they know: to analyze, dissect, catalogue, and place behind glass in museums for all posterity to behold.

This is inevitable, justifiable, even historically and sociologically praiseworthy, but, still, highly regrettable, for such an overdose of intellectualism is all that is needed to hasten the art to a still earlier grave. True, there is instinctive intellectualism in all arts, no matter how folksy, among the artists themselves. That, and inspiration, is what causes creation (1). But that is a forward-surging, healthy kind of intellectualism, while today's tends to follow one of two inconvenient roads: a static clinging to the past, such as is happening in the *Cante,* or an excessive keeping-up-with-the-times, causing a high degree of sophistication wholly out of keeping with the essence of the art, as is happening with the guitar. The first road has smothered all instinct for creation, resulting in precise duplication of the *cantes* of singers of old —down to the length and placement of the «ay's», the vocal mouthing of a word— that is deadly boring to the *aficionado* with even a touch of imagination. The second road is resulting in an empty mixture of international influences far out of keeping with true flamenco. For flamenco, as anyone knows who has heard or seen it when it is worth hearing or seeing, must be instinctive, animal, spontaneous, anything but intellectual, to be great. I keep having the urge to shout to a singer: «Forget how it was sung years ago. Sing in the way you feel it, the way you must to express your own personality, not the way you've sung it six thousand times just because it was sung that way in the past. Put something of yourself into it or you're just a bloody parrot!» But I hold my peace, for the ones I would shout this to are precisely those who are incapable of escaping habit and intellect. Unfortunately, they are the vast majority, and, even more unfortunately, they feel that they are right in their easier, tradition-bound course because most of the mentioned intellectuals encourage, and even insist, that it be that way. The same holds true for the guitarist, who plays unvarying compositions time after time, year after year, or takes the modern course and tinkles away like a player piano (or both), or the dancer of set routines. Intellectualism of this type is natural and even essential in the student, but a grave defect in the veteran artist.

Which brings us to a last paradox in our discussion. As I suggest in various passages in this book, truly great flamenco can only be experienced in the intimacy of the small *juerga.* This was true in the past and it is true today, and is in itself an extremely limiting factor to the number of people who will ever truly understand what makes flamenco

---

(1) In the days when communications were limited to face-to-face conversation, and transportation to beasts of burden, flamenco contained another readymade fountain of «creation». The very non-existence of radios, phonographs, tape recorders, and easy modes of moving around forced the singer (guitarist, dancer) to approximate the *cantes (toques, bailes)* of others as much as possible by memory alone, perhaps after hearing or seeing them only two or three times. As memory is fallible, often these versions would be mistaken, and a new style of the *cante* would be born. In the process, the fancy and passion of the new creator would creep into his mistaken version, for better or for worse, sometimes with the effect of improving upon the style he was copying. This explains, of course, the many only slightly different styles of particular *cantes* that exist today. In present times this fountain of «creation» has dried up. If the singer is caught up in this time-honored process he is firmly put down as mistaken, a man that did not research his material properly.

the exceptional art that it can be. Even in Spain most people are just not interested enough to undertake the complications and expense inherent in *juergas* (see «Private Juergas» appendix). In addition, *juergas* are not considered respectable in Spain. Most Spanish men do not consider taking their wives or girls to one (this is due as much to male egoism as convention; they are freer for whatever comes up when unaccompanied), and many men even snicker boyishly if the subject is brought up. The word *«juerga»* invariably invokes scenes of debauchery, drunkenness, and prostitution in their imaginations, which, true enough, goes on occasionally, depending on who is throwing the *juerga*. The vast majority of times, howerver —we could safely state a percentage well in the nineties— a *juerga* is a most innocent affair, in which a small group of *aficionados* and artists gather together in an attempt to conjure up a few unforgettable moments of gaiety and *duende.*

Let us sum up what we have seen in this chapter. Traditional flamenco is making a strong comeback, but in an intellectual manner not at all in keeping with flamenco tradition. Many new, serious artists are entering the field, most of whom are immediately swept up and tainted by commercialism. The *tablaos,* the *cafés cantantes* of the twentieth century, are holding a prolonged tug-of-war with opposition groups of purists. Private *juergas,* the only artery to the heart of flamenco, are attended by only a small minority.

What conclusion can we draw from this jumble of facts? There is an unfortunate one that comes to me clearly, causing me to predict, without, I am afraid, much risk of mistake, that we have just a few years left, perhaps, with luck, to the end of this century, to savour a living, breathing, significant art of flamenco. After that it will surely continue to exist, but in an academic manner far removed from flesh-and-blood life, a curious and highly-sophisticated reminder of a great folk art of a more primitive age.

Luisa Maravilla emphasizes beautifully the most important aspects of the feminine dance: the arms and hands.

Castanets, traditionally not used in flamenco, besides being unsightly and distracting disturb the natural fluidity and beauty of the hands and fingers.

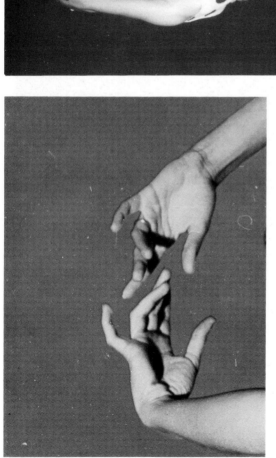

Femine hands: fluidity, grace, character without exaggeration . . . . .

Photo: Elke Stolzenberg
Male lines: virility without affectation. The dancer is El Güito.

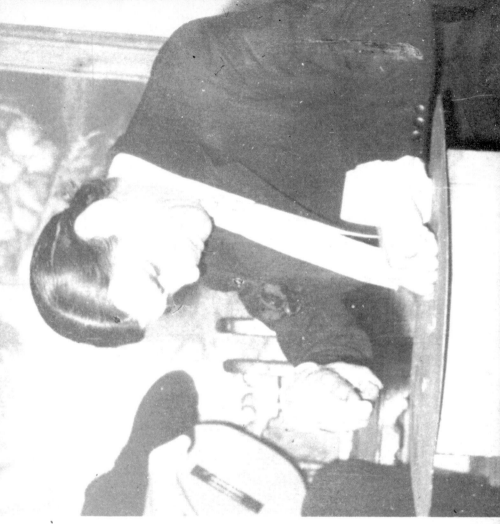

Photos: D.E. Pohren

Traditional gypsy cave attire, including lack of shoes, has been popularized in commercial flamenco circles in modern times by La Chunga and her sister, *La Chunguita* (shown above).

Upper right:

Flamenco is not all tragedy and profound sentiment. Comedy plays a highly-important role, as can be appreciated by the delighted faces of the cuadro supporting *La Coriana's* telling of a tall tale. The chuflas was the flamenco form used.

Photo: Manuel del Rey

This primitive manner of keeping the rhythm (with fingers and knuckles) has been built into an art by a few artists, such as Carmen Amaya, Vicente Escudero, Anzonini del Puerto, and *José María Peña "The Poet of the Hands"* (pictured at right).

Photo: Elke Stolzenberg

The bata de cola, an exaggerated copy of the Andalusian street wear of another age, is still a popular mode of feminine attire in the commercial flamenco circuit, admired for its beauty and difficulty of manipulation. The dancer is *Manuela Vargas*.

Photo: Vicente Ibanez

The use of the shawl (mantón) has been elevated to high art by a few dancers, such as *Blanca del Rey* (above).

Merche Esmeralda has made a study of the old-time female flamenco dance, which she dances well. This photo shows her in an attitude typical of that style.

PART III
THE ENCYCLOPEDIA OF FLAMENCO

DISCUSSION OF THE VERSES OF THE CANTE

The verses included in the Encyclopedia have been selected to be the most representative of each *cante*. The Spanish form has been guarded as closely as possible in the translations, although it was often necessary to translate the verses more or less freely in order to avoid clouding their meaning. The rhyming of the verses had to be sacrificed entirely. These verses, ingenious in their phrasing and symbolism in Spanish, lose somewhat in translation. A considerable knowledge of Andalusia and its philosophy is necessary in order to capture the true fragance of their meaning, something of which I have attempted to give during the course of this book. A brief general explanation follows, which is intended to further crystallize the significance of these verses.

The verses of the *cante* are derived from two sources: the poet, who creates them and passes them on to the people through a published work (and which are often altered to fit the personality of each interpreter), and those springing from the people themselves, created during inspired moments by *cantaores* and *aficionados*. The verses of the professional poet, profound expressions of the feelings and philosophy of the Andalusian people, contain more imagery and symbolism than those created by the people, and, as is natural, are invariably more grammatically correct.

A great majority of the verses presented here are anonymous, stemming from the common people, although some poets are also beautifully represented, including Manuel Machado, José Carlos de Luna, Federico García Lorca, and Domingo Manfredi Cano, all Andalusians, as have been, to my knowledge, all of the widely-heralded flamenco poets.

Perhaps the most colorful verses are those of the gypsies, which are distinguished by their picturesquely incorrect grammatical structure, word choice, and spelling, insertion of gypsy words, and their generally more direct and primitive expression of emotions and ideas.

I have left some of the verses with touches of incorrect spelling, which are meant to be a direct reflection on the mispronunciation not only of the gypsies, but of all the Andalusian masses. There are several unwritten rules for arriving from Castilian Spanish to the Andalusian: h's often become j's; final v's and s's are eaten; s's in the middle of a word may be entirely eaten, but will more often become h's; l's at the end of words or syllables often become r's; v's become hard b's; the

99

d is eaten in all «ado» endings of words, becoming «ao», and in some other instances *(granadina-granaína; vestida-vestía)*; the word «de» becomes «e», and words like «todo» and «para» become simply «to» and «pa»; the ll becomes y, or more often yj *(calle - caye* or *cayje)*; and so forth (1).

Examples:

<table>
<tr><td align="center">CASTILIAN</td><td align="center">ANDALUSIAN</td></tr>
<tr><td>

El día que tú naciste
¡qué triste estaría el sol
en ver que otro sol salía
con mucho más resplandor!

</td><td>

Er día que tú nasihte
¡qué trihte ehtaría er só
en be que otro só salía
con mucho má rehplandó!

</td></tr>
<tr><td>

La muchacha que yo quiero
está llenita de lunares
hasta las puntas del pelo.

</td><td>

La gachiᵃ que yo cameloᵃ
ehtá yjenita e lunare
jahta la punta der pelo.
   ᵃ *Gypsy words.*

</td></tr>
</table>

Generally speaking, however, for the sake of clarity I have stuck more to Castilian than Andalusian Spanish, sprinkling just enough *andaluz* about to remind the reader of the vast difference between reality and the printed page.

The overwhelming majority of flamenco verses deal with all aspects of love (2). Death is perhaps a distant second, followed by many topics, depending largely on the general theme and geographic location of each *cante*. Apart from the grammatical considerations already discussed, the verses are by no means sung exactly as they appear on the printed page. Lines are often repeated, words prolonged, long wails of *aaay* interjected (3). When actually heard and seen interpreted, the verses are infinitely more meaningful. That is another adventure that awaits the *aficionado!*

---

(1) Alonso Zamora Vicente has made a complete study of this in his «Dialectología Española», Ed. Gredos, Madrid, 1967, pps. 287-331.

(2) One folklorist, Francisco Rodríguez Marín, in his «El Alma de Andalucía» (The Soul of Andalusia), had to limit himself to choosing only 1,316 of the 22,000 verses dealing with love that he had gathered.

(3) Take the example of this *Siguiriya* of the legendary Manuel Torre:

Son tan grandes mis penas	*My suffering is so great*
que no caben más.	*I can bear no more.*
Yo muero loco, sin caló de nadie,	*I am dying insane, without warmth of anyone,*
en el Hospitá...	*in the hospital (insane asylum)*

In the actual singing of this verse, it may be changed thus:

Son tan grandes mis penas	*My suffering is so great*
que no caben más	*I can bear no more*
¡ayy!...	*¡ayyy!...*
que no caben más.	*I can bear no more.*
Dios mío,	*My God,*
que yo muero loco, sin caló de nadie,	*I am dying insane, without warmth of anyone,*
en el Hospitá...	*in the hospital...*

GENEALOGY OF CANTE FLAMENCO

The following genealogy is the result of extensive studies of the origins of the components of present-day flamenco. The chart only attempts to trace the basic origins of these components, along with a few of the more important secondary influences. If all of the subtle cross-currents were charted, the result would be an incoherent muddle. It will suffice keeping in mind that the Andalusian influence—predominently gypsy or *payo* depending on the particular *cante* (see Appendix No. 1)— is strong in all of these components as we know them today, regardless of their origins.

Regarding the chart on the next page, I wish to clarify that in truth no one knows which was the originating *cante,* or even if the originating *cante* is still known and sung today. There is a large school that believes that, of those known to us, the *caña* and *polo* share this honor, largely due to early references to them, and to their unique passages that are so similar to early religious chants. Another school believes the *tonás* to be the first, which is certainly a possibility (we could arbitrate and say that the three developed more or less simultaneously, which might easily have been the case). Others insist on the *soleá,* also a possibility, but, in my opinion, less likely, as it has all of the characteristics of being a less ancient offspring, further removed from religious influences, of the *caña* and *polo.*

As all but three *(danza mora, zapateado, rondeña toque)* of the charted components are believed to have been first conceived as songs, the chart has been entitled Genealogy of *«Cante»* Flamenco.

101

GENEALOGY OF CANTE FLAMENCO

Cantes probably derived from religious songs and chants of various origins (Jewish, Muslim, Christian, Gypsy, Indo-Pakistani, etc.).

Cantes probably derived from the folklore of various origins (Celtic, Arabic, Andalusian, Gypsy, Latin American, etc.).

ENCYCLOPEDIA INDEX

P. 104   Alboreás
P. 105   Alegrías
P. 106   Bamberas
P. 107   Bulerías
P. 108   Caleseras
P. 109   Campanilleros
P. 109   Cantiñas
P. 111   Caña
P. 113   Caracoles
P. 114   Carceleras
P. 115   Cartageneras
P. 116   Chuflas
P. 116   Colombianas
P. 117   Danza Mora
P. 117   Debla
P. 118   Fandangos Grandes
P. 120   Fandangos de Huelva
P. 120   Fandanguillos
P. 121   Farruca
P. 121   Garrotín
P. 122   Granaínas
P. 122   Guajiras
P. 123   Jaberas
P. 124   Jaleos
P. 124   Livianas
P. 125   Malagueñas
P. 127   Marianas
P. 127   Martinetes
P. 128   Media Granaína
P. 129   Milongas
P. 130   Mineras
P. 130   Mirabrás
P. 131   Murcianas
P. 131   Nanas
P. 132   Palmares

P. 132   Peteneras
P. 134   Playeras
P. 135   Policaña
P. 111   Polo
P. 135   Roás
P. 135   Romeras
P. 136   Rondeña (toque)
P. 136   Rondeñas
P. 137   Rosas
P. 138   Rumba Gitana
P. 138   Saetas
P. 140   Serranas
P. 141   Sevillanas
P. 142   Siguiriyas
P. 144   Soleá
P. 146   Soleá Corta
P. 144   Soleares
P. 146   Soleariya
P. 149   Tangos
P. 151   Tanguillo
P. 151   Tarantas
P. 152   Taranto
P. 152   Temporeras
P. 153   Tientos
P. 149   Tientos Canasteros
P. 154   Tiranas
P. 154   Tonás
P. 155   Trilleras
P. 156   Verdiales
P. 156   Vito
P. 157   Zambra
P. 158   Zapateado
P. 158   Zorongo Gitano
P. 160   Piropos in Song

ALBOREAS.—*Cante, baile* and *toque chico*.

The word «*alboreás*» is an abbreviation of «*alboreadas*», meaning «dawning, dawn of the day», which has led some theoreticians to believe that the *alboreás* are merely songs sung at dawn. In reality, the *alboreás* are a gypsy wedding *cante*. The word «*alboreadas*» can also be construed to mean «a happening at dawn», which is the time the *alboreás* are often sung to the newly-weds, and which could explain their connection with dawn. More romantically, it could also signify the «dawning of a new life» for the couple.

The *alboreás* are usually done to the *compás* of the *bulerías*.

En un verde prado	*In a green pasture*
tendí mi pañuelo.	*I stretched out my handkerchief.*
Salieron tres rosas	*Three roses appeared*
como tres luceros.	*like three morning stars.*
Padrinito honrao	*Righteous father,*
a tu hija ya la han coronao.	*they have crowned your daughter.*
Ay, novio, mírala bien	*Ay, bridegroom, look well at her,*
que hasta bonitos tiene los pies.	*she is pretty to the tips of her toes.*

The above verses refer to a gypsy ceremony testing the virtue of the bride-to-be. If this «virtue test» is successfully passed, it is in effect the wedding ceremony. The mother of the bride-to-be, and the parents of the bridegroom-to-be, deliver the nuptial handkerchief to an old woman who presides at this ceremony. The old woman takes the girl aside and inserts the handkerchief into her, deftly rupturing the girl's virginity, if existent. If the handkerchief is withdrawn spotted with blood, the wedding in consecrated, and a two or three day celebration ensues. If the handkerchief is withdrawn with no trace of blood, anything might happen, including a pitched battle between the families and their supporters. One thing is certain; the wedding rarely takes place. But considering that gypsy girls marry at the tender age of fourteen (or less), the ceremony has all of the probabilities of turning out well. If so, further rituals are performed (described in Donkey Back, Part I), culminated by the singing of the *alboreás* to the newly-weds.

Of course, more and more gypsies are adopting *payo* customs, including the church wedding ceremony. Only a few gypsy bands still tenaciously cling to their antique customs and rituals in this age when all remnants of regional colour are fast giving way to a fanatical drive to make three billion people look, act, and talk alike in a dull, universal togetherness.

Until just recently the gypsies considered it bad luck to sing the *alboreás* other than at weddings, and within hearing range of non-gypsies. Today, with the *alboreás* having been recorded in anthologies and sung in at least one movie, with no widespread consequences of note, this belief is generally discredited.

ALEGRIAS.—*Cante chico, baile intermedio, toque chico.*

The *alegrías* are the dominant *cante* of a group of *cantes* categorized as *«cantiñas»* (see *cantiñas* section), developed in Cádiz from the more ancient *soleares* and *jaleos*. The rhytmical count and accentuation of the *soleares* and the *alegrías* are identical, although the *alegrías* are faster, and their chord structure stresses the gay major rather than the more melancholy minor chords of the *soleares*. The *cante* and *toque* of the *alegrías* are lively and vivacious (*«alegrías»* translates «gaiety»), the *cante* probably having been influenced to some extent by the *jota*. The *baile* has developed along more *jondo* lines. As a popular *tango* verse states, one should go to the *barrio* Santa María (gypsy quarter) in Cádiz to see the *alegrías* performed with their true flavor.

As I have stated in the «Discussion of the Verses of the *Cante*», the *cantes* of flamenco are by no means sung just as they appear on the printed page. The *alegrías,* for instance, are very flexible. Examples: if we number the lines of each of the first three verses below 1, 2, 3, and 4, they will often be sung thusly: 2, 1, 2, 3, 4, 3, 4. Or, sometimes the last 3 and 4 are omitted, and a type of *remate* inserted, which could be verses four or five as they are, or verses six or seven expanded and sung 1, 1, 2, 3, or even repeating the first line four times, then the 2nd and 3rd only once. (For obvious reasons of over-complexity, I shall not go into this type of explanation for each of the *cantes* that follow in the Encyclopedia).

Aunque ponga en tu puerta	1.	*Even if they put in your doorway*
cañones de artillería,		*artillery cannons*
tengo que pasar por ella		*I would attempt to enter*
aunque me cueste la vía.		*although it cost me my life.*
Dos corazones a un tiempo	2.	*Two hearts*
se han puesto en balanza;		*are being weighed on a scale;*
uno pidiendo justicia		*one asking justice,*
otro pidiendo — venganza.		*the other — vengeance.*
Si yo supiera, compañera,	3.	*Were I to find out, companion,*
que el sol que sale te ofende,		*that the sun that shines offends you,*
con el sol me peleara		*I would fight with it*
aunque me diera la muerte.		*although it cost me my life.*

105

Cuando te vengas conmigo ¿que adónde te voy a llevar? Que a darte un paseíto por la muralla real.	4. When you come with me where am I going to take you? For a little walk alongside the great sea-wall.
¡Cómo reluce mi Cádiz! ¡Mira qué bonito está! Sobre un cachito de tierra que le ha robaíto al mar.	5. How my Cádiz shines. See how beautiful! On a little piece of land stolen from the sea.
Si vas andando rosas y lirios vas derramando.	6. You go scattering, as you walk, roses and lilies.
Ay, Dolores, ¡cómo huele tu cuerpo a flores!	7. Ay, Dolores, how your body smells of flowers!

BAMBERAS.—*Cante chico*, neither danced nor played.

In a few Andalusian towns there still exists a curious medieval tradition of erecting huge swings every spring and summer, as a sort of fair weather sport celebrating the crop harvests. Each neighborhood in the town has its swing, and there are competitions to see who can swing the highest. The swingers are usually full-skirted girls, aided by people on the ground with ropes attached to the swings. In rhythm to the swinging, the spectators sing *bamberas*, which are similar to the other *cantes camperos*, while peeking at the girls' legs. It is claimed that the *bamberas* are of Celtic origin. Their name is derived from the word *«bamba»*, the local name for swing. The Niña de los Peines has been the principal professional interpreter of the many delicious *bamberas* verses.

Eres chiquita y bonita, eres como yo te quiero, eres una campanita en las manos de un platero...	You are petite and pretty, like I want you, a little bell in the hands of a silversmith...
La niña que está en la bamba no tiene padre, ni madre, ni novio que vaya a verla, ni perrito que le ladre...	The girl that is swinging has neither father nor mother, nor boy friend that goes to see her, nor even a little dog to bark at her...
Entre sábanas de Holanda y corche de carmesí está mi amante durmiendo que parece un serafín.	Between Dutch sheets and a red coverlet lies my love, sleeping like an angel.

Eres palmera y yo dátil	You are the palm-tree and I the date,
tú eres alta y yo me enreo.	you tall and I entwined about you.
Eres la rosa fragante	You are the fragrant rose
del jardín de mi deseo.	of my garden of desire.

BULERIAS.—*Cante, baile* and *toque chico.*

The *bulerías* occupy a special and supreme position in the world of flamenco. They are its most flexible form, constantly undergoing change, wide-open to spontaneity, full of humor and yet intrinsically majestic, all of which combine to make them flamenco's run-away festive favorite.

There are many opinions concerning the origin of the *bulerías.* The two most feasible theories are: 1) they were developed from the *alegrías;* 2) they began as a *remate* with which the singer Loco Mateo ended his *soleares.* In my opinion, the answer lies somewhere inbetween. The *bulerías* were likely another *cantiña* (see *cantiña* section), set to the rhythm of the *alegrías,* but generally given the three-line verse form of the *soleá corta.*

There are two basic ways of interpreting the *bulerías.* The most usual today is at a fast, machine-gun-like clip, while the other is a bit slower and more stately, variously called «*a golpe*», «*soleá por bulerías*», or «*bulerías por soleá*». There are several styles within the *cante,* usually referred to by their places of birth (Utrera, Alcalá, Triana, Jerez, Los Puertos, Cádiz). However, these styles are generally intermixed today, and few *cantaores* or *aficionados* presently distinguish between them.

And their name? Again, no one knows, but theories abound. The most popularly accepted, and most likely, is that «*bulería*» was derived from «*burlería*» (from *burlar,* to make fun of). R. Molina and A. Mairena suggest that it may have come from «*bolera*» (19th century dance), by way of *bolera-bolería-bulería.* This would lead to the unlikely conclusion that the *bulerías* originated as a popular 19th century dance. And so forth.

Due to the extreme adaptability of the *bulerías,* they are flamenco's most badly abused *cante,* having to suffer never-ending mixtures and brews both national and international. They are one of the most difficult dances to dominate, as a great deal of *gracia* and sense of rhythm are essential. They are also the most technically intricate and difficult flamenco form for the guitarist, especially at the ridiculous pace they are so often played at today.

With very few exceptions, the *bulerías* only truly come alive under the magic touch of gypsies.

107

The following are typical verses:

Tengo en mi casa un jardín
por si viene un contratiempo
vender yo flores pá ti.

In my house I have a garden
in order to sell flowers for you
if bad times come.

A mi me duele, me duele
la boquita de decirte,
gitana, si tú me quieres.

My mouth hurts me,
gitana, from asking you
if you love me.

Lo he dicho, y lo voy hacé
un teléfono sin hilo
pá sabé de tu queré...

I'm going to make, as I have said,
a wireless telephone
in order to know of your love...

Er queré quita er sentío;
lo digo por esperiensia,
porque a mi m'ha suseío.

Love destroys the senses;
I talk through experience
because it has happened to me.

A mi me daban, me daban,
tentaciones de locura
cuando de ti me acordaba.

I had
crazy temptations
whenever I thought of you.

Cuando pases por mi vera
orvía que me has querido
y no me mires siquiera.

When you pass by me
forget that you have loved me
and don't even glance my way.

En un cuartito los dos,
veneno que tú me dieras,
veneno tomara yo.

If we were in a room together
I would do anything for you,
even take poison.

Tu mare no dice ná;
tu mare es de las aue muerden
con la boquita cerrá.

Your mother says nothing;
she is one of those who bites
with her mouth closed.

CALESERAS.—*Cante chico*, neither danced nor played.

A «*calesero*» is the driver of a horse-drawn buggy. The *caleseras*, now forgotten, were the *cante* that helped these drivers pass the long hours of the open road. The *compás* was to the trot of the horse's hooves, slow or fast as the case may be. Their verses were usually about animals, the country, and love. They were thought to be a much gaier descendent of the *serrana*.

Anda jaquita graciosa
mueve las manos airosa
y que tu gracia y tu brío
sean la estampa del señorío.

Come on, little pony,
raise your hooves high,
and may your grace and dash
carry the stamp of stateliness.

Tengo una yegua rubia,
rubia castaña,
la rubia de Lucena
se llama la yegua.

I have a blonde mare,
a chestnut mare,
she is called
the Blonde of Lucena.

108

CAMPANILLEROS.—*Cante* and *toque chico,* not danced.

The *campanilleros* are a traditional *cante* sung by the members of religious processions called the «Rosario de la Aurora» (Rosary at dawn). These processions leave at dawn from their churches for various religious motives, proceeding through the streets singing the *campanilleros,* en masse, to the accompaniment of the ringing of little bells, and sometimes guitars, carried by the members of the processions. The tradition of the bells is being lost, although a few parishes in Andalusia still respect this colorful ceremony. These processions take place most frequently during Lent, and in the fall of the year.

The *campanilleros* are not usually considered flamenco, as the *cante* has few of the characteristics of true flamenco singing. Nevertheless, they do play an interesting part in the life of Andalusia, and therefore qualify to be mentioned. Also, a few singers have introduced more flamenco-ized versions of the *cante* (Manuel Torre's moving versions on old records), which have had the effect of adding the *campanilleros* to flamenco's repertoire. Their name derived from the tradition of the little bells, which are called «*campanillas*».

En los pueblos de mi Andalucía	*At dawn the campanilleros*
los campanilleros a la madrugá	*wake me with their little bells*
me despiertan con sus campanillas	*and make me weep with their guitar*
y con su guitarra me jasen llorá...	*in the villages of my Andalucía...*
Un devoto por ir al Rosario	*As the Rosary (procession) passed [by*
por una ventana se quiso arrojá,	*one of the devout threw himself [from a window,*
y al decí «¡Dios te sarve María!»	*and on crying «God save you, [María!»*
se jayó en el suelo sin jaserse ná	*he crashed to the ground uninjured.*

CANTIÑAS.—*Cantes* and *toques chicos,* variable in the dance.

The word «*cantiña*» is originally the name given to medieval songs from Galicia, in northern Spain, today extended in meaning to signify «popular song». It is derived from «*cantiñear*», a verb meaning «improvised, spontaneous song». It is said that the term arrived to the port of Cádiz on shipboard, and so swept through the provinces of Cádiz and Sevilla that after a time any song sung in these provinces was called a «*cantiña*». Around Cádiz many of these *cantiñas* were gypsified, put to the *compás* of today's *alegrías,* and baptized with flamenco names: *alegrías, romeras, mirabrás,* and *caracoles,* to name those remaining today. These cantes, therefore, are no longer referred to as «*cantiñas*» (with the frequent exception of the *alegrías,* which many *cantaores* and *aficionados* name «*alegrías*» or «*cantiñas*» interchangeably), although they still fall under that general category.

In Cádiz today a *cantiña* is any miscellaneous melody sung with the «*aire*» and rhythm of the *alegrías,* oftentimes extremely similar to the traditional *alegrías,* and as often as not utilizing *alegrías* verses. The *cantiñas,* therefore, are still «improvised, spontaneous song» to a certain extent, serving as a necessary and praiseworthy outlet for the singer's inspiration (1).

A little further north, around Jerez and the province of Sevilla, the *cantiñas* mostly developed into today's *bulerías,* although they are not exclusively called *bulerías;* a few have retained their original name —the *cantiñas* of «Pinini» and «Juaniquí» are the most famous of these—while others are called such picturesque names as «*fiesta en Jerez*», «*jaleo en Utrera*», or whatever. All of these *cantes,* however, regardless of the name given them, fall within the scope of today's *bulerías;* it seems that it was up to the innovating artist to name his style of *bulerías* as he wished.

The northernmost extremity of the *cantiñas* (within Andalusia and flamenco), this time in the form of *alegrías* instead of *bulerías,* is the so-called «*alegrías de Córdoba*».

A ti muchos te dirán,	*Many will tell you*
«*Serrana, por ti yo muero*»;	«*Serrana, I would die for you;*»
yo nunca te he dicho ná	*I have never told you that,*
que soy el que más te quiero.	*although I love you the most.*
Que con el aire que llevas	*With the air that you have*
que cuando caminando vas,	*when swinging along,*
que hasta el farol de la popa	*you're likely to blow out the lantern*
que tú lo vas a apagar...	*at the poop of the boat...*

And these three savory verses; what a story they tell when sung in this order.

Tienes los dientes	*Your teeth*
que son granitos	*are like grains*
de arroz con leche.	*of rice with milk.*
Eres bonita,	*You're lovely.*
qué pena, morena,	*What a shame, dark one.*
que estés mocita.	*that you're a virgin.*
Vente conmigo.	*Come with me.*
Dile a tu mare	*Tell your mother*
que soy tu primo.	*that I'm your cousin.*

---

(1) Such a catch-all classification would be valuable throughout all of flamenco's categories of *cantes,* as it would serve the all-important purpose of breaking the rigidity of traditional form that so menaces the *Cante* today.

110

CAÑA and POLO.—*Cantes, bailes,* and *toques grandes.*

I have grouped these *cantes* together because of their close similarity in many factors: their *compás,* structure, «ay» passages, and feeling (or lack of it) transmitted. Due to the widely accepted hypotesis of José Carlos de Luna, presented some years ago, the *caña* and *polo* have become known as the most pure and ancient forms of flamenco still in existence today. This theory was passed on from writer to writer and *aficionado* to *aficionado* and, as there is no proof to the contrary, almost became an historical fact though repetition. Today, however, an oppositon group has sprung up, headed by Ricardo Molina and Antonio Mairena, and discussion rages concerning just what flamenco niche the *caña* and *polo* should occupy. Those who say that they are the first outcroppings of gypsy *cante* are countered by the truthful answer that they actually have little in common with the authentic *cante gitano.* They are much too formal in structure, and greatly lacking in primitive emotion, signifying to these *aficionados* that the *caña* and *polo* had a more literate background, very likely religious, probably the Gregorian chant, and as such represent the *cante grande* of flamenco's Andalusian *cantes* (nongypsy). But what about the fact that in the last century, when flamenco began finding its way into print, many of the great interpreters of these *cantes* were gypsies? The answer might be that the gypsies took them up and tried to make them a part of their *cante,* but could never quite succeed in converting them into genuine *cante gitano.*

Were all of this true, where do the *soleares,* the indisputably gypsy *cante* so similar to the *caña* and *polo,* enter the picture? Did they descend from the *caña* and *polo,* as is almost universally thought, the gypsy offspring of Andalusian *cantes?* Or was it the other way around, the *caña* and *polo* descending from the *soleares?* Either way seems feasible, and anything we can say for either argument is mere conjecture. Except for one thing. The *caña* and the *polo* were both mentioned in literature before the *soleares.* This may have some significance.

Two of these early literary references cast light on the naming and pre-flamenco origin of the *caña.* The earliest was written by the Englishman Richard Ford in 1830. He wrote that the *caña,* «which is actually the *guannia,* or Arabic song,» was sung in a *juerga* that he attended. Another early writer, Estébanez Calderón, wrote in 1847 much the same information about the *caña* having derived its name from the «*guannia*», which, he said, signifies «song» in Arabic. He goes on to describe the singing of the *caña* in much the same way as Ford. What does this signify, if these gentlemen are correct? For one thing, that the name «*caña*» came from «*guannia*», and that before becoming flamenco it was an Arabic song. It follows that the *polo* had much the same birth. And something else, more important: that no doubt far

111

more flamenco than theorists like to think had its origins in the Oriental music of Spain's neighbors to the South.

One more historical reference. It is known, through literary references and oral tradition, that at one time there were various styles of both the *cañas* and the *polos*. These *cantes* began falling into disuse years ago, however, before the invention of the phonograph, and only one unvarying style of each has reached modern times. For this reason it is more appropriate to refer to them in the singular.

The outstanding characteristic of both the *caña* and the *polo* is a simple passage, very similar in both, sung totally in «ayes», which almost certainly was borrowed from religious sources, be they Christian or Muslim. These «ayes» can be sung in or out of *compás*. If they are sung rhythmically, they are usually allotted either two or three full *soleares compases*, of twelve beats each. If sung out of *compás*, it is up to the singer. Antonio Mairena, for instance, sings them out of *compás*, allowing them roughly two-and-a-half measures.

There is certain discussion as to whether these *cantes* were always danceable. My investigations point to the fact that their dances were developed not many years ago by theatrical groups in their quest for variation. They are not as readily adaptable to the dance as the *soleares*, due to their rather un-flamenco stiltedness, although the «ay» passages do give them certain unusual possibilities.

The guitar *compás* is identical in the *caña, polo* and *soleares*.

The *caña* and *polo* that we know today are in truth not well regarded by most knowledgeable *aficionados*. They have a formality and «*aire*» very un-flamenco in nature, causing the *soleares* to have far surpassed them in depth, possibilities for *duende,* and that other most essential flamenco characteristic: naturalness. The *caña* and *polo* are already cloaked in burial garments, while the *soleares* is still one of flamenco's most alive *cantes.*

Like most of the *cante grandes,* both the *caña* and the *polo* are characteristically ended by a *macho.*

Caña verses:

Deja que la gente diga	*Let the people say what they wish,*
que te quiero y no te quiero,	*that I love you or don't love you,*
yo soy quien pasa las penas,	*I am the one who suffers the pangs*
y sé que te estoy queriendo	*and I know that I love you...*
El libro de la experiencia	*The book of experience*
no sirve al hombre de ná;	*serves man for nothing;*
al final viene la letra	*the truth comes at the end,*
y nadie llega al final	*and no one arrives to the end...*

112

La mujer y la sombra	A woman and a shadow
tienen un símil:	are much alike;
que buscando se alejan,	on being pursued, they escape;
dejadas, siguen.	on being ignored, they follow.

Polo verses:

Toítos le piden a Dios	Everyone asks God
la salud y la libertad,	for health and freedom,
y yo le pido la muerte	I ask for death
y no me la quiere mandar...	and he will not grant it...
Si el queré era bueno o malo	I asked a wise man
a un sabio le pregunté;	if love is good or bad;
el sabio no había querío	the wise man had never loved
y no supo respondé.	and knew not how to respond.
Clérigos y confesores,	Clergymen and confessors,
obispos y cardenales,	bishops and cardinals,
en la hora de morí	in the hour of death
todos seremos iguales.	we shall all be equals.

This verse indicates the only consolation left to the poor people... equality after death. It will be interesting to see if it works out that way.

And a beautiful *macho:*

Mi cariño	My love
me tiene conmosionao,	has me all muddled up
sin sabé lo que me pasa...	beyond my understanding...
lloro y tiemblo como un niño	I tremble and cry like a little boy
por ti...	for you...

CARACOLES.—*Cante* and *toque chico, baile intermedio.*

The *caracoles,* one of the group of *«cantiñas»* from Cádiz, are rhythmically identical to the *alegrías,* varying mainly in their *cante* and in their chord structures. Today the *caracoles* are considered to be a *cante* of Madrid. In modern times this is true, due to their supposed introduction to Madrid by the 19th century bull ring personalities Curro Cúchares and el Tato, who heard, and were captivated by, the *caracoles* in Cádiz. It is said that the *caracoles* were a majestic and serious *cante* that has, contrary to the usual laws of growing older, become gaier and lighter with the years. Their creation and development involve the names José el de Sanlúcar, Paco el Gandul, Romero el Tito, and Antonio Chacón. It is thought that they may have been in part developed from the 19th century *cantiña* called «la *caracolera».* The word *«cara-*

coles» literally means «snails», but here it is used as an exclamation, much like *«caramba».*

The *caracoles* resemble the already-discussed *caña* and *polo* in one respect: they are also a dying, stilted *cante,* and even in their heyday cannot, in my opinion, have been considered either a very gypsy and/or very flamenco *cante.* They were likely a mere plaything in days past, as they are, in the main, today. Unlike the *alegrías,* the *caracoles* do not adapt themselves well to poetry, and most of their verses are relatively nonsensical. The traditional verses stated below are perhaps some of their best.

Cómo reluce	*How the great street of Alcalá*
la gran calle de Alcalá	*glitters and shines*
cuando suben y bajan	*when the people of Andalucía*
los andaluces.	*pass up and down.*

Alcalá is a principal street in Madrid.

Vámonos, vámonos	*Let's go, let's go*
al café de la Unión	*to the Unión café,*
en donde paran Curro Cúchares	*the meeting place of Curro Cúchares,*
el Tato y Juan León.	*el Tato y Juan León.*

The *Café de la Unión,* in Madrid, used to be the hangout for *toreros, banderilleros,* and other people of the bull ring.

CARCELERAS.—*Cante grande «a palo seco»,* not played, traditionally not danced.

The *carceleras* are *tonás* developed in the atmosphere of Andalusian prisons (*«carcel»* means «jail» or «prison», *«carceleras»* translates «happenings in a prison»). Their original form is not remembered, and today they are sung merely as *martinetes* whose verses refer to jail life.

Other than serving as an emotional outlet for prisoners, the *carceleras* also served a practical purpose. Gypsy prisoners used to sing messages in *caló* (the language spoken by the Spanish gypsies, an impure mixture of *romaní* and Spanish) to relatives and friends outside the walls, much to the helpless annoyance of the uncomprehending guards.

Veinticinco calabozos	*The jail in Utrera*
tiene la cárcel de Utrera.	*has twenty-five cells.*
Veinticuatro he recorrido	*I have done time in twenty-four*
y el más oscuro me queda.	*but the darkest still awaits.*

Ayyy, al subir por la escalera	Ayyy, on climbing the steps
en el primer calabozo	of my first jail
oí una voz que decía:	I heard a voice say:
lástima de tan buen mozo	the pity of it, such a good man
con la libertá perdía.	with his liberty lost.

Ya van tres días que no como
más que lágrimas y pan:
estos son los alimentos
que mis carceleros me dan.

In three days I've eaten
only bread and tears:
that is the food
that my jailers give.

Dame una puñalaíta
y llévame al hospitá,
y dile a la hospitalera
que me acabe de matá.

Jab me with a knife
and take me to the hospital
and tell the head nurse
to finish me off.

Maldita sea la cárcel,
sepultura de hombres vivos
donde se amansan los guapos
y se pierden los amigos.

Damned be the jail,
tomb of live men,
where spirited men are tamed
and friends are lost.

Conocí a un hombre de bien
tan cabal como un reló
y por cosas del querer
en un presidio murió.

I knew a good man,
as faultless as a watch;
through the happenings of love
he died in a prison.

CARTAGENERAS.—*Cante* and *toque intermedio,* not danced.

There are mixed theories about the *cartageneras.* Some say that they grew up in the atmosphere of the mines, like the *tarantas.* Others say no, they are not mining *cantes* but merely a *fandango* from the region of Cartagena, dealing more with the sea and the country than the mines. I would say that, judging by their verses, they are a combination of all of these components of life. One point that is generally agreed upon; they are the most modern of the *cantes* of Levante, probably coming into existence around the end of the last century.

The *cartageneras* were strongly influenced by the *tarantas.* Their musical structure is roughly the same and, like the *tarantas* and all of the *cantes de Levante,* they are free of *compás.* Also like all of the *cantes* of Levante, they are undeniably Andalusian, with a strong Moorish, not gypsy, influence.

Se está quedando la Unión
como corrá sin gallinas:
a unos se los lleva Dios,
a otros los matan las minas.

La Unión *is becoming*
like a farm without chickens:
God takes some,
the mines finish the others.

115

La *Unión* is a mining town in the mountains near Cartagena that had a typically large casualty list in the years of primitive mining.

Obrero, por qué trabajas
si pá ti no es el producto
para el rico es la ventaja
y para tu familia el luto.

Worker, why do you work
if you don't reap the benefits;
for the rich, the rewards,
for your family, the mourning.

Notice the similarity between this verse and the American union songs of the 20's and 30's.

A Cartagena me voy
a ver la mar y sus olas
y a ver los barcos del rey
con la bandera española.

I am going to Cartagena
to see the sea and the waves
and to see the Spanish flags
on the ships of the king.

Al pie de un soberano
llora una cartagenera:
por Dios y por la santa Magdalena

A girl from Cartagena cried,
kneeling before a potentate:
for the love of God and Santa Mag-
[*dalena*

que no se lleven a mi hermano
ayy, al peñón de la Gumera.

don't take my brother away
to the cliff prison Gumera.

CHUFLAS.—*Cante, baile,* and *toque chico.*

A more burlesque form of the *tanguillos,* the *chuflas* are an all-out effort at humor. Developed by the gypsies of the Cádiz region, it is said that only the gypsies have the abandon to dance and sing the *chuflas* well; if not done with true *gracia* and good taste by natural comedians, they tend to become grotesque.

The *chuflas* are often used to convey the public's views of contemporary events, usually in a humorously ironic manner. As in the *chuflas* anything goes, they are probably flamenco's most truly spontaneous component. Their verses are often recited, not sung, or a combination of both, which gives the performer far more leeway for true comedy.

Verses of the *tanguillos* and the *chuflas* can be sung interchangeably, as the rhythm and accentuation are identical.

The word «*chufla*» means «kidding», «horsing around».

COLOMBIANAS.—*Cante, baile,* and *toque chico.*

The *colombianas* have been inspired by the rhythms of Colombian folk music. Their *compás,* accentuation, chording and flavor are strongly reminiscent of the Cuban *guajiras* and the *rumba gitana.* They have been popularized to a great extent, both in and out of Spain, by Carmen

116

Amaya and the guitarist Sabicas. Carmen Amaya sang the following verses:

Quisiera ser perla fina
de esos pulidos arretes
y besarte la boquita
y morderte los cachetes.
¿Quién te manda ser bonita
si hasta a mí me comprometes?

Oh, to be one of the elegant pearls
of your burnished ear rings
and kiss your pretty mouth
and bite your cheeks.
Who told you to be so pretty
that even me you are winning?

Me gusta estar en la sierra
que cuando llega el nuevo día
y me acuerdo de tus amores
y de tu mala partía
me consuelo con las flores
que es mi única alegría.

I like to be in the sierra
when the new day arrives
to remember your love
and your sad departure.
I console myself with the flowers,
that are my only happiness

Quisiera, cariño mío,
que tú nunca me olviaras
y tus labios con los míos
en un beso se ajuntaran,
y que no hubiera en el mundo
nadie que nos separara.

I would like, my sweetheart,
for your never to forget me
and for our lips to come together
in a kiss
and for there to be no one
in the world to separate us.

DANZA MORA.—*Baile* and *toque chico*, not sung.

«*Danza mora*» translates «Moorish dance», and is a direct flamenco adaptation of the Moorish style of music. Rhythmically it is similar to the *zambra*.

The *danza mora* is the flamenco *baile* and *toque* most influenced by the Moors. It is usually danced barefoot, and often with little cymbals on the tips of the fingers which make bell-like sounds when struck together. It is generally more serious and less sensuous than the *zambra*, with an increased use of slow, fluid arm movements, and without the *desplantes* which mark the *zambra*. When danced well the *danza mora* has an air of mysterious beauty which characterizes all serious Oriental dancing. Sometimes verses of the *zambra* are sung to the *danza mora*. This practice is frowned upon, as it is out of keeping with the feeling of the dance.

DEBLA.—*Cante grande «a palo seco»*, not played, traditionally not danced.

The *debla* is one of the more difficult of the many *tonás* that formerly existed. It is said that the *debla* we know today was sung by el Lebrijano and Diego el Fillo, and in more modern times was

117

resuscitated by Tomás Pavón. Until recently its verses were always ended with the curious phrase «*deblica bare*», *caló* for «grand goddess», causing theorists to suspect a connection between the *debla* and some distant gypsy religious rite. As this ritual is not remembered today, howerver, many singers feel that the «*deblica bare*» ending is outdated, and no longer include it in their renditions of the *debla*.

Yo ya no era quien era
ni quien yo fui ya seré;
soy un árbol de tristeza
pegaíto a la paré.
Deblica bare...

I am no longer what I was
nor will I be again;
I am a tree of sadness
in the shadow of a wall.
Deblica bare...

Una mujer fue la causa
de mi perdición primera;
no hay perdición en el mundo
que por mujeres no venga.
Deblica bare...

A woman was the cause
of my first downfall;
there is no perdition in the world
that is not caused by women.
Deblica bare...

En el barrio de Triana
no hay pluma ni tintero
pá escribirle yo a mi mare
que hace tres años no la veo.
Deblica bare...

In the neighborhood of Triana
there is neither pen nor ink
with which to write my mother,
whom I haven't seen for three years.
Deblica bare...

FANDANGOS GRANDES.—*Cante* and *toque intermedio*, not danced.

The *fandangos grandes* are one of the most widely sung, and badly abused, *cantes* of all flamenco. Every singer with the minimum of pretentions attempts the *fandangos grandes;* but the *grandes*, sung as they should be, are not a *cante* for the run-of-the-mill singer. The true *fandangos grandes* approach the *jondo,* and are dominated by only a few singers. One of these, el Gordito de Triana, gives a veritable lesson in their interpretation on the record «*Sevilla - Cuna del Cante Flamenco*».

The origin of the category «*fandangos*», which includes the *grandes* and the *fandanguillos* (also called *fandangos de Huelva*), is thought to have been in the *jota* country of northern Spain (1). The original *fandangos* were lively and danceable, accompanied by guitars, castanets, tambourines, and violins (as is still true of the traditional *verdiales* of the same family). In time one branch of the *fandangos* took on more serious aspects, chiefly because of the influence of Arabic stylings, and grew away from the original *fandangos;* this *jondo* outgrowth is the *fandangos grandes.* Now, due to their completely different natures, it

---

(1) The *jota*, in turn, has been traced to a Moorish heritage. The word signifies «dance» in Arabic.

118

is necessary to differentiate between the *fandangos grandes* (great *fandangos*) and the *fandanguillos* (little *fandangos*).

There are many types of *fandangos grandes,* the most prodigious being those of Triana and Lucena. They are an abstract *cante* without an indicated *compás,* the guitar having to closely follow the singer.

La gente quiere perderte	*The people wish to reject you,*
y voy a salvarte yo,	*but I am going to save you*
porque me duele tu pena	*because your grief saddens me*
como le dolió al Señor	*as the grief of Magdalena*
el llanto de Magdalena.	*saddened God.*
A los racimos de uva	*Your love seems*
se parece tu querer;	*like a bunch of grapes;*
la frescura viene antes,	*the freshness comes first,*
la borrachera, después.	*the drunkenness after.*
Yo como tú no encuentro ninguna,	*I won't find another woman*
mujer, con quien compararte;	*to compare with you;*
sólo he visto, por fortuna,	*I have only seen one*
a una en un estandarte	*on a pedestal*
y a los pies lleva la luna.	*with the moon at her feet.*

This verse refers to a staute of the Virgin Mary, on which she is standing on a ball which could be taken as the moon.

Por su santa voluntá	*God made love blind*
ciego hizo Dios el queré.	*by his saintly desire.*
Yo he visto más de una vé	*I have seen more than once*
perderse a un hombre cabal	*the ruin of a good man*
por una mala mujer.	*over a bad woman.*

And two depressing *fandangos de Triana:*

Una mujer se moría	*A woman was dying*
sus hijos la rodeaban	*her children surrounded her*
y el más chico la decía	*and the smallest said to her*
Mamá mírame a la cara	*Mama look at my face*
no te mueras todavía...	*don't die yet...*
Entré un día en un manicomio	*I entered an insane asylum one day*
me pesa el haberlo hecho	*—it grieves me to have done it—*
yo vi una loca en el patio	*I saw a crazy woman in the patio*
se sacaba y daba el pecho	*take out and feed her breast*
a una muñequita de trapo...	*to a little rag doll...*

119

FANDANGUILLOS.—*Cante* and *toque chico*, mixed dance.

The *fandanguillos* (*fandangos de Huelva*) are thought to have descended from the *jota* of northern Spain. Originally they were accompanied by guitars, violins, tambourines, and castanets. Deep in the Huelva country, where these instruments are scarce, supplemental accompanying instruments have been developed, and are still used, which are: reed flutes, hand-made by the country people from reeds that grow in the country; pieces of partially-split cane that, when skillfully banged between the thumb and forefinger, produce a sound similar to castanets; and crude drums on which they beat out the basic rhythm.

Each village in the province of Huelva has developed its own style of *fandanguillo*. A particularly good time to hear these many types of *fandanguillos* is during the *Romería del Rocío* (religious pilgrimage to the village of Rocío, which lies between Sevilla and Huelva). Once a year el Rocío is the convergent point of oxen carts from all over the province (this *Romería* is, sadly enough, becoming badly cluttered up with automobiles, motos, trucks, etc.). Religious ceremonies are stressed the first two or three days, followed by two or three days more of merriment sparked by countless *fandanguillos* which issue from everywhere and everybody.

The *fandanguillos* have enjoyed immense popularity during this century, much to the disgust of the purists. During a span of thirty on forty years the *fandanguillos* and the *fandangos grandes* were almost all that could be heard of flamenco. This state of affairs, extremely harmful to the art of flamenco, is just today subsiding.

The most famous *fandanguero* remembered is Pepe Pérez de Guzmán, a member of an aristocratic family of Huelva.

The *fandanguillos* are characterized by a never-ending number of poetically beautiful verses of all themes and moods, as follows:

Cuando la vi llorar
que creí de volverme loco,
pero luego me enteré
que ella lloraba por otro,
y entonces fui yo quien lloré.

Me tratas como a un niño
porque te quiero con locura.
Tú me tiras por los suelos.
Qué malamente me miras
tanto como yo te quiero.

When I saw her cry
I thought that I would go crazy.
But later I understood
that she cried for another;
then it was I who cried.

You treat me like a child
because I love you with frenzy.
You drag me through the dirt.
How bad you are with me
as much as I love you.

Se volvieron a encontrar	As they rounded a corner
al revolver una esquina,	they met again,
y como dos criaturas	and like two children
se pusieron a llorar.	they began crying.
El amor no tiene cura.	Love has no cure.
No quiero que hables con nadie.	I don't want you to talk to anyone.
Sólo con tu confesor,	Only to your confessor,
con tu padre,	your father,
con tu madre,	your mother,
con tu hermanita	your sister,
y yo.	and me.
Hasta después de la muerte	I shall love you
te tengo que estar queriendo,	even after death,
que muerto también se quiere.	for the dead can still love.
Yo te quiero con el alma,	I love you with my soul,
y el alma nunca se muere.	and the soul never dies.

FARRUCA.—*Baile* and *toque chico*, rarely sung today.

Domingo Manfredi Cano states in his book *«Geografía del Cante Jondo»* that the port of Cádiz was an important stop-over point for ship travelers in the past. These visitors brought their songs and dances with them, many of which were adopted by the people of Cádiz and converted into flamenco. This, Sr. Manfredi says, is what has happened to the *farruca*, which is nothing more than an Asturian dance strongly influenced by the *tangos* of Cádiz. A dictionary definition seems to back this up: *«Farruca* - Asturian or Galician newly-arrived», which could also account for its name, once introduced into Cádiz. Its name could also have stemmed from another of its dictionary definitions: «brave, courageous», an accurate description of the dance when danced well.

The *compás* of the *farruca* is identical to that of the *tangos*, although the guitar chord structure is different, as are the accentuation and emphasis.

There exist two or three recorded versions of the *farruca*, but in general its *cante* has nearly disappeared.

GARROTIN.—*Cante, baile*, and *toque chico*.

Until recently considered folklore, the *garrotín* is slowly but surely being accepted into flamenco circles, as are the *sevillanas*, *milongas*, *tanguillos*, *campanilleros*, and the *vito*.

There are two schools of thought concerning the origin of the *garrotín*. One states that it has taken the same road as the *farruca*; that is, from Asturias to flamenco via the port of Cádiz. The other

121

school, led by Vicente Escudero, insists that the *garrotín* is a creation of the gypsies of Lérida, in northern Spain. The latter school, I believe, is most likely to be on the right track. There is little mention of the *garrotín* in Cádiz, while there *is* much mention of it around the regions of Lérida and Barcelona.

Regardless of its background, the *garrotín* is a pleasing addition to flamenco, slow and sensual, generally with colorful verses. Carmen Amaya has been its principal popularizer.

Mi marío es mi marío	*My husband is mine*
y no es marío de nadie;	*and mine alone;*
la que quiera a mi marío	*whoever wants him*
vaya a la guerra y lo gane.	*has a fight on her hands.*
Pregúntale a mi sombrero,	*Ask my hat*
mi sombrero te dirá	*and it will tell you*
las malas noches que paso	*of the bad nights that I pass*
y el relente que me da.	*and the cold that I feel.*

GRANAINAS.—*Cante* and *toque intermedio.* Not danced.

The *granaínas* are an adaptation of the *fandangos grandes* which have been strongly influenced by the Moors, rulers of Granada for eight centuries. They have, therefore, developed a more discordant, Oriental quality than the *fandangos grandes.* Although a bit too ornamented to be *jondo* (in my opinion, their immediate descendent, the *media granaína,* far exceeds them in this possibility), certain virtuoso singers can give them a superficial beauty that cannot be denied. They are a free *cante* without a determined *compás.* The term «*granaínas*» is an abbreviation of «*granadinas*», which means to say «songs from Granada».

La que habita en la carrera,	*The Virgin of Anguish,*
la Virgen de las Angustias,	*she who lives in the carrera,*
de esa señora me espante	*may she punish me*
si no te quiero de veras.	*if I don't truly love you.*
Ninguno ya tiene penas,	*No one has grief anymore,*
que todas las tengo yo,	*I have it all myself,*
con una losita negra	*like a black tombstone*
encima del corazón...	*upon my heart...*

GUAJIRAS.—*Cante, baile,* and *toque chico.*

The *guajiras* are a flamenco version of a Cuban rhythm of the same name. They are said to have been brought to Spain in the XVI century by Spanish soldiers returning from the conquests. Most of their verses deal with Cuba and the Cubans, usually in a light vein. Indolent and sensual, they are rhythmically similar to the other flamenco forms influenced by the new world.. It is not unheard of for their verses to be slightly racy.

Yo vi bañarse un cubanito	*I saw a Cuban boy swimming*
entre los cañaverales	*between the cane fields;*
y al mirarme sonreía	*on seeing me he smiled*
y cantándome decía	*and asked me, singing,*
que lo sacara del agua	*to take him out of the water*
porque el agua estaba fría...	*because it was very cold...*
A la Habana me he venio,	*I came to Havana*
a probar el aguacate	*to try some avocado*
y me encontré en el bohío	*and instead found in a grass hut*
un negro de chocolate.	*a chocolate Negro.*
Bajo la fronda de un mate	*Beneath a leafy holly bush*
me dio la rica banana,	*he gave me the savory banana,*
y al cabo de una semana	*and at the end of a week*
el negro pidió mi mano.	*he asked for my hand.*
«Con vos no me caso, hermano,	*«I will not marry you, brother,*
porque no me da la gana.»	*because I don't feel like it.»*

JABERAS.—*Cante* and *toque intermedio.* Not danced.

The *jaberas* are a rarely heard member of the large family of the *fandangos grandes,* more directly associated with the *malagueñas.* They are believed to have originated as an inland *cante* of country people. Like the *malagueñas,* they are a free *cante* with no determined *compás.*

Se despierta un rey celoso,	*A jealous king who wakes up*
coge la pluma y escribe,	*picks up his pen and begins writing,*
y en el primer renglón pone:	*and on the first line he puts:*
quien tiene celos no vive.	*he who is jealous does not live.*
En el pinar del amor	*In the pine forest of love*
estando cortando piñas,	*cutting pine trees,*
del tronco saltó una astilla;	*a splinter flew from a trunk*
se clavó en mi corazón.	*and buried itself in my heart.*
Muerto estoy, llórame, niña...	*I am vanquished; cry for me, love...*
Cuando paso por tu calle	*When I go up your street*
miro siempre tu ventana	*I always look at your window*
esperando ver tus ojos ¡ay!	*hoping to see your eyes, ay!*
pa que alumbren la mañana.	*so that they light up my morning.*

123

JALEOS.—*Cante, baile,* and *toque chico.*

The *jaleos,* thought to have been a more primitive form of the *alegrías,* are said to be the oldest flamenco form from the port of Cádiz.

Viva Cádiz y viva	Long live Cádiz
la muralla junto al mar.	and its sea wall...
Vivan los cuerpos gaditanos	Long live the gaditanos,
que se saben jalear...	experts at hell-raising...
Viva la novia, y el novio,	Long live the bride and the groom,
y el cura que los casó,	and the priest who married them,
el padrino y la madrina	and the godfather, and the godmother,
y los convidaos, y yo...	and the guests, and myself...

LIVIANAS.—*Cante, toque,* and *baile grande.*

According to Domingo Manfredi Cano, among other theorists, the *livianas* is a less difficult descendent of the *tonás,* probably having been first sung in the gypsy forges. He goes on to say that, like the *tonás,* it had no *compás,* and only with time adopted that of the *siguiriyas* and *serranas.* Other theorists, such as Ricardo Molina and Antonio Mairena, see a much closer melodic similarity between the *livianas* and the *cantes camperos.* This hypothesis seems to me to be the closest to the undeterminable truth, for the *livianas,* as sung today, largely lack the force and *rajo* essential in the *tonás,* but do possess the calm, easy-going style and *aire* of the *cantes camperos (trilleras, etc.)* and *nanas.*

The *livianas* (meaning «easing up» in this case) is one of the less difficult and more smoothly flowing of the *cantes grandes,* and as such is often sung directly before the *serranas,* as a kind of introduction, or warming up.

Although the name «*livianas*» has come down to us in the plural, there is in truth only one style of it remembered today.

The following *livianas* verses depict well the difference between the verses of the learned poet, and the people. The first three, full of poetry, philosophy, wisdom, and hard work, are Manuel Machado's. The last two are the more simple observations of less complicated souls.

Quita una pena otra pena,	One sorrow relieves another sorrow,
un dolor, otro dolor,	one pain, another pain,
un clavo saca otro clavo,	one nail forces another,
y un amor quita a otro amor...	and one love is replaced by another...

Crece el fuego con el viento,	Fire grows with the wind,
con la noche el padecer,	suffering with nightfall,
con el recuerdo, la pena,	sorrows with remembrance,
con los celos, el querer...	and love with jealously...
Tengo una copa en la mano,	I have a drink in my hand
y en los labios, un cantar,	and a song on my lips,
y en mi corazón, más penas	but in my heart... more sorrows
que gotas de agua en el mar,	than drops of water in the sea,
y en los desiertos arenas...	or sand in the desert...
Ventanas a la calle	Windows facing the street
son peligrosas, son peligrosas,	are dangerous, so dangerous,
pá la mare que tiene	for the mother that has
sus niñas hermosas.	beautiful daughters...
De canelita fina	I am making,
pá mi morena	for my morena,
estoy jaciendo un camino	a road of fine cinnamon
pá ir a la sierra.	leading to the sierra.

MALAGUEÑAS.—*Cante* and *toque intermedio,* not danced.

The province of Málaga has developed its own very personal world of flamenco. They early decided that the gypsy-style flamenco was not for them, and went on to innovate their own *cantes* to fit their every mood. They have the *verdiales* and *rondeñas* for gaiety, the *jaberas* for light philosophy, and, for their *cande grande,* the *serranas,* and countless styles of *malagueñas,* whose verses encompass the most profound human emotions. For a time, during the last thirty years of the past century, these *malagueñas* swept Spain, picking up quantities of admirers and interpreters who were not from Málaga. The most admirable of these, Antonio Chacón, from Jerez de la Frontera, who created his own difficult, flowing style, and Enrique el Mellizo, from Cádiz, who added the gypsy touch, converting his *malagueña* into the most movingly flamenco of all, came to be ranked alongside of the «king of the *malagueñeros»:* Juan Breva, from Vélez-Málaga. The *malagueñas* of these three artists are those best remembered and most sung today, although there were scores of other fine interpreters and creators within this *cante,* most of whom were from the province of Málaga, as is fitting.

Like so many *cantes,* the *malagueñas* are directly descended from the *fandangos grandes,* and, like them, are a free *cante* without a determined *compás.*

The well-known semi-classical *malagueña* of Lecuona was based on the flamenco *malagueñas*, and at times displays certain faint traces of a flamenco style.

Malagueñas credited to Juan Breva:

A un sabio le pregunté	*I asked a wise man a question,*
y me contestó al momento	*and he responded instantly:*
«Yo también me enamoré	*«I too have fallen in love,*
y aunque me sobra el talento	*and, although I ooze wisdom,*
lloro por una mujer».	*am also crying over a woman.»*
Los siete sabios de Grecia	*The seven wise men of Greece*
no saben lo que yo sé...	*don't know as much as I...*
las fatiguitas y el tiempo	*anguish and time*
me lo hicieron aprender...	*have made me learn...*
¡Ayy! Maresita del Carmen,	*Ayy! Virgin of the Carmen,*
qué pena tan grande es	*what suffering it is*
estar juntito del agua	*to be so near water*
y no poderla beber...	*and not be able to drink...*
En ti puse mi querer	*I gave you my love*
creyendo que ya eras buena	*thinking that you had changed,*
pero yo me equivoqué;	*but I was mistaken;*
tú sigues siendo quien eras	*you are still the same,*
y Dios te lo pague, mujer.	*and may God punish you, woman!*

Malagueñas of Antonio Chacón:

En la tumba de mi madre	*In the tomb of my mother*
a dar voces me ponía,	*I started shouting,*
y escuché un eco del viento;	*and I heard an echo on the wind;*
no la llames, me decía,	*do not call her, it sighed,*
que no responden los muertos.	*the dead do not respond.*
Aquella campana triste	*The mourning bell*
está dando la una;	*tolled one;*
hasta las dos estoy pensando	*until two I thought*
en el querer que me diste;	*of the love that you gave me;*
y me dan las tres llorando...	*as it tolled three I was crying...*

Malagueñas of Enrique el Mellizo:

¿Dónde va a llegar	*Where is it leading us,*
este querer tuyo y mío?	*this love of ours?*
Tú tratas de aborrecerme,	*You wish to destroy me,*
yo cá vez te quiero más;	*and each day I love you more,*
Ayy que Dios me mande a mí la	*Ayy that God send me death...*
[*muerte...*	

126

Ayy yo vi a mi mare veni
en el carrito de la pena, y ̄
se me ocurrió a mí el deci:
«siendo mi mare tan buena,
no se debía de morí.»

Ayy I watched my mother arrive
in the cart of the dead
and found myself blurting:
«My mother, being so good,
should not have had to die.»

MARIANAS.—*Cante* and *toque chico,* not danced.

Although the *marianas* are sometimes called *«tientos de las maria-nas»,* I believe it is safe to assume that they were derived from the *cantes camperos.* Their name has excited some speculation. Some say that Mariana was the name of the creator's sweetheart. A more popular theory claims that Mariana was the name of a performing monkey, whose itinerant gypsy owner, probably Hungarian or Rumanian, sang of her adventures. The following verse supports this theory:

Sube, Mariana, sube,
por aquella montañita arriba sube,
no pegarle más palitos a la
          [Mariana,
porque la pobrecita está manquita
y coja.

Run, Mariana, run,
up that little mountain.
Don't hit Mariana any more
becauses the poor thing is one-armed
and lame.

The *marianas* are a simple, charming Andalusian *cante,* free from a well-defined *compás.* They are well on their way to extinction.

MARTINETES.—*Cante grande «a palo seco»,* not played, traditionally not danced.

When the gypsies were driven off of the open road, many of them entered iron forges and became blacksmiths. Frustrated by their desire to roam and by the hard life to which they had been subjected, they poured out their souls in song while they hammered away at their work. Thus the *martinetes* of the forges were derived from the *tonás* of the open road.

The *martinetes,* probably first developed in the forges of Triana, are extremely difficult to interpret, as they take great physical and emotional capacity. They are often accompanied, traditionally with no attempt at *compás* (in modern times the *compás* of the *siguiriyas* is being increasingly used), by a blacksmith's hammer. The word *«martinete»* is said to have been derived from *«martillo»* — hammer.

The two types of *martinetes* still sung are the *«natural»,* and the *«redoblao»,* longer and more difficult.

I have stated above that the *martinetes* are «traditionally not danced.» Today, however, the only remaining *cante grande* that has not been defiled by theatrical dance companies is the *tonás*. It will not, I predict, hold this distinction for long.

Entre la Hostia y el Cali,	*As I took the sacred Bread and Wine,*
a mi Dios se lo pedí,	*I asked my God*
que no te ajoguen las fatigas	*not to permit misery to choke you*
como me ajogan a mí.	*as it chokes me.*
Así, como está la fragua,	*Like the forge,*
jecha candela de oro,	*my insides glow like gold*
se me ponen las entrañas	*when I remember you,*
cuando te recuerdo, y lloro.	*and I weep...*
Con las fatiguitas de la muerte	*With the weariness of death*
a un laíto yo me arrimé;	*I crept to one side;*
con los deítos de la mano	*with the fingers of my hand*
arañaba la pared...	*I tore at the wall...*
¡Alza la voz, pregonero!	*Shout out, town crier!*
levanta la voz y di;	*Raise your voice and say:*
no hay deuda que no se pague	*there are no debts that are left unpaid*
ni amor que no tenga fin.	*nor love that does not end.*

MEDIA GRANAINA.—*Cante* and *toque intermedio*, not danced.

The *media granaína* is a less difficult, less ostentatious and ornamented sister *cante* of the *granaínas*. As such, it has far more possibilities for profundity. Like the *granaínas*, the *media granaína* has absorbed a strong blend of Moorish and Andalusian influences. Today the *media granaína* is more widely sung than the *granaínas*, probably because it is not only easier, but in better flamenco taste. Both of these *cantes* are from the province of Granada. «*Media*» translates «half».

Una cruz llevas al pecho,	*You carry a cross on your chest,*
engarzá en oro y marfil,	*mounted in gold and ivory,*
deja que me duerma en ella,	*let me sleep upon it,*
crucificándome allí...	*crucifying myself there...*
Gitaniya como yo	*Another gypsy girl like myself*
no la tienes que encontrar	*you will never find*
aunque gitana se vuelva	*although all Christianity*
toíta la cristiandad...	*turns gypsy...*
Dejarme un momento solo,	*Leave me alone a moment,*
quiero hartarme de llorar;	*I wish to satiate my crying;*
déjame que ponga unas flores	*Let me put some flowers*
a esa tumba tan sagrá,	*on that tomb so sacred,*
recuerdo de mis amores...	*memory of my loves...*

128

Ya te tengo prepará,	I have prepared for you
pá cuando quieras vení,	for whenever you want to come,
una cuevecita nueva	a new little cave
jecha en el Albaicín.	in the hill of the Albaicín.
Quiero vivir en Graná	I wish to live in Granada
porque me gusta el oir	because I like to hear
la campana de La Vela	the bell of La Vela
cuando me voy a dormir...	when I go off to sleep...

MILONGAS.—*Cante* and *toque chico*, not danced.

The *milongas*, thought to have originated in Argentina, groped their way into flamenco much in the same manner as the *guajiras* and the *colombianas* although, in truth, they are much less flamenco in nature than either of those *cantes*. Their *compás* is variable: sometimes free (*por fandangos*), sometimes well-defined (*por rumba*). They are of little flamenco value, certainly not to be taken seriously, although they do lend diversity, and are sprinkled with some colorful verses.

Cuando siento una guitarra	When I hear a guitar
me da ganas de llorar,	I feel the urge to cry,
porque me acuerdo de España	because I remember Spain,
la tierra por mí soñada.	the land of my dreams.
Y en la noche clara	In the clear night
hasta el aire canta,	even the air sings,
y de una garganta	and from a throat
yo creo escuchar	I can almost hear
palabras de amores	words of love
muy junto a una reja;	pass through barred windows;
suspiros y quejas	sighs and murmurs
y un beso al chocar...	and a kiss through the bars...

These are obviously the sentiments of a homesick Spanish immigrant in America.

¡Me gustas más que el buen vino	I like you more than good wine
y más que un pavo trufao!	and roast turkey!
¡Más que me gusta el tabaco	And more than tobacco
y que estar siempre tumbao!	and just lazing around!
¡Con decirte que me gustas	I tell you that I like you
más que el acta a un diputao!	more than a lawyer likes court!
¡Y eso que eres un tonel	And this, even though you're a barrel
y tu cutis se ha arrugao!...	and your skin is all wrinkles!...

129

Mas no sé qué gracia tienes	I don't really know what charm
ni qué tienen tus traseras	*you and your buttooks have,*
que te miro y me parece	*that when I look at you it seems*
que das adormideras...	*you've given me opium...*

This immigrant seems to be better adjusted.

MINERAS.—It is uncertain whether the *mineras* were a slight variation of the *tarantas* and *cartageneras,* or a way of calling these very same *cantes* when their verses dealt with mining themes. If the former, the *cante* has been forgotten. If the latter the term is rarely used today. «*Minera*» translates «mining», or «pertaining to mining».

MIRABRAS.—*Cante, baile,* and *toque chico.*

The *mirabrás* were undoubtedly inspired by the *alegrías* or a similar *cante,* as the *compás* and many other characteristics are identical.

A mí qué me importa	What does it matter to me
que un rey me culpe	*whether a king pardons me*
si el pueblo es grande	*if the country is large*
y me adora...	*and the people believe in me...*

This verse has led theoreticians to consider the possibility that the creator of the *mirabrás* was a nobleman, or person of the upper classes, persecuted by the king.

Venga usté a mi puesto, hermosa,
y no se vaya usté, salero,
castañas de Galarosa vendo, camuesa y pero.
Ay Marina,
yo traigo naranjas y son de la China.
batatitas redondas y suspiros de canela,
melocotones de Ronda, agua de la nevería;
te quiero yo
como a la mare que me parió...

Come to my stand, beautiful,
don't go away, salero;
I sell sweet and sour apples
and chestnuts from Galarosa;
I have China oranges,
little round yams and cinnamon sweets,
peaches from Ronda and water like ice.
Ay Marina, I love you
as I loved my mother who gave me birth.

This verse reveals the technique used by the owner of a stand in attempting to entice Marina with the delicacies that he sells. It has inspired the theory that the *mirabrás* came into being when José el de Sanlúcar, a 19th century *banderillero* and *cantaor*, first saw the many colorful stands of delicacies that used to rim the Madrid bull ring. He is said to have put his verses to the music of a *cantiña* called «*El Almorano*», and the *mirabrás* came into existence.

In my opinion, the *mirabrás*, although no doubt a gypsy-developed *cante*, contains little of the true «*aire*» *gitano*. Although its *compás* is identical to that of the *alegrías*, it by no means possesses the rhythm and *gracia* of that *cante*, leading me to believe that it was created, in the never ending commercial quest for variety, for the *café cantante* circuit of the last century. That could explain its awkwardness and superficiality, and the feeling that the *cante* did not come about naturally, but was hastily ground out in the flamenco version of a song writer's studio.

As can be expected under these circumstances, its dance cannot begin to live up to the dance of the *alegrías*.

MURCIANA.—The *cante por murcianas* is shrouded in mystery. To my knowledge, no one knows exactly how it went, nor is it even referred to in modern times. My theory is that the *murcianas* (from the province of Murcia) gave birth to today's *cartageneras* (also from the province of Murcia) and then ceased to exist, or, simpler yet, was merely an earlier name for the *cartageneras*.

NANAS.—*Cante chico*, not traditionally played, not danced.

The *nanas* are cradle songs, sung to the children at bedtime to lull them to sleep. Cradle songs, of course, date back to the first mother and her child, but the cradle songs of Andalusía, sung in a tender flamenco style, are especially irresistible. The *compás* of the *nanas* is the rhythm of a rocking cradle. «*Nana*» literally means «slumber song», «grandmother», «wet nurse», or, less frequently, «mother».

As the *nanas* are not, of course, sung for *fiestas*, nor exploited in any way, they have never known guitar accompaniment. An exception to this is Perico el del Lunar's beautiful accompaniment of Bernardo de los Lobitos' *nana* on the Hispavox Anthology of *Cante Flamenco*.

Un ángel de canela	*A cinnamon angel*
guarda tu cuna,	*watches over your crib,*
la cabeza p'al sol,	*his head towards the sun,*
los pies pa la luna...	*his feet towards the moon...*
A dormir va	*Off to sleep goes*
la rosa de los rosales;	*the rose of roses;*
a dormir, niña,	*sleep, little girl,*
porque ya es tarde...	*it is getting late...*

131

El niño chiquito	The little baby
se quiere dormir,	wishes to sleep,
y el pícaro sueño	but the mischievous sandman
no quiere venir...	just won't come...
En los brazos te tengo,	I hold you in my arms
y me da espanto. ·	and am suddenly afraid:
¿Qué será de ti, niño,	what will become of you, little one,
si yo te falto?	if I fail you?
Clavelito encarnado,	Little pink carnation,
rosa en capullo,	budding rose,
duérmete, vida mía,	sleep, my life,
mientras te arruyo.	while I sing you a lullaby.
Nana, nana... ay... nana,	Slumber song... ay ... slumber song,
duérmete, lucerito de la	sleep, little star of the
mañana...	morning...

PALMARES.—A *cante* that is completely forgotten, the *palmares* were very similar to another country *cante,* also on the verge of disappearing: the *temporeras.* The *fandangos* and *fandanguillos* have replaced these *cantes* in the hearts of the people.

PETENERAS.—*Cante, baile,* and *toque intermedio.*

The legend goes that the *peteneras* were created by a beautiful prostitute who was a great destroyer of men's hearts, and who finally died a violent death at the hands of one of her deceived lovers.

Quien te puso Petenera	Whoever named you Petenera
no te supo poner nombre,	did not name you properly;
que debía de haberte puesto	he should have called you
la perdición de los hombres.	the cause of men's perdition.

The girl, as the verse states, was named Petenera, and is thought to have been from the village of Paterna, near Jerez de la Frontera. The similarity between the names «*paternera*» (girl from Paterna) and «*petenera*» has caused some to think that the *cante* of the *peteneras* derived its name from the mispronunciation of the word «*paterneras*». This is generally discredited.

There are two types of *peteneras* sung today. The older one, lor. ger, more difficult and ornamented and therefore, as is usually the case, less moving, was resuscitated and recorded by the Niña de los Peines. This version, referred to as «*larga*», is rarely sung today, and is again well on its way to being forgotten. The other, called the «*corta*»,

132

has been recorded by Rafael Romero in the Hispavox Anthology of *Cante Flamenco* (thereby helping discredit the «black legend», still believed by many flamencos, that performing the *petenera* brings the interpreter had luck).

It is interesting to speculate on the *peteneras'* past. Friends of mine returning from Turkey and other Middle Eastern countries have met ancestors of the Sephardic Jews who were expulsed from Spain at the end of the XV century (1492). These people not only still speak the Spanish language as it was spoken at that time, but conserve many of their old Spanish customs and traditions. Among these, they sing songs very similar to many of flamenco's *cantes,* including the *peteneras.* The possibility exists, of course, that these people learned the *peteneras* while on tourist visits to Spain, or from records, but the very people who sing them claim not. They say they are passed down from generation to generation within their own tightly-knit group. Hipólito Rossy, in his book *«Teoría del Cante Jondo»,* cites this same curiosity, referring to the Sephardic Jews now living in the Balkans. They, he writes, sing the *peteneras,* including the verse of the Petenera being the *«perdición de los hombres»,* a verse still widely sung today in flamenco circles.

Sr. Rossy reasons, as have other theorists, that the verse concerning Rebeco and the synogogue (below) also helps date the *peteneras,* for the synagogues disappeared in Spain, togeher with the Jews, in 1492. He thinks that it could easily be that this verse existed at that time, and even that the *peteneras* was originally a song of the Sephardic Jews. He goes on to say that that could explain the *peteneras'* striking dissimilarity to the rest of the *cantes* of flamenco.

When the Petenera was killed, the following verse became popular:

La Petenera se ha muerto,	*La Petenera has died*
y la llevan a enterrar,	*and they are taking her to be buried;*
y en el panteón no cabe	*all of the followers of the procession*
la gente que va detrás...	*will not fit into the mausoleum...*

Other popular verses:

Ven acá, remediaora,	*Come here, girl of remedies,*
y remedia mis dolores,	*and remedy my affliction;*
que está sufriendo mi cuerpo	*my body is suffering*
una enfermeá de amores...	*the sickness of longing...*
Al pie de un árbol sin fruto	*At the foot of a fruitless tree*
me puse a considerar	*I sat down to contemplate*
qué pocos amigos tiene	*how few friends one has*
el que no tiene que dar...	*who has nothing to give...*

133

¿Dónde vas, bella judía,	Where are you going, beautiful Jewess,
tan compuesta y a deshora?	after hours and so fixed up?
Voy en busca de Rebeco,	I go looking for Rebeco,
que está en una sinagoga...	who is in a synagogue...

PLAYERAS.—The *playeras* are believed to have been the most plaintive form of the *siguiriyas*, derived from the verb *«plañir»* (to mourn, grieve, bewail). Except for the content of their verses—those of the *playeras* are traditionally even more pessimistic and black with death than those of the *siguiriyas*—they are identical to the *siguiriyas*. In modern times a distinction between them is rarely made.

It is said that the *playeras* were originally a *cante* of mourning, sung during the procession to the graveyard, and at the gravesite itself. It is curious to note that professional mourners were often hired who had a knowledge of the songs and rituals of mourning, and who interpreted them movingly and well. This burial singing may well have been the earliest outcropping of flamenco on a professional level.

El carro e los muertos	The cart of the dead
pasó por aquí;	passed by;
como llevaba la manita fuera	I recognized her
yo la conocí...	by her dangling hand...

From *«The Venta de Los Gatos»*, by Becquer, this verse tells of the tragic end of denied love, in which a boy, unaware of the death of his forbidden sweetheart, recognizes her by her hand protruding through an opening in the funeral cart. The boy, so the story goes, went insane from grief. The singer Silverio made this verse famous over a century ago, shortly after the tragedy is thought to have occurred.

Una noche e trueno	One stormy night
yo pensé morí,	I felt death
como tenía una sombra negra	like a black shadow
ensima e mí.	upon me.

La muerte llamo a voces,	I cry for death
no quiere vení,	but it will not come;
que hasta la muerte tiene	even death
lástima e mí.	finds me unworthy.

Cuando yo me muera,	When I die
mira que te encargo	I ask of you
que con la cinta de tu pelo negro	to tie my hands
me amarres las manos...	with the ribbon of your black hair...

134

This verse reflects a custom formerly practiced in Andalusian villages of tying the hands of the dead person together when preparing him for burial.

POLICAÑA.—José Carlos de Luna, in his book «De Cante Grande y Cante Chico», mentioned in passing a cante, no longer sung, called the «policaña». Domingo Manfredi Cano («Geografía del Cante Jondo») elaborates on the theme, speculating that the policaña may have been a mixture of the caña and the martinetes. I would say, judging solely from its name, that it seems more reasonable to assume that it was a combination of the polo and the caña, perhaps being a step in the development of the soleares.

ROAS.—Gypsy ceremonial dance and song, not generally considered flamenco.

The roás are a song and dance which have been conserved from an ancient gypsy religious (mystic) ceremony. They are believed to have been brought by the gypsies from the East, and to be a descendent of one of the primitive rituals such as sun, moon, or wind worship. The roás is an abbreviation of «rodadas» (to wander about, to roll), which is thought to have resulted from the constant wandering of gypsy caravans. They are usually accompanied by tambourines, and the dance and cante are accomplished by an entire circle of gypsies simultaneously. In Spain this ceremony is practiced mainly in the Granada area; outside of Spain the roás, by a different name, are said to be practiced by gypsies in Hungary, Yugoslavia, France, and in other countries where gypsies are found.

ROMERAS.—Cante, baile, and toque chico.

The romeras, a form of the cantiñas of Cádiz (see cantiñas section), are a cante that falls short of reaching the true «gracia» and flowing ease so characteristic of Cádiz' cantes. As I have written of the mirabrás, the romeras also strike me as a hastily-conceived cante, possibly innovated to add variety to the café cantante circuit. I understand that they were never in much demand, and well on their way to extinction when rescued by el Chaqueta and recorded in the Hispavox Anthology of Cante Flamenco. Because of this recording the romeras are today making a comeback, and are enjoying some popularity.

There are various versions as to how the name «romeras» came about. One is that they were named after their creator, a gaditano singer known as Romero el Tito. Another is that they received their name from a phrase of one of their popular verses: «Romera, ay mi romera...»

135

Regardless of the dubious merit of the melody line of the *romeras,* their traditional verses are sometimes quite delightful.

Romera, ay mi romera,
no me cantes más cantares,
como te coja en el hierro
no te salva ni tu mare.

Romera, ay my romera,
don't tell me more lies,
because if I catch you in another
even your mother will be unable to
                                    [*save you.*

Debajo de los laureles
tiene mi niña la cama
y cuando sale la luna
viene y la llama.

My little girl has her bed
under the laurel trees,
and when the moon rises
it comes and calls her.

Qué disparate,
qué disparate,
~ue yo te quiera
igual que antes.

What foolishness,
what silliness,
for you to think that I love you
as before.

Estoy por decí,
estoy por decí,
que no quiero a naide,
na más que a ti.

I want to say,
I want to shout,
that I love no one,
only you.

RONDEÑA (TOQUE).—*Toque intermedio,* rarely danced, not sung.

The little know *rondeña* differs completely from the *rondeñas,* which are a form of the lively *verdiales.* The *rondeñas* is an emotional, discordant *toque,* strangely reminiscent of the haunting mountain country near Ronda (much of the discordant effect of the *rondeña* is caused by the re-tuning of two of the strings of the guitar). It is said to have been a *toque* of the *bandoleros* (bandits) of the rugged sierra near Ronda; Ramón Montoya is credited for developing it into the complex *toque* that it is today. The *rondeña* is not widely played, and the first and only interpreters of the *baile rondeña,* to my knowledge, have been Carmen Amaya and Luisa Maravilla. It is rhythmically similar to the *baile* and *toque taranto.* It can safely be said that the *rondeña* is one of the most beautiful of flamenco's *toques* and *bailes.*

RONDEÑAS.—*Cante* and *toque chico,* group dance.

The *rondeñas* are the *verdiales* of Málaga removed to the rugged mountain country of Ronda. They are a gay, optimistic *cante,* very similar to the *verdiales* in rhythm and temperament, but much less frequently heard. The name «*rondeñas*» is generally believed to have stemmed from «*rondar*», to serenade, which would indicate that they were originally songs for serenading.

136

¡Rondeñas vienen cantando!
Sobre la cama me siento,
porque en oyendo Rondeñas
se me alegra el pensamiento...

They come singing Rondeñas!
I sit on my bed to listen
because my thoughts become gaier
when I hear them...

Después de haberme llevao
tóa la noche de jarana
me vengo a purificar
debajo de tu ventana
como si fuese un altar.

After having spent
the night in revelry
I come to purify myself
beneath your window
as if it were an altar.

Navegando me perdí
por esos mares de Dios,
y con la luz de tus ojos
a puerto de mar salí.

Navigating I became lost
in God's stormy seas,
and with the light of your eyes
I found my way to port.

Vive tranquila, mujer,
que en el corazón te llevo,
y aunque lejos de ti esté,
en otra fuente no bebo
aunque me muera de sé...

Live tranquilly, woman,
because in my heart I carry you,
and although I may be far from you
from another fountain I shan't drink
although I die of thrist...

ROSAS.—The term «rosas» has nearly disappeared today. Most books on flamenco do not so much as mention them, or if they do, limit themselves to stating that the rosas were a variation, now forgotten, of the alegrías.

However, through questioning many old-time flamenco artists and aficionados, I have been able to arrive at a fairly well-defined idea of just what constituted the rosas. They were, in effect, alegrías played more slowly, utilizing the graver key of mi instead of the usual key of la, whose verses tended towards despondency and melancholy instead of the gaiety essential in the alegrías. This explanation abolishes the incongruity of including the following disconsolate rosas verses within the category «alegrías».

Pá que pases por mi pena
que Dios te mande el castigo
que la persona que quieras
se te vuelva tu enemigo.

May God punish you
for all you have made me suffer
by causing the person you love
to turn against you.

Qué me importa a mí que pases
por mi puerta y no me hables,
si yo no como ni bebo
con los buenos días de naide.

What do I care if you
pass by my door without speaking?
Your salutations will neither
feed me nor quench my thirst.

137

Ni el Pare Santo de Roma
ni el que inventó los tormentos
está pasando las ducas
que está pasando mi cuerpo.

Neither the Pope in Rome
nor the creator of anguish
is enduring the pangs
that my body is suffering.

RUMBA GITANA.—*Cante, baile,* and *toque chico.*

Borrowed from the Latin American rumba, the *rumba gitana* has retained all of the sensuality and charm of its source in becoming flamenco's sexiest dance. When danced well, it is certainly most suggestive and gaily infectious while never having to resort to vulgarity. The guitarist can actually use the slapping techniques of the Latin American guitarist, while inserting flamenco *falsetas* and *rasgueado* as desired. The singing is gay and colorful. Rhythmically the *rumba* is in the family of the *tangos* and the *colombianas,* although varying in the accentuation.

Hazme con los ojos señas
que en algunas ocasiones
los ojos sirven de lengua...

Make signs to me with your eyes
for on many occasions
the eyes can speak...

Yo me la llevé a mi casa,
se la presenté a mi gente,
y le pusieron corona
por ser gitana decente.

I took her to my house
and presented her to my people;
they crowned her
for being a decent gypsy.

El sol le dijo a la luna
«apártate, bandolera,
que a las seis de la mañana
¿qué hace una mujer soltera?»

The sun told the moon,
«go home, little tramp,
what is a single girl doing out
at six in the morning?»

SAETAS.—*Cante grande «a palo seco»,* neither danced nor played.

The *saetas* are sung as chants worshipping the figures of the Virgin Mary and Jesus Christ during Holy Week religious processions. Traces of the *saetas* date back centuries, before they evolved as a part of flamenco. In the mountain areas of Granada, especially, these early *saetas,* generally agreed to have been of Jewish origin, are still remembered and sung in their original form, which is less powerful and moving than present day *saetas,* although perhaps more lyrical. The flamenco *saetas,* only innovated in this century, are sometimes sung with a free rhythm (strong influence of the *martinetes*), other times to the *compás* of the *siguiriyas.* These flamenco *saetas* are known as «*saetas por martinetes*» and «*saetas por siguiriyas*».

The Spanish Holy Week processions, with their corresponding *saetas,* have excited international interest. Barefoot penitents of each

138

church carry their Virgin Mary, or Christ, on heavy, richly-ornamented platforms through the streets of the cities, followed by hundreds of candle-bearing worshippers, also often barefoot, dressed in pointed hoods, and capes. These snail-like processions are marked by a band monotonously repeating a religious type of march. At intervals the platforms pause to rest and the band stops playing, which is the opportunity for the singers to sing to Jesus and the Virgin. This is a very emotional moment for the devout. In many Andalusian towns, such as Sevilla, it has become traditional for the *saetas* to be sung by a particular *saetero* (singer of *saetas*) from pre-established balconies, under which crowds of people gather waiting for him, or her, to sing. More often than not the crowds will cheer on the *saetero* just as they do at a *juerga*, reducing the whole matter to an exhibition during which, of course, the true significance of the *saetas* is largely lost.

For this reason many people prefer to spend at least part of Holy Week in a small town, where the atmosphere is far more authentically religious. In some out-of-the-way villages they still stage traditional medieval plays in the village plazas, which depict the biblical events of each day of Holy Week. Processions, on a minor scale, also take place, with the corresponding singing of *saetas*. These villages and small towns invariably achieve a more truly religious atmosphere than the larger towns, as the towns and cities get caught up in competitions between churches (who has the prettiest, most richly-dressed and ornamented Virgin, the best processions, etc.), and attract milling crowds largely composed of curiosity-seekers, rowdies, and the irreverent, whose attitude and actions strongly detract from the essential (if this pageant is to be at all meaningful) religious intensity of Holy Week.

Saetas are sung of the suffering, death, and majesty of Jesus Christ, and of the grief of the Virgin Mary.

Jazmines de luna nueva	*White lights of a new moon*
le nacieron a la Cruz,	*shone like jasmine on the Cross,*
y claveles, a la tierra	*and carnations covered the ground*
que echaron las manos buenas	*thrown by good hands*
en la tumba de Jesús...	*on the tomb of Jesus...*
Míralo por onde viene	*Look at him come*
agobiao por er doló,	*bent with pain,*
chorreando por las sienes	*his brow dripping*
gotas de sangre y suor.	*with blood and sweat.*
Y su mare de penita	*And his suffering mother*
destrosao er corazón.	*with her heart broken.*
Los judíos te clavaron	*The Jews nailed you to the cross*
por decir que tú eras Dios,	*for saying that you were God;*
que no quisieron creerlo,	*they did not wish to believe it,*
como me lo creo yo...	*as I myself do...*

Ayy una soga lleva en su garganta,
que otra lleva en su cintura,
y otra en sus manos santas;

son tan fuertes ligaduras
que hasta las piedras quebranta.

Ayy he has a rope around his throat,
and another around his waist,
and another around his saintly
[*hands;*
they are tied so tightly
that they would crush rock...

And a *simpática* gypsy *saeta:*

De las flores más bonitas
voy a jacé una corona
pa ponérsela a María,
hermosísima paloma...

I am going to make a crown
of the prettiest flowers
to put on María,
beautiful dove...

SERRANAS.—*Cante, baile,* and *toque grande.*

The *serranas* are said to have originated as a *cante* of the smugglers who plied their trade on the southern Mediterranean coast. When they had brought in a large haul they would hide in caves in the nearby mountains to the south of Ronda for long periods of time. Their *cante* thereby derived its name and mood from the life of these smugglers and their compatriots, the *bandoleros* (bandits), in the sierra (the word *«serrana»* means «mountaineer», «people of the sierra»).

The following verses, the first and third originals of José Carlos de Luna, the second popular, tell a little story of a shepherd turned outlaw.

No me jayo en la choza
con los pastores;
quiero ser bandolero
de los mejores;
y por el día
pasear a caballo
la serranía.

I won't be penned up in a hut
with the shepherds;
one of the best bandits
I must be;
and by day
ride my horse
through the mountains.

Por la Sierra Morena
va una partía
y el capitán se llama
José María.
No será preso
mientras su jaca torda
tenga pescuezo.

Through the Sierra Morena
rides a band
whose leader is
José María.
He won't fall captive
as long as his dapple pony
remains proud.

Al llover en la sierra
por primavera,
toman coló de sangre
las torrenteras.

When the spring
rains fall
the bursting ravines
turn the color of blood.

140

Y entonces pienso:	*And then I think:*
Así será mi llanto	*that will be my fate*
si caigo preso.	*if they catch me.*

The *serranas* are spotted with verses, such as the ones above, referring to the life of bandits, as well as others about love, and mountain life in general. They possess the same *compás* as the *siguiriyas,* and show signs of having been influenced by the *siguiriyas, livianas,* and *caña* (the «ay» sections in the *serranas* and *caña* are very similar, among other things). José Carlos de Luna, in fact, is of the opinion that the *serranas* are a direct adaptation of the *caña.*

The *serranas* are generally played slower and in a graver tone than the *siguiriyas.* Nevertheless, they are not as gypsy as the *siguiriyas,* nor do they reach such profound depths. They are generally ended by a *siguiriyas macho,* usually those of María Borrico, a *cantaora* of the 19th century.

Silverio Franconetti, among the professional *cantaores,* was a great interpreter and creator within the *serranas.* One of his verses, perhaps that most widely sung today, is:

Yo crié en mi rebaño	*I brought up in my flock*
una cordera,	*a lamb*
de tanto acariciarla	*who turned vicious*
se volvió fiera.	*from too much caressing.*
Y las mujeres,	*And women,*
contra más se acarician	*the more they are pampered*
fieras se vuelven...	*the more difficult they become...*

SEVILLANAS.—*Cante, baile,* and *toque chico.*

This infectious rhythm, typical of Sevilla although extremely popular throughout all of Andalusia, was derived from the ancient *seguidillas manchegas,* of Castile, in central Spain. The colorful dance, danced by couples, and the *cante* are performed by men, women, and children alike during Sevilla's annual week-long fair, considered the gaiest in Spain. It is a time when traditional dress is donned, work is ignored, and the *sevillanas* are danced at all hours in the streets, bars, and wherever groups congregate. One group of guitarists traditionally sets itself up in a plaza of the typical neighborhood of Santa Cruz and offers its accompaniment to all, much to the delight of passing celebrants.

Like the *fandanguillos,* the *sevillanas* is an alive *cante,* to which new styles are constantly being added. These styles are differentiated in various ways: some in their verse content, some in their points of accentuation, others in their melody line. The *compás,* of course, always remains the same.

141

Un moreno garboso ronda mi calle y dice que me quiere más que a su mare. Esta es la vía; que aquel que más promete más pronto olvía.	A handsome dark boy paces my street saying that he loves me more than his mother. But that's life; he who promises the most forgets the quickest.
En el río de amores nada una dama, y su amante en la orilla llora y la llama; ¡ayy que te quiero! y como no me pagas de pena muero...	In the river of love a lady swims, and from the edge her lover weeps and cries to her: ayy how I love you! As you don't return my love I am dying...
A mí me gusta pegarte sólo por verte llorar.	I like to hit you just to se you cry.
¿Para qué quiero llorar si no tengo quien me oiga?	Why do I wish to cry if there is no one to hear me?

SIGUIRIYAS.—*Cante, baile,* and *toque grande.*

Most *aficionados* agree that the *siguiriyas,* including its most desolate form, the *playeras* (see «*playeras*» section), are the most profoundly emotional element of flamenco. That is, when they are performed with true feeling and unfalsified emotion, for the *siguiriyas* is a release of pent-up hates, persecution, denied liberty and love, tenderness towards a companion-in-misery, and above all, of relentless, stalking death. I have seen and heard the *siguiriyas* unleashed («performed» is not the word) in a way that makes one's insides tighten with a momentary glimpse of the world's hopelessness and cruelty. Not often, to be sure, and never in a commercial atmosphere. The truth is, the *siguiriyas* are completely out of place in commercial surroundings (like the Lord's Prayer in the local gin mill). Usually the singer toys with them in an unfeeling act, the guitarist is being busily virtuoso, and the dancer contrives to destroy whatever emotion remains. Favorite commercial methods of abuse are ending the *siguiriyas* with *a bulería* or a *tango,* and the use of castanets in the dance.

The *compás* of the *siguiriyas* is identical to that of the *serranas* and the *livianas.* To the uninitiated it appears a difficult, vague *compás,* but in reality is composed of twelve beats, as are the *soleares, alegrías, bulerías, fandanguillos,* and many other rhythmical flamenco forms (1).

---

(1) It does not occur to many aficionados to think of the *siguiriyas* as having twelve beats. If they count them at all it is generally while learning to dance, or play the guitar, and then they are usually taught to count to an irregular five or seven beats, holding some

The *siguiriyas,* perhaps the most gypsy *cante* in flamenco today, is also one of the most richly varied. There are many styles, most of those presently sung dating from the last century, when every singer with a grain of pride created his own version. They demand a great physical and emotional outlay from the singer, which is even more pronounced when they are ended by a *macho.* It is probably the most difficult of the *jondo* dances to dance well, due to its character and necessarily slow-paced *compás.* The dancer must be able to captivate solely by an exceptional personality and dance of the upper torso, for any type of theatricalism or artificiality, including prolonged speeding up the *compás* to «relieve the boredom», immediately and thoroughly destroys the essence of the *siguiriyas.* For the guitarist of good taste it is a *toque* of great potential for emotional outlet.

Three-line *siguiriyas* verses exist, but the huge majority, like those below, contain four lines. *Siguiriyas* verses (in Spanish) contain an oddity that distinguish them on paper from four-line verses of other *cantes:* a third line that is quite a bit longer than the other lines. This is due to the structure of the *siguiriyas'* cante.

No quiero que se entere	*I don't want her to know,*
quien sólo era mía,	*she who was only mine,*
que en mis profundos suspiros por	*that in my profound sighs for her*
[ella	
se me va la vía...	*my life is wafting away...*

counts longer than others. This is a perfectly acceptable means to an end. I personally had never considered counting to twelve counts in the *siguiriyas* until one occasion, when I was rehearsing a commercial *soleá* with a dancer.

There is a *zapateado* in the *soleares* that also fits perfectly well into the *siguiriyas,* during which the guitar is usually silent until nearly the end of the footwork. Now during the period when the guitarist is just sitting there, he may start thinking about wine or girls or something equally as important and distractedly begin following, in his mind, the footwork *por siguiriyas* instead of *por soleá,* the consequences being, of course, that when the footwork reaches its rapid climax and the guitarist has to break in, he may do so, as I did, in the wrong form.. On this particular occasion the dancer followed the guitar, and we ended a dance flawlessly *por siguiriyas* that we had started *por soleá.*

It came as a shock to all of us that the *siguiriyas* and the *soleares* are so similar in *compás* and even accentuation, and we began analyzing the situation. Bob Haynes, an American *aficionado* present, was the first to hit on the solution and put it on paper. It was simply that the *compás* and accentuation are identical in the two forms, but are started in different places. To demonstrate. The line of numbers below is one full *compás* of the *soleá.* The blacker numbers signify points of accentuation. Count this out slowly, at the speed of a normal *soleares,* emphasizing the blacker numbers.

1 2 3 4 5 6 **7** 8 9 **10** 11 **12**

Now count twelve beats, starting at the number eight, at about twice the speed as you did the *soleares,* bearing in mind to also accentuate the blacker numbers (**8** 9 **10** 11 **12** 1 2 3 4 5 6 **7**), This will give you a perfect *siguiriyas.*

This little gem of information brings to mind any number of possibilities. For one, the *soleares* and the *siguiriyas* are not as far apart as they appear and are thought to be. It is not unlikely, in fact, that when someone decided to put the *cantes* of the *tonás* group to *compás,* they merely chose the *compás* of the *soleares* (or perhaps of the *caña* or the *polo* at that time, if the *soleares* had not yet fully developed), inadvertently or purposely disguised it, and the primitive *siguiriyas* was born. Another: that all of the rhythmical *cantes grandes,* and a good many of the *cantes chicos,* have an identical *compás* structure and accentuation, varying only in the points at which the various forms are entered into (i. e. the number diagram above). A third: that flamenco is not quite as complex a business as it is generally throught to be.

Anhelaba vivir	I longed to live
por verte y oirte;	to see you and hear you;
ahora que no te veo ni te oigo,	now that you're not here,
prefiero morirme.	I prefer to die.

Me faltaba entereza:	I lost all reason:
yo sólo veía	I only saw
que era la mujer a quien adoraba	that the woman I adored
la que se moría.	was dying.

Si te enteras que he muerto,	If you hear of my death,
pide a Dios por mí,	pray to God for me;
pues de ese modo, en la otra vida	if you do this, in the other life
yo pediré por ti.	I shall pray for you.

No temo a la muerte,	I'm not afraid of dying,
morí es naturá;	dying is natural;
lo que siento es la cuenta tan [grande	what bothers me is the huge list of [sins
que a Dios voy a dá.	that I have to present to God.

Me asomé a la muraya,	I climbed to the top of the wall,
me respondió er viento:	and the wind said to me:
¿pa qué das esos suspiros,	what is the use of sighing
si ya no hay remedio?	if there is no remedy?

Le dije a la luna	I asked the moon
del altito cielo	high in the heavens
que me llevara siquiera una hora	to grant me if only an hour
con mi compañero.	with my companion.

No pegarle a mi pare,	Don't hit my father,
soltarlo, por Dios,	for God's sake release him;
que ese delito que ustedes le [acusan	that crime of which you accuse him
lo había hecho yo.	I myself committed.

The *cabales* of el Fillo:

Desde la Polverita	From the Polverita
hasta Santiago	to Santiago
las fatiguitas de la muerte	the anguish of death
me arrodearon.	surrounded me.

SOLEARES (SOLEA).—*Cante, baile,* and *toque grande.*

The word «*soleá*» is a gypsy abbreviation of «*soledad*»; the word «*soleares*» is an improper gypsy pluralization of «*soledad*» (it should be «*soledades*»). Thus both «*soleares*» and «*soleá*» signify the same thing, «loneliness», and can be used interchangeably.

The *soleares* have been described as the «mother of the *Cante*.» This, of course, is a poetic allusion, more likely referring to the role that the *soleares* play in flamenco —there is no doubt that they are the central figure, the matriarch, around which all of flamenco revolves— than to any belief that the *soleares* have given birth to flamenco.

There are countless theories concerning the antiquity and development of the *soleares*. It is thought certain that in some form, most probably not that which we know today, the *soleares* have existed for many centuries. Poetry identical to today's *soleá corta* verses, particularly, pops up frequently in past literature, including examples in the works of Cervantes (XVI century). The first *soleares* that have reached us, however, are those of Triana, which date back only to the first half of the last century. From Triana they spread through the provinces of Sevilla and Cádiz (and, in diluted forms, to some other centers, including Córdoba), and many styles of *soleares* were born.

Many theorists, myself included, feel that the «*aire*» and essence of the *soleares* is serious, and that they should inspire verses dealing with serious themes — not desolate, like the *siguiriyas* and *playeras,* but at least leaving the frivolous and insignificant to the far-more-appropriate *cantes chicos.* As Ricardo Molina and Antonio Mairena point out, however, in practice this is not always the case. Many *soleares* verses do deal with inconsequential themes — some insignificant event, or trivial comment or complaint — which incites one to seriously consider another of the mentioned gentlemen's viewpoints: that the *soleares* have developed over the past one hundred years from a fast, gay *cante,* that served basically to accompany the dance, to the slower, more serious form presently in existence. Were this correct, it would explain the phenomenon of the many inane *soleares* verses, so out of keeping with the form as it is known today, as well as why the earlier *soleares* of even this century were performed at a faster tempo.

The *cante por soleá* is broken down into three categories: the *soleá* «*grande*» (great, profound), the *soleá* «*corta*» (short), and the «*soleariya*» («little» *soleares).*

Soleá Grande.

The *soleá grande* is thought to be the most recent form of the *soleares* to have developed. It differs from the *soleá corta* and the *soleariya* in two ways: its verses contain four lines instead of three, and are therefore longer and more difficult to sing; and the *soleá grande* is characterized by increased solemnity, and as such is more sprinkled with wisdom, philosophy, and death than its shorter counterparts. Examples:

Quisiera por ocasiones
estar loco y no sentir,
que el ser loco quita penas.
penas que no tienen fin.

Aquer que fue poca cosa
y que cosa llega a ser,
quiere ser tan grande cosa
que no hay cosa como él.

La muerte a mi cama vino
y no me quiso llevá;
no estaba cumplío mi sino
y al irse me eché a llorá.

Estoy viviendo en el mundo
con la esperanza perdía;
no es menester que me entierren
porque estoy enterrá en vía.

Cuando murió la Sarneta
la escuela quedó serrá
porque se llevó la llave
del cante por Soleá.

*Sometimes I would like
to be crazy and not feel,
for being crazy takes away grief,
grief that has no solution.*

*He who was no one
and becomes someone
wishes to be the biggest someone,
bigger than all the rest.*

*Death came to my bedside
but did not wish to take me,
as my destiny was not complete;
on its departure I began to weep.*

*I am living in the world
devoid of hope;
it is not necessary to bury me,
as I am buried alive.*

*When la Sarneta died
her school was lost
because she took with her
the secret of the Soleá.*

The above verse became popular after the death of the famous singer and creator of *soleares*, Merced la Sarneta. The «school» refers to her style of *soleá*.

Y si he caío en desgracia
que le hemos de jasé.
Santitos que yo pintara
demonios se han de volvé.

Er querer es cuesta arriba,
y el orvidar, cuesta abajo;
quiero subir cuesta arriba
aunque me cueste trabajo.

Florecillas silvestres
se menean cuando paso
yo te quiero a ti solita
y a ninguna le hago yo caso.

*If I have fallen into disgrace
what can be done?
Saints that I paint,
demons become.*

*Love is uphill,
forgetting, downhill;
I want to climb uphill
even though I end up suffering.*

*The wild flowers
shimmy when I pass
but I love you only
and walk on unheeding.*

Soleá Corta and Soleariya.

These two forms of *soleares*, composed of three-line instead of four-line verses, are shorter and therefore less difficult to sing than the *soleá grande*. They differ from each other in only one respect: the first line of a *soleariya* verse is extremely brief, while the corresponding line of the *soleá corta* is of normal length.

In talking about these *cantes* the very name «*soleá*» (loneliness) is misleading, for the *soleá corta* and the *soleariya* (and, of course, to a certain extent the *soleá grande*) form one of flamenco's principal *cantes* of ardor and romance. The vast majority of their verses push death and other such considerations aside, and the more immediate problems of love take over.

These shorter *soleares* are sung at a variety of tempos: sometimes slowly, like the «*grandes*», other times at varying cadences which can get quite fast, developing into what is known as the «*soleá por bulerías*». The tempo, profundity of interpretation, and verse content are entirely up to the individual singer (1). In the mouths of some singers, such as Manolito de María, Fernanda de Utrera, Joselero de Morón, and Juan Talegas, the *soleá corta* leads love to profound depths, while other singers make love their playground. In this respect, these *soleares* serve as an insight into the character of the individual singer.

The *soleá corta* and the *soleariyas* are better suited than the *soleá grande* to the *baile*. Their tempo, as we have seen, is more flexible, and their verses appropriately deal with love. As love is many-sided, the dance *por soleá* can absorb many more touches of gaiety and insertions of technique than, for example, the always desolate *siguiriyas*. I would say that it should depend on the content of the verses sung whether the dance develops in a *jondo* manner, or whether it can be ended gaily with the customary *bulerías a golpe*. If it is optimistic, the *bulerías* ending is somewhat appropriate, as long as it does not get wildly out of hand; if pessimistic, the *bulerías* ending is incongruous. In practice, of course, the dancer rarely patterns his dance on the *cante,* as obviously should be the case. The dancer and singer are too often wrapped up in their own worlds, and perform emotionally independently from one another.

As for the guitar, the *soleares'* simple, straightforward *compás* (see footnote, *siguiriyas* section), makes it pregnant with *jondo* possibilities. It also makes it an ideal virtuoso *toque* Consequently, little of value is heard guitar-wise *por soleá*

Lo gitano	*That which is Gypsy*
va en la masa de la sangre	*is found in the surge of blood*
y en las rayas de las manos	*and in the grooves of hands.*

---

(1) The singer is often influenced, as is natural, by the tradition prevalent in his area. Example: the verse content of the *soleares* of Cádiz is generally lighter and more inconsequential than that of the province of Sevilla.

Por tu vera paso de noche y de día, buscando mi compañera...	I pass by your side day and night searching for my mate without recognizing you...
Por ti las horitas de la noche me las paso sin dormir.	I pass the hours of the night without sleep because of you.

The above three verses are characteristic of the *soleariya* because of their short first line. The following verses are *soleás cortas*.

Ay pobre corazón mío... por más gorpes que le doy nunca se da por vensío...	Ay my poor heart... despite the bad times I gives you you never give up...
Yo me agarro a las paredes cuando te encuentro en la calle, chiquilla, pá no caerme.	I cling to the wall when I meet you, chiquilla, for support for my fluttery legs.
Me va faltando er sentío. Cuando estoy alegre, lloro; cuando estoy triste, me río.	I am losing my senses. When I am happy, I cry; when sad, I laugh.
¿De qué me sirve dejarte, si dondequiera que mire te me pones por delante?	It is useless to leave you if wherever I look you are there.
Tienes cuerpo de chiquilla y carita de mujer llenita de picardía.	Your body is a little girl's, but your face that of a woman full of mischief.
Dejo la puerta entorná por si alguna vez te diera la tentación de empujá.	I'll leave the door ajar in case one day you have the temptation to enter.
Unos ojos negros vi... Desde entonces en el mundo todo es negro para mí.	Her eyes were black... since then the whole world is black for me.
Tu calle ya no es tu calle, que es una calle cualquiera, camino de cualquier parte.	Your street is no longer your street it is any street anywhere.
Voy como si fuera preso; detrás camina mi sombra, delante, mi pensamiento.	I go as a prisoner; behind me my memories, ahead, my thoughts.
No siento en el mundo más que tener tan mal sonío, siendo de tan buen metal.	Nothing saddens me more than I, being of such good metal, having such a bad sound.

Le dijo el tiempo al querer:
«esa soberbia que tienes
yo te la castigaré».

Time said to Love:
«I shall destroy
this cocksureness that you have.»

TANGOS (TANGOS FLAMENCOS) (TIENTOS CANASTEROS).—
Cante, baile, and toque chico.

There are various *tangos* scattered throughout Andalusia. There are those of the Malagueñan singer Piyayo, for instance, others of Frijones de Jerez, others from Triana, but the *tangos* that have most captured the hearts of *aficionados* are those from Cádiz. At their best, the Gaditanan *tangos* are a gay, contagious example of the lively spirit of that port-city; combined with a few glasses of wine, they are a sure remedy for all ailments. However, all *tangos,* even those from Cádiz, are not happy. An inverse case of the *soleares,* which incongruously contain frivolous and even humorous verses, some *tango* verses are most melancholy. To me, this phenomenon signifies one of two things: a serious *tango* past, from which the sad verses are remnants, or the insensitivity of some of the old-time *tango* interpreters (1).

The *tangos,* considered one of the oldest and most basic gypsy *cantes,* have an unknown origin, but theories abound. Argentineans claim that they are a brother of the Argentine *tangos.* Others theorists dissect the word «*tango*», tracing it to Latin, or demonstrate the similarity between «*tango*» and the names of various musical instruments. Still others find its roots in ancient songs of northern Spain, while Fernando Quiñones has recently presented the possibility that the suffix «ngo» may be associated with Negro Africa.

The *tangos* are also called «*tientos canasteros*», which means to say «gypsy *tientos*» («*canasteros*» is a flamenco term for «wandering gypsies», and also, less likely in this case, for «basket weavers»), and has led some to think that the *tangos* came about as merely a more gypsified version of the *tientos.*

The dance *por tangos* is sensual and exciting, more subtle and therefore more effective than the *rumba gitana.* It's *toque,* driving and rhythmical, is straightforward and exciting.

---

(1) In many cases «ignorance» and/or «limitedness» are better words than «insensitivity», for in days past there were many «specialists» who sang only one *cante* (or danced one *baile,* or played one *toque*). Let us say that this *cante* is *por tangos,* or *por bulerías,* both characteristically gay *cantes.* Now obviously our specialist is not always going to be bubbling with joy, and, being a flamenco singer, when some tragedy befalls him he must also give vent to it through song. If it is death, and he only knows the *tangos* or *bulerías,* he must sing of death in his chosen *cante.* He will undoubtedly slow it down to a minimum, of course, and sing it with great emotion, but, nevertheless, the verse dealing with death may remain within the traditional *tangos* or *bulerías* verses. Inversely, if he can only sing *por soleá* and he wins the lottery, he will sing a wildly rambunctious *soleá,* which verse may also stick. Fortunately, this state of affairs has largely disappeared today. The one-*cante* specialists of days of yore now know at least two *cantes,* one of each type (*tangos-tientos, bulerías-soleá,* etc.), and presently there is little need, or excuse, to mix the intrinsic emotion and essence of the various *cantes.*

¡Con el ay, caray, caray!
Mirusté qué fiestas
va a haber en Cái.
Luego, qué jambre
se va a pasá...
Ay, caray, caray, cará...

Las fiestas de mi tierra
son de canela,
y está el Ayuntamiento
de enhorabuena.

Dolores, Dolores,
¿con qué te lavas la cara
que tanto te huele a flores?

Péinate tú con mis peines,
que mis peines son de azúca;
quien con mis peines se' peine,
hasta los deos se chupa.

Cuatro casas tengo en Londres,
que me las dejó mi tía,
y rentan cuatro millones
de dinero tós los días.

Si alguna vez vas por Cái
pasa por barrio Santa María,
y allí verás los gitanos
cómo se bailan por alegrías.

A tós los ojitos negros
los van a prender mañana,
y tú que negros los tienes
échate un velo a la cara.

Yo a ti te pondría
un puente pa que pasaras
de tu casita a la mía.

Vales más millones
que los clavelitos grana
que asoman por los balcones.

El vecino del tercero
a mí me mira con seriedá,
porque dise que yo tengo
con la vecina amistá.

With an ay, caray, caray!
Just think of the fiestas
that Cádiz is going to have.
And afterwards, the hunger
that will come...
Ay, caray, caray, cará...

The fiestas of my land
are of cinnamon,
and the City Hall
is to be congratulated.

Dolores, Dolores,
what do you wash your face with
that it smells so much of flowers?

Comb yourself with my comb
as it is made of sugar;
if you use my comb you will
end up sucking your fingers.

I have four houses in London
that my aunt left me,
and they rent for four millions
of money every day.

If you are ever in Cádiz
go to the barrio Santa María,
and see how the gypsies
dance por alegrías.

Tomorrow all black eyes
are going to jail!
And you, whose eyes are black,
cover them with a veil!

I would build you a bridge
for you to more quickly pass
from your house to mine.

You're worth more millions
than all the scarlet carnations
cascading from the balconies.

The neighbor on the third floor
looks at me quite seriously
because he says that with his wife
I have become a bit too friendly

150

TANGUILLO.—*Cante, baile,* and *toque chico.*

The *tanguillo* (little *tango*) is considered by many as Andalusian folklore, outside of flamenco, and by others as a *chico* component. Those who consider it non-flamenco are justified, as the *cante* has few of the characteristics of good *cante chico* (like the *sevillanas*), and is usually sung in a popular vein. The *baile* and the *toque,* on the other hand, are more flamenco in nature. The *tanguillo,* a cross between the *tangos* and the *rumba,* has a mischievous, airy rhythm, an innocent sensuality (unlike the provocative *rumba gitana*), and a lack of any attempt at depth (unlike the *tangos*). The *tanguillo* was developed in Cádiz from the *tangos.*

Niña, asómate a la reja	*Niña, come to your balcony,*
que te tengo que decir	*I want to whisper something*
que te tengo que decir	*to whisper something*
un recadito a la oreja.	*in your ear.*
El recadito consiste	*The message is*
que no te quiero ni ver	*that I want to lose you from sight,*
que los besos que me diste	*and that I've only come to return*
te los vengo a devolver...	*the kisses you gave me...*

TARANTAS.—*Cante* and *toque intermedio,* not danced.

The *tarantas* are basically a *cante* of miners. Thought to have originated in the province of Almería, they spread to wherever there are mines in southern Spain: in particular, to the provinces of Jaén (Linares) and Murcia. They are a resigned *cante,* well reflecting the atmosphere in which they developed.

The *tarantas* are similar to the *cartageneras* in feeling and structure and, like them, are a *cante* free from *compás.* They are descended from the *fandangos grandes,* but with a far more discordant Moorish influence. Their verses usually reflect mining themes.

Clamaba un minero así	*A miner cried out*
en el fondo de una mina;	*in the bottom of a mine;*
¡Ayy en qué soleá me encuentro!	*ayy what loneliness I have!*
y en mi compaña un candil	*and although I have a lamp*
y yo la salía no encuentro.	*I cannot find my way out.*
Dices que te llamas Laura,	*You say that you are Laura,*
Laura de nombre,	*that Laura is your name,*
si no eres de los laureles,	*but you're not of the laurels,*
que los laureles son firmes.	*for the laurels are firm.*

151

En diciendo ¡gente ar torno!
todos los mineros tiemblan
al vé que tienen su vía
a voluntá de una cuerda.

In saying, line up to enter!
all of the miners tremble
to see that their fate
hinges on a rope.

No se espante usted, señora,
que es un minero quien canta;
con el jumo de las minas
tiene ronca la garganta.

Don't be frightened, señora,
it's just a miner singing;
with the smoke of the mines
his voice has turned hoarse...

TARANTO.—*Cante* and *toque intermedio, baile grande.*

The *taranto* is the danceable form of the *tarantas*. Unlike the *tarantas*, which have no set *compás*, the *taranto* has a steady, beating *compás* similar to a slow *zambra*. Its *cante* and *toque* are very similar to the *tarantas* in construction. The dance of the *taranto* is majestic and *jondo*, with great opportunities for expression due to its discordant Arabic beauty. Most of its present-day dance interpreters have a tendency to underestimate the emotional potentiality of the *taranto;* they insist on dancing it too rapidly and commercially, much like they dance the *zambra,* and they are consequently at odds with the somber mood set by the *cante* and the *toque* (this is, of course, the principal objection to all of the *bailes grandes* as danced today).

The *cante por taranto* originated in the province of Almería. *Tarantas* and *taranto* verses can be sung interchangeably.

TEMPORERAS.—*Cante* and *toque chico,* not danced.

A descendent of the *serranas,* the *temporeras* are a country *cante* that originated around the area of Cabra, near Córdoba. They have the peculiarity of being sung by various people in a group taking turns, each singing a different verse. The originating voice calls *«voy»* (I begin); when he ends, another singer calls *«voy»* and sings; this goes on until they have all sung, and finally the originating singer announces *«fuera»* (out), and sings the last verse. The *temporeras,* nearly disappeared, are very similar to the *fandanguillos.*

Las uvitas de tu parra
están diciendo comerme,
pero los pámpanos dicen
que viene el guarda,
que viene...

The grapes of your vine
are asking to be eaten,
but the vine leaves warn
that the watchman is coming,
is coming...

152

Los surcos de mi besana	The furrows of my land
están llenos de terrones,	are full of mounds,
y tu cabeza, serrana,	and your head, mountain girl,
está llena de ilusiones,	is full of illusions,
pero de ilusiones vanas.	but vain illusions.

This verse, originally a *temporera*, is often sung presently as a *fandanguillo*.

TIENTOS.—*Cante* and *toque intermedio, baile grande.*

The *tientos* are very similar to a slow *tango flamenco*, so much, so that few flamencos presently distinguish between them. True, the *compás* and structure of the *tientos* is identical to that of the *tangos*, and their *cante* verses can be sung interchangeably. There is a difference, however, which consists mainly in the way the guitar accentuates the rhythm. Traditionally the *tangos* are played without noticeable accentuation, while in the *tientos* some beats are prolonged, others are cut short. This lends the *tientos* a certain air of remoteness, of profundity, not possessed by the *tangos*. Few guitarists, however, stress this difference today, and more and more a slow *tango* and the *tientos* are becoming molded into one, as undoubtedly they were in the beginning.

It is theorized by some that the *tangos* are a gaier descendent of the age-old *tientos*. Others state exactly the opposite: that the *tientos* are a more *jondo* descendent of the *tangos* — are, in fact, nothing other than a slow *tango,* innovated by the Gaditanan singer Enrique el Mellizo in the latter part of the last century. Still others claim that the *tientos* were a creation of Diego el Marrurro, a singer from Jerez de la Frontera. Actually, all of this conjecture, and the blind stands taken one way or the other, will lead us nowhere, for, in truth, no one knows.

The dance of the *tientos,* one of the most majestic, rhythmic, and sensual of flamenco, has an advantage over most other *jondo* dances. It can be as profound as the interpreter wishes to make, it, while at the same time the movement and *gracia* inherent in the *tientos* should never permit it to become tedious, as is often the case with other *jondo* dances when not danced by truly gifted artists. Inexplicably, the *tientos* is rarely danced today.

¿Qué pájaro será aquel	What bird would that be
que canta en la verde oliva?	that sings in the green olive grove?
Corre y dile que se calle,	Run and tell him to be quiet,
que su cante me lastima...	as his song saddens me...

Yo no le critico a nadie	I cannot criticize anyone
que le domine el queré,	who is dominated by love,
porque a mí me está dominando,	because I myself am dominated
y no me puedo valer.	beyond help.

153

Te voy a meter en un convento
que tenga rejas de bronce,
que la gente no te vea,
ni a la ropita te toque...

I am going to put you in a convent
that has heavy bronze bars,
so that people cannot see you
nor touch your clothing...

Tú serás mi prenda querida,
tú serás el pájaro cuqui
que alegre canta de madrugada;
Ayy lo que te quiero,
¿sin ti mi vía pá que la quiero?

You will be my cherished belonging
the cucu bird
that happily sings at dawn;
ayy how I love you,
without you why would I want to
[live?

Te quiero yo,
te quiero yo
más que a la mare
que a mí me parió.

I love you,
ah how I love you,
even more than the mother
that gave me birth.

TIRANAS.—The *tiranas*, today completely forgotten, was a *cante* very similar to the *malagueñas*.

TONAS.—*Cante grande «a palo seco»*, neither played nor danced.

Professor M. García Matos, who publishes his findings and theories in the *«Anuario Musical»* of the Instituto Español de Musicología, proposed in 1950 what appears to be the most acceptable theory concerning the origin of the *tonás*. He believes that under the name *«tonadas»* they were songs relating stories and events, which were sung by wandering minstrels from village to village throughout Spain. It is probable that these songs were adopted and fomented by the gypsies, and the *«tonás»*, a form thought by many to have been flamenco's earliest, or at least one of the earliest, was born. When the gypsies were driven off the roads, they took the *tonás* with them into blacksmiths' forges, with the resultant development of the *martinetes* of the forges, a form similar to the *tonás*. The *deblas* and the *carceleras* are also offspring of the *tonás*. The original story-telling *tonás* have nearly disappeared, although García Matos states that some of the early folkloric versions still exist in Extremadura, more particularly in the provinces of Cáceres and Salamanca.

The flamenco *tonás* developed into a profund *jondo cante*, one of the most difficult of flamenco that was on the verge of disappearing when flamenco made its comeback in the 1950's. The *tonás* are completely devoid of *compás*, and are not accompanied.

It is said, probably exaggeratedly, that there were at one time some thirty types of *tonás*. Now only three are remembered: the *tonás grande*, the *tonás chica*, and the *tonás del Cristo*.

Ayy no te rebeles, gitana,	Ayy do not fight it, gypsy girl,
yo tengo hecho juramento	I have sworn
de pagarte con la muerte.	to pay you with death.
Vinieron y me dijeron que tú	They came and told me
había hablao mal de mí,	that you have talked badly of me;
y mira mi buen pensamiento.	and imagine my opinion of you
que no le creía de ti.	that I didn't think you capable of it.

This verse, a *tonás chica*, reflects a normally violent gypsy reaction.

O pare de almas y ministro de	O father of souls and minister of
[Cristo,	[Christ,
tronco de nuestra iglesia santa	heart of our saintly church
y árbol del paraíso.	and tree of paradise.

This verse, the «*tonás del Cristo*», may reflect the contrition felt by the gypsy after his impetuous act.

TRILLERAS.—*Cante* and *toque chico*, not danced.

The *trilleras* are a song of the country, traditionally of the wheat grinders. In Spain the ancient method of grinding wheat is still used, which consists of a man, seated on a small platform resting on shining blades of steel, being pulled by two horses round and round over the wheat spread on the ground. While this monotonous process goes on hour after hour, the rider may divert himself singing the *trilleras* to the *compás* of the beating hooves. His song is joyful and optimistic, and his verses are usually *piropos* (flatteries) to his horses, his girl, someone else's girl, his village, the sun and the birds. Unfortunately, the *trilleras* have nearly disappeared.

Qué mula, vamos a ver,	What a mule, gee, git up...
a esa mula de punta la gusta el	that one up front that likes grain so
[grano,	[much;
aligera y no comas	Gee now and hurry, don't eat any
	[more!
que viene el amo...	Here comes the boss!...

Esa yegua lumanca tiene un po-	That spotted mare has a little colt
[trito	
con una pata blanca	with one white hoof
y un lucerito;	and a star on his forehead,
bueno... buenooooo...	bueno... woa... woooa...

VERDIALES.—*Cante, baile,* and *toque chico.*

The *verdiales,* said to have been named after a tiny village, Los Verdiales, in the province of Málaga, are thought to be the oldest of the existing *fandangos* in Andalusia. They are a gay, lively predecessor to the *malagueñas;* the *malagueñas* of Juan Breva was the intermediate stop between the *verdiales* and the present - day *malagueñas.*

The *verdiales* are accompanied by guitars, tambourines, violins, and certain other crude instruments in sprees of singing and dancing that can go on for many hours and even days in the mountain country behind Málaga capital. When performed more reasonably, time-wise, they are Málaga's festive answer to the *sevillanas.*

The dance, very folksy and undoubtedly ancient, is danced by couples and groups. The *verdiales* has only recently been developed as a guitar solo.

Yo soy de la Triniá...	*I am from Trinidad...*
Viva Málaga, mi tierra	*Long live Málaga, my land,*
el huerto de los claveles,	*home of carnations*
y el puente de Tetuán...!	*and the bridge of Tetuán...!*

La Trinidad is a neighborhood in Málaga.

Quién te pudiera traer,	*That I could carry you,*
pueblo de los Verdiales,	*town of the Verdiales,*
metido en la faltriquera	*in my pocket*
como un pliego de papel.	*like a folded piece of paper.*

VITO, el.—*Cante, baile,* and *toque chico.*

According to Hipólito Rossy, who in turn quotes other writers, the *vito* is an extremely old folk form that surged to the surface in the first half of the last century as a dance accompanied by song. Again it was nearly lost, and again came to the surface with the first theatrical folkloric groups of this century, in part due to the efforts of García Lorca.

Until very recently, however, the *vito* has not been considered fla-menco. At present it is usually performed on stage to the *compás* of the *bulerías.* When sung alone it is often *compás*-less.

Yo me subí a un pino verde	*I climbed a green pine*
por ver si la divisaba	*to see if I could spot her,*
y sólo divisé el polvo	*and all I saw was the dust*
del coche que la llevaba.	*of the carriage that carried her away.*

Anda, jaleo, jaleo;	Anda jaleo, jaleo;
ya se acabó el alboroto	that ends the hullabaloo
y ahora empieza el tiroteo.	and now starts the shooting.
En la calle de los Muros	In the street of the Ramparts
mataron a una paloma.	they killed a dove.
Yo cortaré con mis manos	With my hands I shall cut
las flores de su corona. -	the flowers for her crown
Anda, jaleo, jaleo;	Anda jaleo, jaleo;
ya se acabó el alboroto	that ends the hullabaloo
y ahora empieza el tiroteo.	and now starts the shooting.

The dove in this verse is thought to be the speaker's sweetheart.

ZAMBRA.—*Cante, baile,* and *toque chico.*

Hipólito Rossy writes that there are references to a dance called the *zambra* that date back to the XV century, and that in the XVII century it ranked alongside such popular dances as the *fandangos, zapateado,* and *zarabanda.* He claims that its name came from «*zamra*», Arabic for «flute», and that the *zambra* was originally a lively Moorish dance.

Presently the *zambra* is identical to the *tangos* in *compás,* although it employs a different chord structure. It is practiced mainly by the gypsies of the Sacromonte (Granada). When performed well, in the atmosphere of a cave illuminated by firelight and shining copper, the *zambra* can be a very exciting experience.

No te metas con la Adela,	Don't provoke Adela
la Adela gasta cuchillo	for Adela has a knife
pa quien se meta con ella.	for whomever meddles with her.
Que nos miren desde el puente,	Let them goggle us from the bridge
y que la envidia nos siga,	with all of their envy;
que queriéndonos tú y yo,	as long as we love each other,
deja que la gente diga.	who cares what people say.
Gitana, si me quisieras	Gitana if you should love me
yo te compraría en Graná	I would buy you in Granada
la mejor cueva que hubiera.	the best cave ever.
Vente conmigo y haremos	Come with me and we'll make
una chozita en el campo	a little hut in the country
y en ella nos meteremos.	and there we'll stay.

157

ZAPATEADO.—*Baile intermedio, toque chico,* not sung.

Another ancient Spanish dance, mentioned, among others, by Cervantes, that has surely reached us in a completely varied form, the *zapateado* today is a virtuoso dance strictly for showing off footwork. Originally a man's dance, it has been adopted by *bailaoras* in recent years to the extent that it is now considered a necessary componet of both the male and the female repertoire. For this dance the female usually dons tight-fitting men's ranch wear (*traje corto,* boots, *cordobés* hat, ruffled shirt), or less frequently, women's ranch wear (a *traje corto* with a long slit skirt instead of pants, boots, *cordobés* hat, ruffled shirt). In my opinion the development of the female *zapateado* has contributed a great deal to the decadence of the feminine dance. The *bailaor* can make the *zapateado* a virile, exciting dance; the *bailaora* merely demonstrates the results of hours of practice.

The *zapateado* is danced by both the male and the female in a rigid attitude, grasping with both hands the bottom of their *traje corto* jacket throughout most of the dance.

The guitarist plays a difficult accompanying role in the *zapateado,* as he should follow to perfection the stops, starts, and accentuations of the intricate footwork. Usually the arrangement between the dancer and the guitarist is worked out in advance. Recently guitar solos have also been developed for the *zapateado* by concert guitarists in their effort to increase the scope of the flamenco guitar. Rhythmically it is played to the *compás* of the *tanguillo,* although with a more stern approach, and utilizing a different set of chords. The most popular music for the present day *zapateado* was composed by the Spanish classical composer Sarasate, followed by an arrangement by Monreal. When the dance is accompanied by the piano, the arrangement is played directly from the sheet music; when by the guitar, the arrangement is based on the classical, but usually some flamenco touch, some innovation or improvisation, will creep in.

El Raspao, a dancer of the 19th century, later Antonio de Bilbao, and more recently the late Estampío, have been legendary interpreters and developers of the *zapateado.* The arrangements of footwork most danced today are based on those of Juan el Estampío.

ZORONGO (ZORONGO GITANO).—*Cante, baile,* and *toque chico.*

The *zorongo,* another of the old folk songs resuscitated by Federico García Lorca, has only recently become a part of flamenco. Since its rediscovery by García Lorca it has been popularized largely through theatrial flamenco dance groups. The following verses were all composed by García Lorca.

158

La luna es un pozo chico,	*The moon is a little well,*
las flores no valen nada,	*flowers are worth nothing;*
lo que valen son tus brazos	*what are of value are your arms*
cuando de noche me abrazan...	*when at night they embrace me...*

This verse is the theme of the *zorongo,* carrying the *compás* of a slow, sensual *tango,* and is repeated alternately after each of the following verses:

Las manos de mi cariño	*My loving hands*
te están bordando una capa	*are embroidering a cloak for you*
con agremán de alhelíes	*with the cape of jasmine*
y con esclavina de agua.	*and the collar of clear water.*

Cuando fuiste novio mío,	*When you were my sweetheart,*
por la primavera blanca	*during the white spring*
los cascos de tu caballo	*the hooves of your horse*
cuatro sollozos de plata.	*were like four silver sighs.*

These are two verses of the many that are done to the *compás* of the *bulerías.*

PIROPOS (COMPLIMENTS) IN SONG

A large slice of Andalusian life is devoted to making the Andalusian woman *feel* like a woman. She may be as beautiful as sunrise, ugly as sin, *simpática,* bitchy, gay, dull, but one thing she is not: ignored. It is not surprising, then, that the *cante* flamenco is sprinkled with charming *piropos,* oftentimes expressed so poetically that the most determined woman must weaken.

The following are a few such *piropos,* mostly verses that originated with the populace, not the professional poet. When one stops to think that until recent years the common people in Andalusia were largely illiterate, with no formal education whatsoever, one cannot help being overwhelmed by the verses (especially, of course, when read in Spanish), and by the feeling that Andalusia must be a land of lovers.

Although, as we have seen, the *soleares* is basically flamenco's *cante* of love, it by no means has the corner on that market. These verses can be adapted to most of flamenco's appropriate *cantes* by prolonging a word here, repeating a line there.

So attention, lovers!

De rosas y claveles
y de alhelíes
se te llena la boca
cuando te ríes.

Your mouth fills
with roses and carnations
and jasmine
when you laugh...

Ya no se llaman dedos
los de tus manos,
que se llaman claveles
de cinco ramos...

The fingers of your hands
are not like fingers,
they are more like
a bouquet of five carnations

Es tu pecho redoma
llena de olores,
donde se purifican
todas las flores.

The flowers
are scented
by the perfume
of your breasts.

Sin duda que tu padre
fue confitero,
pues te hizo los labios
de caramelo.

Your father doubtless
was a confectioner,
for he made of your lips
two lollypops.

160

Es tu cara una rosa
que colorea,
y tu cintura, el tallo
que la menea.

Eres alta y delgadita
como junco de ribera;
has de tener más amores
que flores la primavera.

Cuatrocientos contadores
se pusieron a contar
las gracias de tu hermosura;
no pudieron acabar.

Te vi por la serranía:
¡pintores no te pintaran
bonita como venías!

El día que tú naciste,
¡qué triste estaría el sol,
en ver que otro sol salía
con mucho más resplandor!

El día que tú naciste
nacieron todas las flores,
y en la pila del bautismo
cantaron los ruiseñores.

¿En qué jardín te has criao,
linda maseta de flores,
que no tienes quince años
y ya robas corazones?

De tu cara sale el sol;
de tu garganta, la luna:
bonitas he visto yo,
pero como tú, ninguna.

La gachí que yo camelo
está llenita de lunares
hasta las puntas del pelo.

¡Bendito Dios, morenita,
qué buena moza te has hecho:
delgadita de cintura
y abultadita de pecho!

Your face is a
reddening rose,
and your waist
the fluttering stem.

You are tall and thin
like a rush at river's edge;
you must have more loves
than springtime has flowers.

Four hundred accountants
could not finish
counting the graces
of your beauty.

I saw you in the mountains:
painters could not have painted you
as pretty as you were.

How sad the sun must have been,
the day that you were born,
to see that another sun now rises
with more radiance and splendor.

All flowers were born
the same day as you,
and in the baptismal fountain
sang the nightingales, too.

In what gardin were you cultivated,
beautiful flower,
that before your fifteenth year
you already steal hearts?

From your face rises the sun,
from your throat, the moon:
I have seen pretty girls,
but none as pretty as you.

The girl that I love
is covered with beauty spots
to the tips of her hair.

For goodness sakes, morenita,
what a doll you have become:
with your narrow waist
and blossoming chest!

161

Eres
la emperatriz de las flores,
la reina de las mujeres.

La iglesia se ilumina
cuando tú entras
y se llena de flores
donde te sientas.
Y cuando sales,
se revisten de luto
todos los altares.

Esa madeja de pelo que
te cuelga por las espaldas,
de día, por hermosura;
de noche, por almohada.

A tu cara le llaman
Sierra Morena,
y a tus ojos, ladrones
que andan por ella.

Al revolver de una esquina,
tus ojitos me asaltaron,
tus cabellos me prendieron
y a la cárcel me llevaron.

Tus ojitos, *morena*,
tiene tal virtud
que a los mismos que matan
le dan la salud.

Tienes un hoyo en la barba
que parece una cunita:
¿quieres que me meta en él
y me cantas la nanita?

Eres y eres
la flor y nata de las mujeres.

You are
the empress of flowers,
the queen of women.

The church is illuminated
when you enter
and fills with flowers
where you sit.
And when you leave,
the altars return
to mourning.

That bouquet of hair
that cascades down your back.
By day, how lovely;
by night, what a pillow!

They call your face
the Sierra Morena,
and your eyes, bandits
that roam over it.

On rounding a corner
your eyes assaulted me,
your hair captured me,
and they led me to my imprisonment.

Your eyes, dark one,
possess such magic
that even while they devastate
they restore health.

The dimple in your chin
looks like a crib:
if I climb in will you
sing me a lullaby?

You are and you are
the blossom and cream of womanhood.

For further *piropos*, consult the other verses included in the Encyclopedia, particularly those of the *alegrías, bamberas, bulerías, cantiñas, soleariyas* and *soleás cortas*, and *tangos*.

PART IV
APPENDICES

APPENDIX NO. 1

BREAKDOWN OF THE CANTE, BAILE, AND TOQUE

Breakdown of the Cante.—The following is a list of the *cantes* that can still be heard today, broken down into the major categories *grande, intermedio,* and *chico.* The *cantes grandes* are those of a profound nature, of extremely difficult interpretation, all of which stem from religious antecedents. The *intermedios,* still profound, are a little less so than the *grandes,* and less difficult to interpret. Mostly derived from folkloric origins, they are the *cantes* with perhaps the strongest Arabic influence. The *chicos* are a gayer breed, least difficult of all to interpret, stemming from both folkloric and religious origins. Included among the *chico cantes* are several still considered by some theoreticians as folklore, not flamenco. I have included them among the *chicos,* however as they are thought of as flamenco by the large majority of *aficionados.* They are the *garrotín, sevillanas, tanguillo, vito, campanilleros,* and *milonga.*

The (G) or (A) following a *cante* indicates whether the *cante* is believed to have been originally and basically gypsy (G) or Andalusian (A)—developed. Those that are followed by an (R), signifying «rarely heard», are well on their way to extinction.

CANTE GRANDE

with guitar accompaniment (danceable):

Caña (A)	Polo (A)	Siguiriyas (G)
Livianas (G)	Serranas (G)	Soleares (G)

without guitar accompaniment (termed *a palo seco,* not traditionally danced):

Carceleras (G) (R)	Martinetes (G)	Saetas (A)
Debla (G)	Tonás (G)	

165

CANTE INTERMEDIO

all *cantes intermedios* have guitar accompaniment:
not danced:

Cartageneras (A)	Jaberas (A)	Tarantas (A)
Fandangos Grandes (A)	Malagueñas (A)	
Granaínas (A)	Media Granaína (A)	

danceable:

Peteneras (A)	Tientos (G)	Taranto (A)

CANTE CHICO

with guitar accompaniment (danceable):

Alboreás (G)	Garrotín (A)	Tangos (G)
Alegrías (G)	Guajira (A)	Tanguillo (A)
Bulerías (G)	Mirabrás (G)	Verdiales (A)
Cantiñas (G)	Romeras (G)	Vito (A)
Caracoles (G?)	Rondeñas (A)	Zambra (G)
Chuflas (A)	Rosas (G) (R)	Zorongo (A)
Colombianas (A)	Rumba Gitana (G)	
Fandanguillos (A)	Sevillanas (A)	

with or without guitar accompaniment (not danced):

Bamberas (A) (R)	Milonga (A)	Trilleras (A) (R)
Campanilleros (A)	Nanas (A)	
Marianas (A) (R)	Temporeras (A) (R)	

Breakdown of the Baile.—The *Baile flamenco* is unlike the *Cante* in that each *baile*, or danceable *compás*, does not have traditional characteristics that have to be adhered to. Each *cante*, on the other hand, has a definite structure and other characteristics that belong only to that *cante*, as is true, to a lesser degree, with each *toque*. In the *Baile*, the rhythm largely determines the dance, and between *bailes* with very similar rhythms and moods there will be no inherent difference in the dance. Therefore, all of the possible *bailes* have not been listed, as were the *cantes*, as it would lend a deceptive scope to the *Baile*. Instead, only the *bailes* having a distinct *compás* and feeling are listed, with a separate listing below of other very similar *bailes* which could be danced in exactly the same emotional and technical manner.

BAILE GRANDE

Caña	Siguiriyas	Taranto
Serranas	Soleares	Tientos

BAILE INTERMEDIO

Alegrías	Peteneras	Zapateado

BAILE CHICO

Alboreás	Farruca	Tangos
Bulerías	Guajira	Zambra
Chuflas	Rumba Gitana	Zorongo
Danza Mora	Tanguillo	

GROUP DANCES

Fandanguillos	Sevillanas	Verdiales

Other dances not listed due to their close similarity to some of the above are as follows: the *polo,* similar to the *caña;* the *livianas,* similar to the *siguiriyas;* the *romeras, caracoles, mirabrás, rosas,* and *cantiñas,* similar to the *alegrías;* and the *colombianas* and *garrotín,* similar to the *rumba gitana* and *guajira.* It may be argued that the *soleares* and *caña* are also similar, as are the *siguiriyas* and the *serranas,* but I believe that the inherent emotional qualities in each of these *bailes* should cause a distinction in the dancer's interpretations.

The *aficionado* will notice that the *alegrías* and the *zapateado,* considered by many as *bailes grandes,* are listed under *bailes intermedios* due to what I consider a lack of adequate *jondo* qualities. On the other hand, I have elevated the *taranto,* relatively new to the *Baile,* to the *baile grande* section because of its obvious *jondo* attributes.

MODERN THEATRICAL DANCE INNOVATIONS

A new trend in the world of theatrical *Baile flamenco* is the performance of such never-before-danced forms as the *martinetes, deblas* and *carceleras.* That these *cantes* are traditionally abstract and rhythmless stops no one; they merely put them to the *compás* of the *siguiriyas,* and then enact theatrical scenes, at their best in keeping with the verses sung, but more often quite independently from the singing. In its desperate groping for material the theater will, it seems, stop at nothing.

167

Breakdown of the Toque.—The following are the *toques* most used for solo playing:

TOQUE GRANDE

| Caña | Serranas | Siguiriyas | Soleares |

TOQUE INTERMEDIO

Granaínas y Media	Malagueñas	Tientos
Granaína	Tarantas y Taranto	
Rondeña (toque)	Peteneras	

TOQUE CHICO

Alegrías	Farruca	Tanguillo
Bulerías	Guajira	Verdiales
Caracoles	Rosas	Zambra
Colombianas	Rumba Gitana	Zapateado
Danza Mora	Sevillanas	Zorongo
Fandanguillos	Tangos	

Besides the *toques* listed above, the really well-rounded guitarist has to be able to accompany all of the *cantes* and *bailes* listed elsewhere in this appendix, with the exceptions of those denoted «without guitar», which are the five *cantes* «*a palo seco*». Nevertheless, if the guitarist learns to accompany the singing and dancing for those forms listed above (with the addition of the *fandangos grandes*), he will have a reasonably complete mastery of the flamenco guitar, and will certainly be able to accompany those *bailes* and *cantes* most often performed.

APPENDIX NO. 2

FLAMENCO RECORDINGS OF SPECIAL INTEREST

In the 1984 edition I wrote that LPs of flameco were out, and that anthologies were in. In the six year interim, the reverse has again come to pass. In the last edition I wrote up six excellent anthologies. Only one remains on the market that I can find, the *Magna Antologia del Cante Flamenco*, which, due to its importance, I shall re-review later in this section.

Some fine LPs have replaced the anthologies, if you can find them. They are usually issued in small quantities and therefore go out-of-print quickly, and fewer and fewer record and music stores these days carry much in the way of serious flamenco. The relative purity of the sixties, seventies and first half of the eighties has dissipated, and flamenco has reverted to a large extent back to the *cante bonito*, to the lads with the high-pitched, fluty voices crooning pseudo flamenco ballads. Records of these singers, headed by Chiquetete, are everywhere.

But, as I said, there are fine records available of serious flamenco. In continuation I shall list a few of the locales that stock them.

Madrid, Opera Tres, Plaza Isabel II, 3, 28013 Madrid, Tel: 5426600, Fax: 5426475. This large music store has the best selection of good flamenco LPs that I have found in Madrid. They mail order both nationally and internationally, will send a list of their records, and other specified merchandise, upon request.

Córdoba, Librería Lucano, Calle Lucano 8, 14003 Córdoba, Tel: 472885. Owner Manuel Sánchez Rabadán is a rabid aficionado, stocks a large selection of flamenco LPs, as well as an impressive number of books about flamenco (and Andalusian culture in general). He mail orders both nationally and internationally, will send out lists of both records and books upon request.

Sevilla, The Casa Damas, Calle Sierpes 61, 41004 Sevilla, Tel: 223476, has long prided itself on its selection of flamenco records.

169

Magna Antología del Cante Flamenco, Hispavox, Twenty LPs or cassettes, accompanied by a lengthy and thorough explanatory booklet in Spanish by José Blas Vega which includes a listing of all the verses sung. This massive anthology is intended to be, and is, the definitive in-depth work in flamenco. Twenty are a lot of LPs, and here one can find just about any cante that is remembered today, including some that were on the verge of disappearing,To accompolish this, Blas Vega relied heavily on such veteran singers as Bernardo de los Lobitos, Agujetas Viejo, Jacinto Almadén, Aurelio Sellé, Pericón de Cádiz, Antonio Mairena and, above all, Pepe Núñez de la Matrona, one of whose 22 cantes on the anthology is the tonás grande attributed to Tío Luis el de la Juliana, flamenco's first documented singer (c.1760-1830). Other singers, in order of number of bands, are Enrique Morente (22), Gabriel Moreno (14), Antonio Mairena (12), Pericón de Cádiz (12), Antonio Piñana (8), Aurelio Sellé (6), Ramón Medrano (5), Pepe el Culata (5), El Chozas de Jerez (4), El Borrico (4), Sernita de Jerez (4), Terremoto de Jerez (4), Jacinto Almadén (4), Agujetas Viego (3), Antonio Ranchal (3), Romerito (3), El Flecha de Cádiz (3), Juan de la Loma (3), Flores el Gaditano (3), Manuel Mairena (2), Niño de las Moras (2), Antonio Chocolate (2), Bernarda de Utrera (2), El Sordera (2), La Perla de Cádiz (2), Manolo Vargas (2), Pepe de Algeciras (2), and so forth.

Guitar accompanists. Some singers are accompanied by their favorite accompanists (Pepe de la Matrona mostly by Manolo el Sevillano, Antonio Mairena and Caracol principally by Melchor de Marchena, Pepe de Lucía by brother Paco de Lucía, Terremoto by Morao, the old Zambra singers by Perico el del Lunar, most Jerez singers by Paco Cepero, most of the Levante singers by Antonio Piñana (hijo). Other accompanists include Pepe Habichuela, Niño Ricardo, Paco Anteqera, Andrés Heredia, Marote, José Luis Postigo, Pepe Martínez, Luis Maravilla, Juanito Serrano, Victor Monge "Serranito", Antonio Vargas, and a few others, but the guitarist who truly carries the load, accompanying 68 bands, is Félix de Utrera. The closest accompanist to Félix in number of bands is Melchor de Marchena, with 23. If you are a Félix fan, this is just fine. If not, it is a little unfortunate.

As for the cantes included, prepare yourselves for true depth. One entire LP is devoted to romances (fanciful stories, usually of an historical nature, told in song. They are not particuilarly flamenco in nature, are today considered more gypsy folklore than flamenco), the largest number ever compiled; there are 13 bands of cantes "a palo seco" (6 tonás, 5 martinetes, 1 debla, 1 carcelera); included are the incredible number of 34 siguiriyas, 6 from Los Puertos, 11 from Jerez, 8 from Cádiz port, and 9 from Sevilla. Represented are siguiriyas of Manuel Molina (4), el Marrurro, Paco la Luz, El Loco Mateo, Antonio Chacón, Frijones, Manuel Torre, El Planeta, El Nitri, Diego el Fillo, Enrique Ortega, María Borrico, Curro Dulce (2), Enrique el Mellizo (2), Frasco el Colorao, Cagancho, Silverio (3), Tomás Pavón, La Niña de los Peines, and so forth; there are 21 soleares, from Cádiz, Utrera, Jerez, Alcalá, Triana, Córdoba, etc.; 3 cañas and polos; 5 peteneras; 15 bulerías; 12 tangos; 10 tientos; 4 alegrías; 9 cantiñas; 7 livianas, serranas and alboreás; 14 cantes from Málaga, other than malagueñas; 24 malagueñas and granadinas; 13 mining cantes (tarantas, tarantos, mineras, cartageneras, murcianas); 7 fandangos de Huelva; 19 personal fandangos of creative singers of the past; 16 bands of diverse cantes (sevillanas, bamberas, farruca, garrotín, the *pregón* de Macandé, Christmas bulerías and songs, campanilleros, 3 saetas), and 8 bands of cantes of Latin American influence (guajiras, guajiras por bulerías, guajiras festeras, milongas (2), colombianas, rumbas flamencas vintage 1914, and a popular rumba).

As you can see, this anthology is by far the most ambitious in scope ever put together. The only possible criticisms I can anticipate are two: 1) only 30% of the material of this anthology is new, signifying that 70% has been taken from older Hispavox recordings (Antología del Cante Flamenco, the two-record sets of both Pepe de la Matrona and Manolo Caracol, and various LPs). The aficionado with a collection of past Hispavox recordings will, therefore, have considerable repetition on acquiring this anthology; 2) another possible criticism is that some of the bands have been recorded by what we might call studio artists instead of by singers and guitarists from the region of origin of each cante. This, to my way of thinking, converts the process into more of an intellectual than an emotional exercise. That is to say, instead of recording artists raised with the forms of the particular region, in which the cante or toque is second nature to them and in which they have strong emotional binds, the studio artists are called upon to interpret forms basically alien to them. Thus we have Félix de Utrera accompanying 68 bands, and relatively young men like Enrique Morente and Gabriel Moreno singing some cantes they accomplish well intellectually but have not lived. But this is by no means true of the anthology in general; the large majority of cantes and toques are interpreted by appropriate artists.

In summation: this anthololgy is an extraordinary opportunity for all serious aficionados, but far too much for the casual fan, who will be better off with a selection of smaller offerings.

APPENDIX NO. 3

THE JUERGA

The "Juerga" has played such an important role in flamenco's history and development that I believe it deserves an appendix of its own.

The dictionary definition of juerga is a "spree" or "fling." A juerga flamenca, therefore, is a spree built around flamenco. That is clear enough, but complicated by several factors. For one, most flamencos avoid using the term due to its having acquired bad connotations in the past. Spanish society remembers only too clearly when a juerga flamenca was often an all-out blast involving prostitutes (often taking place in their very houses of commerce), in which flamenco-soaked, drunken debauchery frequently lasted for days. Syphilis ran rampant, livers inflamed, pay checks were spent in their entirety, marriages collapsed, all in the name of the juerga flamenca. Thus, it is not surprising that society frowns seriously upon both the term and the action, nor that flamencos today often avoid the term juerga, substituting for it the terms "fiesta" (party) or "reunión" (reunion). These terms are not only less provocative but are frequently accurate, for although the term juerga can be, and is, extended to mean "any intimate gathering involving booze and revolving around flamenco" (and as such precludes all gatherings in which flamenco is of secondary importance), the term "fiesta flamenca" perhaps better describes a type of quite respectable flamenco gathering fashionable today.

Nevertheless, in this book I prefer to employ the extended meaning of the term juerga, for describing a flamenco gathering as a party (fiesta) seems to me to belittle the whole concept.

Brief History of the Paid Juerga. Throughout most of flamenco's history, the paid juerga has been a rarity. Prior to 1850, flamenco existed solely as a way of life. No money was involved. The flamencos were aficionados earning their living however they could, and their singing, dancing and playing were strictly for their own enjoyment. No one, including the flamencos, attached any importance to flamenco other than as their main form of expression and diversion.

The café cantante period (1860-1900) created the flamenco professional. Aficionados were suddenly called "artists," and they found, much to their amazement, that people were willing to pay for their art. The commercial flamenco artist and the paid flamenco juerga came into being, raising flamenco to unprecedented popularity and the flamencos to an elevated standard of living. But only briefly. The forty years of the "Golden Age" passed quickly, and just as the flamencos were getting used to the good life it was snatched away from them. The cafés cantantes closed, and flamenco went terribly commercial, culminating in the "ópera flamenca," while true flamenco crept, bruised and beaten, back to the villages. During this period (1900-1960) even the greatest of the pure artists could not gain a decent living from pure flamenco. They suffered, and their art suffered, for the caliber of flamenco and prolificacy of creation dropped sharply. Paid juergas were hard to come by, and those that were held were generally patronized by two groups: the hell raisers who wanted a flamenco back drop for their debauchery, and, paradoxically, the prosperous commercial flamenco artists, many of whom hated what they were doing and spent much of their earnings on the pure artists and the pure art.

Around 1960 the whole scene miraculously began reversing itself. Commercial artists started losing ground, and the pure artists began surging to truly unprecendented popularity and affluence, far more so than during the café cantante period, for today they not only have commercial establishments and paid juergas vying for them, but lucrative record contracts, flamenco festivals, and foreign lands as well.

But watch out. Putting to one side the inevitable loss of artistic purity caused by over-exposure to commerce and sophistication, another more immediate and unfortunate phenomenon is occurring. So much prosperity has entered the flamenco picture that it is threatening its very foundation, the flamenco way of life. Andalusian villages and towns are being left flamenco-less deserts as more and more artists are lured to the commercial establishments of the big cities, there to live anything but the traditional way of flamenco life. With steady jobs, and money in their pockets, these big city flamenco artists shun juergas, the only group vehicle to moments of true emotion that flamenco has to offer. They point out that a juerga takes so much more out of them than their tablaos or their teaching, and all that drinking and those late hours . . . and if they do deign to even consider accepting a juerga offer, they demand exorbitant amounts of money, enough to discourage the idea in all but the most wealthy aficionados.

For the time being, paid juergas are still possible in Andalusian towns, where the remaining artists are not as yet dipped in gold, and are still enough involved with the flamenco way of life to enjoy a good juerga. However, it is far tougher than before. There are fewer artists available, and with competition slight those remaining can afford to demand larger and larger sums of money.

The trend is definitely towards the disappearance of the paid juerga, and quite possibly, in time, of all juergas as flamenco eventually becomes just another big city business with fixed hours, weekly paycheck, and at home the little woman waiting with dinner on the table and the seemingly irresistible lure of history's most effective hypnotic: television.

The reference to TV is not just an irrelevant attack on an industry. The fact is, television is playing a major role in the extinction of the flamenco way of life, and not only indirectly through captivation of the interest of the public; it is even used effectively as a direct weapon. Let me explain. Until the days of widespread TV, many spontaneous juergas came about because the flamencos were simply bored. They would be standing around in their favorite tavern having a few drinks, and what could be more natural than to start singing and rapping out a compás on the bar. Today, even if the flamencos have the urge their favorite tavern will undoubtedly have a TV set placed prominently, forever turned on blaring away at top volume. The worst part is, bar owners will rarely turn off the TV to make way for a session of flamenco. They have their reasons. The law considers places that encourage flamenco potential trouble spots as, in truth, flamencos drinking, releasing their art, and raising hell in general have been known to get overly rambunctious. Physical violence is rare, but the din of their singing, shouting and wild laughter not infrequently causes a neighbour who has to work the next day to call the police, who in turn will stop the juerga. If the tavern is a repeater, the owner will probably be fined and perhaps his place even be closed down for a time. (This is the principal reason for the "Prohibido el Cante" signs displayed in most Andalusian bars.) To circumvent this situation, bar owners purposely set up the TV barrier. Some, however, who are aficionados, provide special, enclosed rooms for juergas. This helps, but does not nearly solve the problem. Like manipulation of birth control before spontaneous love-making, just the special effort demanded formalizes the situation and often kills the moment. In the case of the spontaneous juerga, additional reasons exist for not wanting to retire to the special room. Flamencos love the idea of being expansive in the middle of a ready-made audience, and, no small consideration, they know that they will be charged more for their wine once seated in the special room. They also know that once in the room there will be pressure to perform in a more formal, superior manner than if just standing up at the bar having fun. So too often they just figure the hell with it, and let themselves be beaten by the box.

APPENDIX NO. 4

COMMERCIAL FLAMENCO ESTÂBLISHMENTS

As has been seen during the course of this book, flamenco is not at its best in a tablao atmosphere. Dyed-in-the-wool aficionados, in fact, rarely frequent these establishments unless there is some extremely special lure to draw them in.

Several insolvable problems arise in the tablaos. A main one is that most of the artists in these places are bored silly. To them, the night after night deadly routine is only bearable as a means of supporting their families. The more imagination they have, and therefore more artistry they are capable of, the more this is true. The public does little to alleviate this boredom, for most of it is there strictly for social purposes, and the huge majority does not understand what is going on anyway. So the artists tend to take the easy way out, entertaining themselves as best they can by horseplay, impurities, and, in general, duende-less flamenco. The main exceptions to this are the short termers, those who occasionally work in tablaos but do not spend long periods of time in them.

Another problem, from the purist's point of view, lies in the managements of the tablaos themselves, who demand from the artists a type of flamenco they believe will best go over with the public. This is, an overdose of rumbas, sex, legs, cuplés, and above all, exaggerated showmanship and flashy arrangements; in general, what can be termed "commercial flamenco." The unfortunate fact is, the managements are on the right track, as can well be appreciated by the sad fate of one Madrid tablao. This tablao, La Cueva de Nerja, decided to experiment with the pure. They brought in from all over Andalusia the great, unsophisticated artists, unglamorous and uncommercial, and began giving shows of *real* flamenco. The flamenco world loved it, going time and again and having a ball. The public, however, did not understand, and the place finally had to close down.

Actually, we may not have the choice in the future of whether or not to attend a tablao if things continue as they are going, for today most tablaos are having a tough time of it, even those who draw good houses and should be making a great deal of money. Apparently they are not, due to several factors; taxes on tablaos are extremely high; the management must pay into the social security fund for each artist and all other employees, which is a substantial percentage of their base pay and a serious drain on profits; the tablaos must charge high prices to cover these costs, and a decreasing segment of public ops to pay them, including many tourists, the principal supporters of tablaos.

Result; in recent times various tablaos have had to close their doors, and others at present are considering following suit. Thus, a few years ago it occurred to various enterprising aficionados that another approach to the presentation of flamenco had to be undertaken, the idea being to cut costs drastically and still make a profit. The first efforts along this line were in Madrid. Non-luxury sites were chosen, and artists were reduced from the 15 or 20 offered in tablaos to some 3 or 4. The most costly element of flamenco presentation, the dancing, was suppressed, thus alleviating the need of a large dancing space, dressing rooms, special taxes and a special license. Two or three singers and a guitarist were the sole artists, and these were paid according to the gate. Two such places opened in Madrid - the Café Silverio, and the Café Burrero - and both died at a young age. The art was fine, the gate was zilch. It seems neither place attracted the much-needed tourists, precisely due to the lack of dancing (legs, sex), and the overdose of all that wailing and seriousness. These places were conceived for true aficionados, and it turns out there are not enough true aficiondos around to support them.

Not long ago another establishment decided to try it out, to date with considerable success. The place itself has a large, very attractive bar-restaurant area out front, which in itself is a money maker, and a good-sized tablao behind closed doors in back. Reasonably priced (at present) flamenco recitals are offered beginning at midnight on Thursday, Friday and Saturday nights, usually featuring only a well-known singer and a guitar accompanist, but sometimes a dancer with his group. The place is usually packed, and looks like it is here to stay. Try it out. It is called *Casa Patas*, on the Calle Cañizares, 10, in Madrid, Tel. 2285070. Nearest metro; Antón Martín.

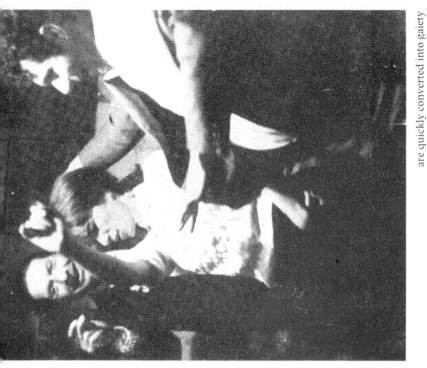

THE JUERGA

are quickly converted into gaiety

The artists are (L. to R.): (left) the late Bernardo de los Lobitos, Paco de Valdepenas, Paco del Gastor; (above) the late Manolito de la María, Luisa Maravilla and Paco de Valdepenas.

The juerga: (left) unidentified singer; (above) Fernandillo de Morón dances to the accompaniment of Paco del Gastor.

The juerga: Diego del Gastor wills La Fernanda de Utrera on to greater expression, exclaims in delight at the result.

The juerga: Antonio Mairena (above), por siguiriyas, and the local fish vendor (below), por chuflas, enrapture this juerga group.

Photo: D.E. Pohren

As wine warms the frosty crevices his voice becomes stronger and more sure, and his duende deepens.

Recitation plays an important role in *juergas*, and more so when sparked by excellent moments of dancing. This gypsy reciter-dancer is Manolo el Poeta, from Alcalá de Guadaira.

A gypsy woman and her child enjoy their own little *juerga* as the boy leans the pitos (finger-snapping).

A form of popular *juerga*: dancing sevillanas during the Seville fair.

APPENDIX NO. 5

FLAMENCO FESTIVALS AND CONTESTS

'Today, the most overwhelming influences in the realm of flamenco are Spain's flamenco festivals and contests. Such phenomena are not necessarily unique in flamenco's history — there was the famous Granada contest in 1922, and a few other widely-spaced events, mostly in the 1920's and mostly, strangely enough, outside of Andalusia (i.e. Madrid) — but today these events are far more than occasional shots in the dark, as they were previously. Presently, to my way of thinking they represent the actual re-blossoming of flamenco in flamenco's places of birth themselves — Andalusia, and the mining districts of south-eastern Spain.

People from all over Andalusia who just a few years ago could not stomach flamenco are now flocking to these events. The reasons are varied. Number one, it is flamenco on a respectable level. Number two, the events appeal to their patriotism, a kind of "I'm an andaluz and I'm with it, too" type of thing. Number three, all classes of society attend, and they are good places in which to be seen and make contacts. Number four, the flamenco artists offered are usually top quality. Number five, they are within almost everyone's means, whereas the private juerga, the only previous alternative, is not.

Two important points to consider are: (1) Are these events good for flamenco? And (2), are they good flamenco?

(1) Good *for* flamenco they are and are not. In the twenty-five years since their modern outbreak (1956) flamenco has made a comeback in Andalusia that has been incredible to behold. I think it can safely be said that these events have played an important role in this comeback. On the other hand, the very act of bringing flamenco from the back rooms into the limelight has created circumstances that have been extremely debilitating to authentic flamenco, as we see under the "Festival" heading later in this section.

(2) Good flamenco they are and are not. Potentially good flamenco, yes, because there is no denying that many of the best flamenco artists take part. But they are sadly lacking in another respect. Flamenco, in its pure and traditional form, simply is not suited for such spectaculars; the hundreds of people squirming in their seats, or chomping away at one of the "food festivals" while the show goes on. Cold, mechanical, intellectual flamenco can be heard and seen, but these events, by their very nature, are largely lacking in the elements that make flamenco worthwhile: the duende; the true

177

gracia, that can only be true at close quarters; the personal contact between artists and spectators (the drinking, laughing, joking together, and the slow, mutual arrival to the "moment of truth"); and the excitement of spontaneity.

This is no one's fault or oversight. These events cost a lot of money, and must play to big crowds. We must think of them in perspective; for the multitudes, they are far better than nothing.

Besides the general points already discussed, each type of event has its own peculiar virtues and handicaps, which we shall briefly discuss now.

Contests. A maze of developments tend to water down the results of flamenco contests, such as small, non-representative turnouts, local favoritism, private business interests, possible inadequacy of judges, and the very idea itself of flamenco being submitted to a contest.

Small turnouts occur because professional artists have a tendency to avoid contests. They realize that they have little to gain and much to lose, as they stake their professional prestige and standing against a comparatively small monetary prize and increase in prestige. They also well realize that the contests are not usually decided on the basis of merit alone. In view of this, professionals have to be enticed into participating by offers of certain guarantees; namely, a prize and/or prize money (participants have been known, often at the insistence of the organizers, to divy up behind the scenes: one gets the prestige, the other the purse), or at least a guaranteed sum as remuneration for his performance. In the latter instance, the man just considers it another job he is hiring out for. All of these factors, including the awarding of prizes and prize money, are often decided long before the contest takes place.

Even in the rare straight contest, who is going to judge, and by whose standards? Will only traditional versions of cantes be accepted (must it be sung exactly as it was by such and such a singer fifty years ago?), or will the individual contestant's personality and creativity be taken into consideration?

Oftentimes sitting in as judges are men who have been chosen on the basis of their prestige or personality rather than on their knowledge of the Cante. Others are good aficionados, which in itself, paradoxically, can also be a drawback, as these men are usually well acquainted with the participating artists, and are wide open to favoritism.

In truth, the results of flamenco contests, and all contests, for that matter, that are organized and judged by human beings, cannot be taken seriously. They can be helpful, however, to flamenco's aficionados and beginning professionals. Monetary prizes aside, energetic and imaginative publicizing of a prize award can bring an artist to the attention of agents and night club owners, and greatly increase his prestige in the eyes of the gullible segment of the public. That is one of the few useful features of flamenco contests.

Festivals. Festivals are more fun than contests, and almost always better flamenco-wise. The atmosphere is less formal, more relaxed, and therefore a little more flamenco. But there remain the problems of hundreds of people, the need to use amplifying equipment (invariably screeching at all the wrong

178

moments), batteries of local and regional radio mikes that tend to obstruct the view of the performers, the interminable presentation of the program by one or several of Andalusia's most garrulous and self-important gentlemen, and the general glaring unauthenticity of the atmosphere that all this makes for.

Despite these problems, during the height of flamenco's resurgence (the 1960's and 1970's), the very novelty of the festivals caught the public's fancy, and they multiplied like rabbits. Every Andalusian town of any size wanted its own. At the beginning this was all well and good. Flamenco artists were delighted with the new and unexpected source of income and charged reasonable fees, fees that were directly reflected in the initially low admission prices. Everyone was happy for a time, the public, the artists, the organizers. Then inevitably, greed and prima donna-ism entered the picture. Artistic heads swelled and they began demanding more and more money even as they performed fewer and fewer numbers. This practice drove up the price of admission to the point where many aficionados decide it simply is not worth it. The resultant half-empty houses often lose money for the organizers, who sometimes conclude that they are not going to be the sole losers, and pay the artists correspondingly less. After such failures the organizers often decide against future festivals, and the short-changed artists against performing at them even if they do continue.

All of the above, combined with the fact that the novelty is now wearing thin, has caused a decline in the big flamenco spectaculars. The large auditoriums, outdoor parks and bullrings are being replaced by smaller halls and theaters featuring considerably fewer artists, arrangements which are far less costly and more practical. But even this movement can work in the long run only if the artists are willing to accept less and put out more, for the average aficionado is getting quite fed up with having his leg pulled.

Trends in the Art. The type of flamenco offered has also affected, and been affected by, the course of the festivals. From flamenco's initial comeback (1956) through the late 1970's, purity of expression was prevalent. Every singer worth his salt felt he or she had to sing por siguiriyas or soleá or martinetes, with the result that spectators had to sit through a multitude of somber cantes when what most really wanted was to drink and be sociable and be entertained. When festival organizers realized this, they began inserting a larger variety of cantes, with a goodly percentage of bulerías, alegrías and others of a light vein. This worked for a while until that too became old hat, which is when the impure first began creeping in, in form of verses from popular and folkloric songs sung por bulerías. From there it was only a step to flamenco-ized versions of entirely non-flamenco songs, which draw considerably more applause than the serious cantes and which produce idols (Chiquetete, Manzanita, Turronero, etc.) whose popularity far exceeds that of any of the serious flamenco singers.

Thus, the theoretically worthy concept of presenting pure flamenco to the masses through festivals has degenerated, in a matter of twenty-five years, to the point where festivals are playing an important role in the destruction of

179

pure flamenco. Take Sevilla's "Half-Month of Flamenco and Andalusian Music" ("Quincena de Flamenco y Música Andaluza"), held yearly the first half of December. During the fifteen day period in 1982 a few potentially excellent flamenco programs were presented (five to be exact), but there were far more of a dubious nature. Those that were undisguisedly Andalusian were fine — two nights for Manolo Escobar, a piano recital of classical Andalusian compositions – but then we were confronted with the mixtures of flamenco and Andalusian and World. Consider Rock Flamenco, the sole offering one of the days. The fact that Sevilla, progenitor of pure flamenco, even recognizes the existence of rock flamenco is a long step down, much less put it on the program. Another day Manzanita (at one time considered a great promise as a flamenco guitarist) offered "New Forms of Flamenco," which is a way of describing his singing of flamenco-ized pop songs. Then there was Chiquetete (a fine flamenco singer when not selling out) mixing it up and really confusing the audience, singing flamenco pop with orchestra, some flamenco with guitar. Even Juan el Lebrijano joined their ranks by singing some far-out stuff to the accompaniment of a Moorish orchestra.

Why do they do it? Ask any of them and they'll sum it up in one word: MONEY.

Now, I respect pure flamenco, I respect pure Andaluz, I even respect pure pop and pure rock. It is the mixing of them that is beginning to tear flamenco apart at the seams, much as did the "ópera flamenca" during the first half of this century. Opera flamenca burned itself out and the pure returned with a vengeance. We can only hope that the same will happen with flamenco rock and flamenco pop and flamenco whatever, and that we relearn that true flamenco is an in-group expression not understood, nor particularly wanted, by outsiders. When it *is* offered to them they immediately set about adapting it to their tastes in order to make it at least reasonably palatable.

Or this time has the authentic truly outlived its day? I am often reminded that flamenco inevitably must change with the times. Perhaps rock flamenco, jazz flamenco, pop flamenco, go-go flamenco, cuplé flamenco, Mexican ranchera flamenco are acceptable? Where is the line drawn, or is there no line?

One comforting thought is that the authentic cannot disappear. It is all recorded, readily available for the day of tomorrow, when the nonsense has died down a bit, for a new generation of singers to rediscover. Meanwhile, no one is forcing aficionados to attend the destruction; one is perfectly free to listen to the real thing in the quiet of one's home.

Where and When. The where and when of festivals are evasive points. Host towns usually make the decision as to when at the last minute, depending on when nearby towns decide to have theirs, the availability of artists, and so forth. July and August are definitely the big months, followed by June and September. The aficionado traveling in Spain can check the Andalusian newspapers, and the bars for posters, and usually find something every Saturday night not too far away. That has been the case, at least, for a number of years. During the period of decline it will be more difficult.

APPENDIX NO. 6

LEARNING FLAMENCO

This appendix has been subdivided as follows:

1. Flamenco Instruction in Spain.

A. Song

B. Dance. Dance Instructors.

C. Guitar. Guitar Instructors.

D. Summer Guitar and Dance Courses in Andalusia.

E. Basic Advice.

2. Flamenco Instruction Outside Spain.

3. Flamenco Methods, Sheet Music, Periodicals, and Bibliography.

A. Methods.

B. Sheet Music.

C. Periodicals.

D. Bibliography.

1. FLAMENCO INSTRUCTION IN SPAIN.

In this section I shall generalize a bit about learning flamenco, and list as well some of the best maestros, and courses, presently available to the student. All of the maestros speak Spanish, of course. I shall also denote those who speak passable or fluent English, a detail that may be of utmost importance to students who speak little or no Spanish. For information about each maestro, you might wish to consult "Lives and Legends of Flamenco."

A. SONG. The Cante is by far the most difficult element of flamenco to learn, above all for the non-Spanish-speaking aficionado. A perfect speaking grasp of Spanish is essential, preferably of idiomatic Andalusian. And that is only part of the struggle. The truth is, one just about has to be born into the Cante, no matter how much one studies and how much one works. Very few singers will even attempt to teach flamenco singing to a Spaniard, much less to a foreigner. I have known two or three non-Spaniards who have become adequate flamenco singers after much striving, but only adequate at best. So why not take up dancing or the guitar, far more amenable fields for the non-Spaniard.

B. DANCE. Choosing a dance instructor is a complex business, for within flamenco there are various styles of dance, and corresponding maestros. There are many maestros who specialize in the folkloric dances such as sevillanas, fandangos and verdiales, which are fine for those students out to get some exercise and learn a few dances for party fun or the Sevilla fair. Other maestros, the majority, are oriented towards teaching those who wish to dance professionally in tablaos or theatrical groups. These instructors know through experience what appeals to the popular public (flashy arrangements, fancy footwork, sex, a great deal of agitation and moving around, etc.), and they know how to teach it. In stating this, I do not intend any malicious reflection on these instructors. Most of their pupils are aspiring professionals, and must be prepared for the well-defined demands inherent in commercial dancing. For the remainder of students, who wish to dance in a more pure style, for personal satisfaction, concentrating on a more subtle dance emphasizing the arms, hands, wrists, posturing, and gracia, still different maestros should be sought.

The reader may ask: cannot a pure-style dancer also make it commercially? It is possible, but rare. Even if given the opportunity, the style of the dancer will undergo subtle changes until it is no longer pure. The instinct for crowd approval, the showman's craving for applause, almost invariably triumphs. Who would not fall if put in the position of watching inferior artists consistently draw more applause merely because they play up to the crowds by use of tricks and banality? (And how many times I have heard these same compromising artists, those equipped with sensitive natures, that is, scorn the crowds for its lack of perception and taste, actually despise it for driving them to their loss of art and integrity.)

. There are various ways of locating an instructor that is to your taste. You can tour the dance studios (listed in continuation) and attempt to sit in on classes so as to judge the maestros. This is relatively accepted practice. And/or you can frequent the tablaos and theaters, single out an artist whose dance you particularly like, and ask him/her about instruction. The chances are that artist will not teach, but will recommend someone adequate (probably his/her ex-maestro). When searching, keep in mind that knowing how to dance, and knowing how to teach and choreograph dance, are quite distinct. Except for the self-taught, the teaching of flamenco dance boils down to just a few maestros, most of them in Madrid and Sevilla.

DANCE INSTRUCTORS — MADRID

There are four principal centers in Madrid where studios can be rented for dancing, and where flamenco is taught. They are listed below, together with names of the more prominent instructors who presently teach in each of them. The person in charge of each locality will be able to inform you of the teaching schedules of each teacher, his/her home phone number, and so forth.

Estudios Amor de Dios, Calle Amor de Dios 4, Madrid-14. Tel. 4673690. Metro Antón Martín. The studios in this former monastery are the most deficient and run-down in Madrid. They are also the most traditional, most active, and cheapest. Due to the heightened activity, Amor de Dios offers the opportunity of observing several dance instructors in action, enabling the student to judge which fits him/her best. Most of the maestros permit potential students to stand-in on group classes, during which time you can size up the professor, judge whether the material taught is to your liking, whether too advanced or not advanced enough, and so forth. At present, very worthy flamenco instructors teaching at Amor de Dios are (in alphabetical order): *Ciro* (speaks English), *María Magdalena, Paco Fernández* (speaks English) and *Rosa Mercé.* Other good instructors also teach there during periods they are free from performing, including *La Tati* and *Merche Esmerlada.*

Estudios Madrid, Calle Ballesta 6, Madrid-13. Tel. 2221347. Metro Callao. These studios are relatively new, clean and with good floors and mirrors. *Rosario,* of Rosario and Antonio, is part owner, and uses Estudios Madrid as her base for teaching. *Luisa Maravilla* (fluent English) also teaches here.

Estudios Calderón, Calle Atocha 21, Madrid-12. Tel. 2390067. Metro Sol. These studios, clean and in relatively good condition, are owned by a professional dancer names Miguel Antonio Novella (of Lina and Miguel). Maestros who teach here include (in alphabetical order): *Angel Torres* (speaks English), *Cintia Serva Jones* (fluent English), *Luisa Maravilla* (fluent English), *Paco Fernández* (speaks English), and *Tomás de Madrid.*

Estudios Libertad, Calle Libertad 15, Madrid-4. Tel. 2228440. Metro Chueca. Old quarters, but superior to Amor de Dios. The principal maestros are *Martín Vargas* and *Merche Esmeralda.*

Estudios Mercedes y Albano, Plaza Tirso de Molina 20 bajo, Madrid-12. Tel. 2305102. Metro Tirso de Molina. Fernando de Triana, in his famous book "Arte y Artistas Flamencos," raved about a ten-year-old dancer, *Merceditas León,* who was already achieving considerable success back in 1935. Daughter of La Quica and Frasquillo, Mercedes came to Madrid with her mother many years ago, and long ago established her own dance academy. Guitar-husband *Albano* accompanies her classes.

DANCE INSTRUCTION — SEVILLA.

Dance instruction in Sevilla is more complex than in Madrid. Instead of

183

general studios that instructors rent for their classes, each instructor in Sevilla provides his/her own studio, often located in his/her home. It is, therefore, more difficult in Sevilla than in Madrid to sit in on classes in order to size up the instructor, and extremely difficult to rent a studio for practicing what one learns; rental studios simply do not exist, to my knowledge, so the student must practice wherever he or she can. Another drawback: what with unemployment running rampant in Andalusia, Sevilla has become Spain's capital for muggers and thieves only too obviously plying their trades; car break-ins (often when you are in them) and purse snatching are routine, anything of value is highly risky. Nevertheless, there are excellent instructors in Sevilla and the city is beautiful, which perhaps make the hardships worthwhile. Some of the instructors are:

Manolo Marín. With the recent death of Enrique el Cojo, Manolo Marín has become Sevilla's most popular dance instructor. Calle Rodrigo de Triana 101, in Triana. Tel. 272385.

Carmen Albéniz (an excellent dancer who retired years ago from active performing due to marriage; aunt of the Carmen Albéniz dancing today). Taller de Expresión Artística on the Calle Salado.

Matilde Coral and *Rafael el Negro*. Calle Castilla 82.

Other professional flamenco dancers who also teach include *José Galván, Eugenia, Ana María Bueno, Manuela Carrasco, Caracolillo, Milagros Menjibas, Isabel Romero, Angelita Milla, Margarita y Mancilla (Gitanillos de Bronce), Pepita Rabay,* and *Rocio Albéniz.* If interested, inquire with the local flamencos in the tablaos for their whereabouts.

C. GUITAR. The guitar beginner could study with most any adequate guitarist in Spain and obtain a reasonably good foundation on the flamenco guitar. After learning the basics, however, say after several months, he will have to perk up his ears and try to calculate just which style of playing he would like to continue in. Upon so doing, he should then attempt to study with a guitarist whose playing he particularly likes, and who has a knack for teaching.

There are two basic methods of instruction: memory and cifra (cryptograph). Memory instruction means exactly what it says; it consists of memorizing the material given by the instructor, and practicing it until it can be played reasonably well. At the end of a long period of memory study the student will be familiar enough with flamenco to be able to begin improvising his own material, take material from records, and perform passages from memory that he may have heard only two or three times, In this method the student will find that his memory will be improved considerably, as well as his musical sense and his instinct for improvisation,

The cifra method is that which utilizes a simplified form of musical notation, This method has the advantage that the lesson is written down, and cannot be forgotten, It has the disadvantage that it can become a crutch, A flamenco artist cannot carry reams of musical notation about with him, and when he does not have it, he is lost, His memory does not develolp properly and his creative ability remains nil, The student will find that after an initial easy period he will be hindered in his advancement, In the long run, I believe the memory method gives the best results, Or, of course, a combination of both, with the memory method playing the leading role,

A valuable modern aid to either method is the use of a tape recorder, The willing instructor can help greatly by recording the material taught at the end of a series of lessons, say at the end of each toque learned, The tape recorder is far better than any system of musical notation, for it is the only way in which the *aire* of a toque can be captured, On the other hand, it is not wise to use the tape recorder overly much, for it will become a nuisance both to the instructor and the student and, as in the cifra method, the student will not give his memory the desirable freedom to develop, ·

Some of the main difficulties the studémnt may run into while studying the flamenco guitar are discussed in the section "Flamenco añd the Non-Spaniard,"

C, GUITAR INSTRUCTORS,   The following maestros are experienced teachers with fame of being patient, knowledgeable and thorough,'

Madrid, (In alphabetical order);
Andrés Batista (speaks English), Calle Libertad 32, Madrid-28004, Tel, 5213918, Metro Chueca,
David Serva Jones (fluent English), Calle Duque de Alba 11, Madrid 28012, Tel, 2391327, Metro Tirso de Molina,
Luis Maravilla, Guitarras Maravilla, Calle León 4, Madrid 28014, Tel, 4295730, Metro Antón Martín,
Rafael Nogales, Calle O'Donnell 42, Madrid-28009, Tel, 2744628, Metro General Mola,

Sevilla,
José Luis Postigo teaches in his guitar shop, located in the

Barrio de Santa Cruz (Calle Rodrigo Caro 8).

Córdoba. In recent years Córdoba has surged into prominence in
the flamenco guitar world, largely due to the efforts of one excellent
guitarist and instructor, Rafael Rodríguez "Merengue de Córdoba".
Merengue and his dancing wife, Concha Calero, opened an academy of
flamenco some 16 years ago. Since then Merengue has produced some
exceptional local guitarists, such as Paco Serrano, Vicente Amigo, José
Antonio Rodríguez, and José Manuel Hierro, who are rapidly becoming
known far beyond the bounds of Córdoba. Merengue's Academia de Flamenco
is located on the Calle Isabel Losa.

 D. SUMMERTIME GUITAR AND DANCE COURSES IN ANDALUSIA.

Córdoba.
 Flamenco guitarist Paco Peña is working hard at making his
hometown a major center of summertime flamenco instruction and
activity. For the past several years he has organized annual flamenco
guitar and dance courses, both for beginners and the advanced, as well
as classical guitar instruction, concerts and recitals by prominent
soloists of both flamenco and classical guitar (Sabicas, Mario
Escudero, John Williams, and a long etc.), an annual flamenco festival
or two, and other artistic activities. The action takes place during
the month of July. For information write: Centro Flamenco Paco Peña,
Plaza del Potro 15, 14002 Córdoba. Tel. 479329.
 A newcomer on the Córdoba scene is the "intensive summer dance
course" conducted by flamenco dancer Manuel Moreno. After a summertime
beginning, it appears the course will now be held in October. For
information contact: Manuel Sánchez Rabadán, Librería Lucano, Calle
Lucano 8, 14003 Córdoba.

 Jerez de la Frontera.
 The *Cátedra de Flamencología* has organized guitar and dance
courses each summer for over two decades in this most flamenco of
towns, which are greatly enhanced by lectures, poetry readings, guitar,
dance and singing recitals, festivals and fiestas flamencas. They are
usually held in the month of August. For information write: Cursos
Internacionales de Verano, Cátedra de Flamencología, Calle Quintos 1,
Jerez de la Frontera (Cádiz).
 In 1989 a new flamenco institution was founded in Jerez, the.
Fundación Andaluza de Flamenco. Palacio Pemartín, Plaza de San Juan 1,

11403 Jerez de la Frontera (Cádiz), Tel. 349265.   This foundation plans on hosting annual dance and guitar courses each July and/or August. In 1989 the dance teacher was Matilde Corral, the guitar instructor Manolo Sanlúcar.

But that is not all. The Foundation is open the year around from 10 a.m. to 2 p.m., during which period it offers impressive libraries of flamenco-related books, video tapes, cassettes and records, with facilities for reading, seeing, hearing them. All that is necessary is to purchase a "user's card", good for one month and very reasonably priced.   The Foundation will also advise one as to flamenco instructors, and other flamenco matters.
     In addition, the Foundation offers a list of flamenco-related books that can be purchased by mail order. Specify "Kiosco Flamenco" on your request.

     Sanlúcar de Barrameda. The course in this Atlantic coastal town, only thirty kilometers from Jerez, is strictly guitar-orientated, concentrating largely on solo playing. Manolo Sanlúcar teaches advanced students, Manolo's brother the less advanced. August is usually the month. For information write to: Curso Internacional de Guitarra Flamenca, Excmo. Ayuntamiento, Sanlúcar de Barrameda (Cádiz).

     E. BASIC ADVICE. Regarding lessons in flamenco, always be sure to agree on the cost before beginning classes. Also, be wary of paying by the arrangement (dance or guitar arrangement, or one cante); it is generally adviseable to pay a set amount per lesson, or the student may end up paying a mighty large sum for a mighty short arrangement. When weighing the cost of classes, the formality of the instructor must be considered, as well as his abililty as a teacher and artist. Many instructors who charge less more than make up for the lower price by abbreviated and badly taught classes. Unless the instructor is way out of line on price, formality and teaching ability should be the student's chief criteria when looking for an instructor.

2. FLAMENCO INSTRUCTION OUTSIDE SPAIN.
     An often effective method of discovering guitar or dance instructors in your area is to inquire at your local music or dance stores or studios, as well as in stringed instrument repair shops, particularly if they handle and/or construct flamenco guitars.

In addition, consult the periodicals listed in continuation (Section 3), two of which contain directories of instructors in various parts of the English-speaking world.

Also in Section 3 you will find methods and sheet music, aids that can prove very helpful to students, above all those living outside of Spain.

3. FLAMENCO METHODS, SHEET MUSIC, and PERIODICALS.

A. and B. *Flamenco Methods and Sheet Music.*.   In the last edition I reviewed a number of methods and a goodly amount of sheet music. Mostly in vain, I have come to realize, for such material becomes unavailable so quickly it is just a practice in frustration for both writer and reader. So this time my only advice is to visit the music stores and see what is available.

If you get to Madrid, however, and are in search of sheet music, methods and other music books, one stop is a must: The *Real Musical*, Carlos III, 1, 28013 Madrid, Tel. 5413007, Metro Opera, claims to be the world's best-stocked supplier of such materials. Catalogue sent on request.

C. *Periodicals.* Over the years aficionados in Spain have started up various periodicals dedicated exclusively to flamenco, all of which have withered and died due to lack of support. All, that is, except two, both exemplary, serious magazines, written in Spanish, of course, that I am sure are hanging in there by the skin of their teeth. They are:

Sevilla Flamenca has been around since 1980, may well be here to stay. The magazine is written with insight, depth and emotion by aficionados who truly understood and love flamenco. Each issue contains some twenty varied articles, including one or two generally excellent feature interviews with old-timers who invariably invoke the days of yore, when the flamenco way of life roared unchecked. I consider this magazine a must for all Spanish-reading aficionados. Published every two months. Subscriptions: José Hurtado Alvarez, Apartado de Correos 79, 41530 Morón de la Frontera (Sevilla).

El Candil, also issued each two months, generally has a somewhat more intellectual, less earthy approach to flamenco than the *Sevilla Flamenca*, causing the two magazines to complement each other to a certain extent, and combine to give the reader a fine overall view of flamenco. Subscriptions: *El Candil*, Revista de Flamenco, Peña Flamenco de Jaén, Calle Maestro 16, Jaén,

The following are English-language periodicals dealing wholly or in part with flamenco:

Jaleo, Box 4706, San Diego, California 92104, The aficionado's search for flamenco knowledge, instruction and/or companionship will be greatly facilitated by this newsletter, dedicated entirely to flamenco on both a local and international level. A useful feature in each issue is a directory of flamenco guitar, dance and cante instructors throughout the USA.

Guitar International, Manor House, Mere, Wiltshire BA12 6HZ, England, This monthly magazine is devoted mainly to the classic guitar, but generally includes at least one flamenco feature in each issue, *Also* offered is a Directory of teachers (classical, flamenco, folk and jazz) throughout the United Kingdom and other English-speaking countries.

Guitar Review, Society of Classic Guitar, 409 E. 50th St., New York City 10022, This irregularly issued magazine, although principally devoted to the classic guitar, usually runs ads for flamenco instructors, and occasionally devotes an issue wholly to flamenco.

Dancemagazine, 1180 Ave. of the Americas, New York City 10036, This monthly is devoted to all styles of dance, flamenco coming in a distant last,

D. BIBLIOGRAPHY. At the time of research for the first edition of this book, back in the late 1950's and early 1960's, very few books were available about flamenco in Spanish, and none, to my knowledge, in English. As flamenco surged to popularity, something of a market for flamenco books came into being, and throughout the second half of the 1960's, and during the 1970's and 1980's, it was possible to enter a large bookstore and find a selection of five or six flamenco books at one's disposal. Most of these books, however, were printed in very limited editions - 200 copies was not uncommon, 500 copies normal, 1000 copies a large edition - and when sold were rarely reprinted, Many dozens of such books, and hundreds of articles and essays, have come and gone in recent years, a complete listing of which seems pointless (and impossible) to print here.

Instead, I shall mention just a few I believe the reader will find particularly informative and/or entertaining, and recommend, for those wishing to delve further, two books devoted exclusively to flamenco's bibliography: "Bibliografía Flamenca," by Anselmo González Climent (Escélicer, Madrid, 1965), and "Segunda Bibliografía Flamenca," by González Climent and José Blas Vega * (El Guadalhorce, Málaga, 1966). These bibliographies list over 9000 books, articles, brochures and other writings either wholly or partly about flamenco, dating back to when flamenco first began appearing in print. Most of the listing will be extremely difficult to find. The two bibliography books, in fact, will be hard to track down: only 300 copies were printed of the "Segunda Bibliografía Flamenca."

However, for those with infinite patience with old-time bureaucracy, the Madrid National Library (Biblioteca Nacional, Paseo de Recoletos 20, Madrid 28001) theoretically has a copy of every book ever published in Spain, available for consultation in the library (books cannot be taken out).

Besides the National Library, two rays of light have recently illuminated the scene. The *Librería Lucano*, Calle Lucano 8, 14003 Córdoba, Tel. 472885, presently has in stock nearly 200 books dealing with Andalusian culture, many of them about flamenco. They mail order, and will send their catalogue on request.

For serious researchers, a trip to Jerez de la Frontera may be in order. As mentioned previously in this appendix, Jerez' *Fundación Andaluza de Flamenco* (Palacio Pemartín, Plaza de San Juan 1, 11403 Jerez de la Frontera, Tel. 349265) has an excellent library of flamenco books, some 2000 in all, they claim, available for reading weekdays from 10 a.m. to 2 p.m. If you wish their mail order list of flamenco books available, specify "Kiosco Flamenco" on your letter.

* Visitors to Madrid may wish to drop in at Blas Vega's bookshop, called the Librería del Prado, Calle Prado 5, Tel. 4296091. The shop specializes in rare books about Spain in general, usually has for sale a good stock of both used and new books about flamenco. One of flamenco's most knowledgeable and prolific flamencologists, Blas Vega personally tends shop mornings.

BIBLIOGRAPHY

In English:

Gerald Bakus;	The Spanish Guitar, 1977,
David George;	The Flamenco Guitar, 1969,
Paul Hecht;	The Wind Cries, 1968,
Gerald Howson;	The Flamencos of Cádiz Bay, 1965,
Ivor Mairants;	My Fifty Fretting Years, 1980,
D.E. Pohren;	The Art of Flamenco, 1962,1967,1972,1984,1990,
	Lives and Legends of Flamenco, 1964, 1988,
	A Way of Life, 1980,
Walter Starkie;	Don Gypsy, 1936,

In French:

Danielle Dumas;	Chants Flamencos, 1973,
Alain Gobin;	Le Flamenco, 1975,
Georges Hiliare;	Initiation Flamenca, 1954,
D.E. Pohren;	L'Art Flamenco, 1963,
Louis Quievreux;	Art Flamenco, 1959,

In German:

Christoff Jung;	Flamenco-Lieder, 1970,

In Spanish:

Carlos Almendros;	Todo lo Básico Sobre el Flamenco, 1973,
Manuel Barrios;	Ese Dificil Mundo del Flamenco, 1972,
	Cante Flamenco,
J.M.Caballero Bonald	El Baile Andaluz, 1957,
	Luces y Sombras del Flamenco, 1975,
Augusto Butler;	Javier Molina, Jerezano y Tocaor, 1964,
Carlos y Pedro Caba;	Andalucía, Su Comunismo Y Su Cante, 1933,
S.Estébañez Calderón;	Escenas Andaluzas, Colección Austral No. 188,
Domingo Manfredi Cano;	Geografía del Cante Jondo, 1955, 1964,
	Gente de Bronce y Seda, 1965,
	Cante y Baile Flamenco, 1973,

A. González Climent;   Andalusia en Los Toros, El Cante y La Danza,
                         Cante en Córdoba, 1957,
                         Oido al Cante, 1960,
                         Antología de Poesía Flamenca, 1961
                         Bulerías, 1961,
                         Flamencología, 1964,
                         Bibliografía Flamenca, 1965,
                         Segunda Bibliografía Flamenca, 1966,
Eugenio Cobo;   Pasión y Muerte de Gabriel Macandé, 1977,
Antonio Moreno Delgada; Aurelio, Su Cante, Su Vida, 1964,
Vicente Escudero;   Mi Baile, 1947,
E. Molina Fajardo;   Manuel de Falla y el Cante Jondo, 1962,
Félix Grande;   Diverse works,
Agustín Gómez;   La Voz Flamenca, 1988,
Rafael Lafuente;   Los Gitanos, El Flamenco y Los Flamencos,1955,
Federico García Lorca;   Obras Completas,
José Carlos de Luna;   De Cante Grande y Cante Chico, 1935,
                         Gitanos de la Bética, 1951, 198?,
Antonio Machado y   Primeros Escritos Flamencos, 1869-71, 1981,
   Alvarez "Demófilo"   Colección de Cante Flamencos, 1881,1947,1975,
F. Rodríguez Marín;   El Alma de Andalucía en Sus Mejores Coplas
                         Amorosas, 1929,
Manuel García Matos;   Cante Flamenco, Anuario Musical, 1950,
Ricardo Molina;   Misterios del Arte Flamenco, 1967,
  with Antonio Mairena; Mundo y Formas del Cante Flamenco,1963,1971,
J.L.Ortiz Nuevo;   Las Mil y Una Historias de Pericón de
                         Cádiz, 1975,
                         Pepe de la Matrona; Recuerdos de un Cantaor
                         Sevillano, 1975,
Teresa M. de la Peña;   Teoría y Prática del Baile Flamenco,1970,198?,
Juan de la Plata;   Flamencos de Jerez, 1961,
D.E.Pohren   El Arte del Flamenco, 1970,
Núñez de Prado;   Artistas Flamencos, 1895,
Fernando Quiñones;   De Cádiz y Sus Cantes, 1964,1974,
                         El Flamenco; Vida y Muerte,
                         Antonio Mairena; Su Obra, Su Significado,198?,
Hipólito Rossy;   Teoría del Cante Jondo, 1966,
Manuel Rios Ruiz;   Introducción al Cante Flamenco, 1972,
                         Rumbos del Cante Flamenco,
                         De Cante y Cantaores de Jerez, 1989,
                         Diccionario Flamenco, 2 vols, 1988,

A. García Ulecia;   Las Confesiones de Antonio Mairena, 1976,
José Blas Vega;   Segunda Bibliografía Flamenca, 1966,
                     Las Tonás, 1967,
                     Temas Flamencos, 1973,
                     Conversaciones Flamencas con Aurelio
                       de Cádiz, 1978,
                     Vida y Cante de Don Antonio Chacón, 1986,
                     Diccionario Flamenco, 2 vols, 1988,

APPENDIX No. 7

THE GUITAR

This appendix covers the following subjects:

1. Difference between the classical, concert flamenco and traditional flamenco guitars.

2. Old versus new guitars.

3. Care of the guitar.

4. A thumbnail history of modern flamenco guitar construction.

5. Flamenco guitar constructors today.

A General review.

B Experimentation.

1. DIFFERENCES BETWEEN THE CLASSICAL, CONCERT FLAMENCO, AND TRADITIONAL FLAMENCO GUITARS.

Madrid luthier Manuel Contreras had a very interesting brochure printed up in 1980, segments of which I am reproducing in this section by his kind authorization. On the following two pages Contreras has broken his classical guitar down into its component parts, with an explanation of the woods he uses and an excellent visual idea of his construction techniques. I in turn have added the woods used for his flamenco guitars where they differ from the classical (if no differences are depicted, they are the same for both types of guitars). It must be noted that a hybrid guitar variety is also becoming common: that used by many flamenco concertists, in which are employed all classical woods but flamenco construction techniques. The differences in the construction techniques will be discussed in this section following the diagrams.

NECK: Central American cedar reinforced with ebony.

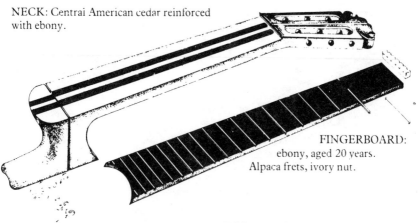

FINGERBOARD: ebony, aged 20 years. Alpaca frets, ivory nut.

BACK: Brazilian rosewood, aged 15 years minimum, for classics and concert flamencos. Aranjuez cypress, aged 10-15 years, for traditional flamencos. Supports of American cedar.

TOP or SOUNDBOARD: German pine or Canadian cedar, aged 10 years. 1. Brackets, 2. Under the bridge support, 3. Upper bout support, 4. Sound hole support, 5. Tail block. 6. Fan bracing, curved for increased strength, 7. Triangular supports.

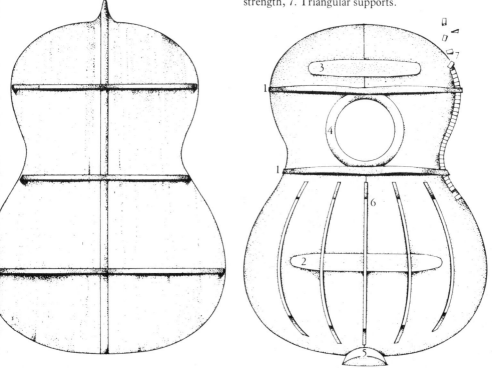

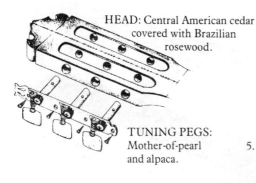

HEAD: Central American cedar covered with Brazilian rosewood.

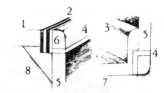

Detail of top and back joint to sides. 1. Top, 2. Sycamore fillets, 3. Reinforcement (supports). 4. Side, 5. Border, 6. Cypress, 7. Back, 8. Small triangle supports.

TUNING PEGS: Mother-of-pearl and alpaca.

BRIDGE: Brazilian rosewood Ivory nut.

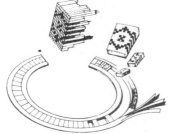

ROSETTE: Sycamore fillets stained and inset.
Approximately 170 pieces for each square centimeter, or about 2,500 pieces for each rosette.

STRINGS: silk and wound metal for bass, nylon for treble (formerly gut).

Horizontal connecting supports of American cedar or especially treated Hungarian beech. Vertical supports of rosewood for the classics; none for the flamencos.

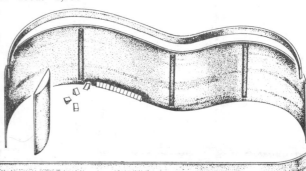

SIDES: Brazilian rosewood, aged 15 years, for the classics and concert flamencos. Aranjuez cypress for the traditional flamencos.

Other than the distinct woods used, as depicted on the previous two pages, we might point out the following differences between flamenco and classical guitars:

Flamenco Guitar	*Classical Guitar*
a. The flamenco guitar weighs far less than the classical. Not only is cypress lighter than rosewood, it is shaved much thinner, the supports are considerably finer, and the box is smaller; classics are up to one inch deeper than flamencos, and are generally wider and longer as well.	a. Larger guitar box, heavier and thicker wood and bracing.
b. Tuning is traditionally done by wooden pegs (rosewood or ebony), although in modern times mechanical tuning has become more popular.	b. Mechanical tuning.
c. Low bridge, which does not normally exceed one fourth inch in height. The bridge bone should also be low to the bridge. This causes the strings to lie much closer to the neck, which in turn necessitates a gradual inclination (cutting down) of the top of the neck as it approaches the mouth of the guitar. This inclination permits the strings to lie close to the neck and to the guitar proper without causing undue vibration, and produces an easier action. This is one of the more difficult techniques in flamenco guitar construction.	c. A much higher bridge than the flamenco guitar, with a high bridge bone, causing the strings to pass well over the neck and the guitar proper. This alleviates the necessity of cutting down the top of the neck, and leaves the guitar with a harder action, suitable for the classical guitarist, but unwieldly in the hands of a flamenco guitarist.
d. White or transparent tapping plates are placed over the vulnerable areas of the flamenco guitar as protective coverings.	d. None

Due to the discussed differences in construction, the classical guitar ideally results clear and ethereal in tone, the traditional flamenco raspier and more earthy, and the hybrid (rosewood) flamenco in between the two in both tone and weight, although still considerably more flamenco than classical. It should be stated that these differences are applicable only in quality guitars. Cheaper guitars, with a few exceptions, come in all sizes and are neither classical nor flamenco.

2. OLD VERSUS NEW GUITARS.

Many guitarists find it desirable to obtain a well-broken in guitar, preferably one at least several years old (1). This is because with age the guitar, like the violin, gains certain qualities that new guitars cannot possess, such as a complete maturity of the wood, a beautiful, deep mellowness of tone, a settling of the construction into its permanent state, and a definite knowledge that the guitar is, or is not, one of the great ones.

However, it is not always easy to find a good used guitar at an accessible price. Since the "rediscovery" of flamenco, beginning in the early 1950's, the flamenco guitar's supply-demand chart has gone through three distinct phases.

1). Prior to, say, 1960, flamenco was still pretty much an in-group art. Very few new flamenco guitars were being made, not only because there were fewer flamenco guitarists (compared to today), but also due to the abundance of good used flamenco guitars then available. Nearly every guitar shop had several for sale, and many the widow's household contained a guitar or two taking up space, the value of which the widow was likely to have no idea. I remember the opportunities that came knocking in the mid-fifties, when guitars would be offered to anyone known as an aficionado at give-away prices. What collections could have been made if one had had just a bit of extra money. Unfortunately, I did not, but I did manage to scrape together enough to acquire both a Santos Hernández and a Domingo Esteso. That sound glorious, and was, but think of the various Manuel Ramirez' and Marcelo Barberos, other Santos' and Estesos, etc., I had to turn down, not to mention the two Antonio Torres' I had a shot at.

(1) Desirable, that is, if the guitar is going to be played in solitude or in small groups for one's own pleasure. The professional flamenco, however, who must play in noisy places over the babble of voices, or work in a cuadro with dancers and singers, often prefers the piercing shrillness of a new guitar, as it will frequently be the only way he can be heard.

2). 1960-1980. Along came the flamenco craze. Flamenco guitarists began springing up like wild grass in a rainy season both in and out of Spain, and soon had snapped up the used flamenco guitar supply. The demand then turned to new flamenco guitars, which sent the guitar-makers into a frenzy of looking for cured cypress. The luthier's trade changed nearly overnight from a quiet, leisurely, low-income profession to one of stress, wheeling and dealing, and big money.

3). The craze began dying down in the mid and late 1970's as the faddists, after experiencing that flamenco is not so easy, lost interest and stopped playing, or turned their attention to newer "in" movements: other exotic stringed instruments (sitar, oud, etc.). or, if they stayed with the guitar, expressions such as jazz, folk and, above all, classical, for the classical guitar has reached enormous and unprecedented popularity in the last years. Spanish guitar constructors have had to turn nearly all their energies to constructing classical guitars, while the flamenco guitar demand has dropped to just a fraction of what it was fifteen years ago. (This has not broken the luthiers' hearts; not only are flamenco guitars more difficult to construct, the classicals bring in considerably more profit per guitar. The theory, once correct, is still that the flamencos are a poor lot, while players of classical are from the wealthy upper strata.)

The decreased demand for flamenco guitars is not entirely due to fewer people playing flamenco at present. Another prominent reason is that during the flamenco fad so many guitars were constructed they glutted the market, and are still nearly sufficient, circulating as they are and combined with the return to the market of older used guitars, to satisfy the demand.

The used guitar is again, therefore, playing an important role in the flamenco guitar's supply-demand cycle.

3. CARE OF YOUR GUITAR.

In his guitar brochure, Manuel Contreras suggests guitar owners take the following into consideration for the best care of their instruments:

"Due to the age of the wood used in guitar construction and the humidity factor at the time of construction — Madrid is relatively dry: between 50% and 60% — try to maintain as best you can the 'original environment' with a margin of, let's say, not below 45% and not above 75%.

"If the guitar is to be transported from one place to another, you must take every precaution to avoid subjecting it to drastic changes in temperature and humidity. Keep it away from windows, radiators, and other heating systems. In this way our beloved instrument will certainly age and perform better.

"Take care that the sound hole is covered with a chamois or, preferably, a natural silk cloth because as the interior of the guitar is not varnished it tends to absorb easily any humidity in the room, which the cloth helps to retain in case of a brusque lowering of the humidity factor (thus avoiding possible cracking and/or warping). In case of such a humidity drop — say from 80% to 50% or less — besides the cloth it is convenient to place a container full of water in the room, which will help offset the humidity loss." (Humidifiers, where available, represent an excellent modern method of avoiding this problem.)

"Keep the strings of your guitar if not in tune at least taut, except, of course, when travelling by plane, in which case the strings should be considerably loosened (but not completely).

"When changing strings, do not take them all off at one time. To avoid altering the normal tension on the neck, you should take off and replace each string one at a time.

"If, on plucking an open string you notice that it buzzes, it could be due to a change in climate which has affected the neck and fingerboard. If this is the case, you will notice that the action is easier. To solve this problem you should acquire some small wooden fillets of varying thicknesses. Take off the strings and place one or more fillets under the ivory pieces either at the head or the bridge or both. Always begin with the thinnest fillet first, graduating to a thicker one if necessary, until you reach the desired height and the buzzing stops."

4. A THUMBNAIL HISTORY OF FLAMENCO GUITAR CONSTRUCTION.

It is not certain when the flamenco guitar, as an instrument somewhat distinct from the old-time Spanish guitar, came into existence; the first references to it I have been able to find date back to the first half of the last century. At that time the guitar in Spain, an instrument that had flourished during earlier periods, was at low ebb. Stringed instrument craftsmen earned their livelihood far more from violins, bandurrias, mandolins, and even lutes, than guitars. Then came the café cantante period and flamenco's rapid surge to popularity (1850 on), and a steady demand for "Guitarras de tablao" was initiated. Soon a few craftsmen were able to specialize in flamenco guitars, which remained true even throughout flamenco's period of decline during the years 1900-1950. The classical guitar, however, lay dormant until Francisco Tárrega showed Spain, and Andrés Segovia showed the world, its vast possibilities, causing the classical guitar to gradually gain in popularity throughout this century.

The following is a list of the guitar craftsmen most influential in the development of the modern flamenco guitar. The photos included in this section give a pictorial history of many of these same gentlemen.

Antonio Torres (c.1817-1892). This guitarrero, from Almería, was the creator of the modern style of Spanish guitar. He was not happy with the small, muddy sound of the traditional "guitarras de tablao," and began experimenting. As the "guitarras de tablao" were terribly shallow — something like two inches deep, some even less — he considerably increased their depth of box. He also revised the curves of the guitar, somehow realizing, perhaps mathematically, that the old guitars were out of proportion and were thus losing volume and resonance. After much calculation and trial and error he ended up narrowing and shortening the bottom part of the feminine form, and widening and prolonging the breast part, making for a better balanced and more mathematically correct instrument in which the sound could escape through the mouth unimpeded by collisions within the box.

Other major innovations of Torres included: experimentation in the use of lighter, more flexible woods; a less cumbersome style of inner bracing; a reduction in the thickness of the top and body woods; and improved varnishing techniques, all innovations that have since been universally accepted as fundamental in the construction of today's guitars, both flamenco and classical.

Because of the far superior tone and volume produced by Torres' guitars, he attracted the small demand for classical guitars that then existed, and eventually a good deal of his production was directed towards the classical field. He then had the opportunity for further experimentation, and developed concepts concerning differences that ideally should exist between flamenco and classical guitars. He recognized that one art is earthy and the other ethereal, and he experimented in the use of materials and building techniques that emphasized this difference. Thus Torres not only was the creator of the modern Spanish guitar, but was also the first constructor to begin successfully differentiating between flamenco and classical guitar construction techniques.

Although Torres did not have any direct disciples who achieved fame, he exerted a vast and lasting influence on most of Spain's luthiers. The most successful of those to adopt his techniques during that period was Manuel Ramírez, in Madrid.

Francisco González (c.1830-1880). Francisco González was the first of the line of Madrid guitarreros who have since converted that city into the flamenco (and classical) guitar capital of the world. He was a man of diverse interests — businessman (guitar constructing alone would not support him in those days), inventor, guitar constructor — and did not, therefore, devote much time to the guitar. When he did build he specialized in "guitarras de tablao" for the flamenco professionals who played in the Madrid café cantante circuit at that time. His most talented apprentice was José Ramírez I, whom we shall discuss in continuation.

González is as well remembered for his inventions as for his guitar craftsmanship. One of them was Spain's first car, built in 1870 and propelled by levers. As José Ramírez III tells the story, the car worked fine on level ground, but could not quite make the steep hills. People ridiculed González for what they considered his failure, and he died an embittered man.

José Ramírez I (c.1857-1923). José Ramírez I replaced his maestro, Francisco González, as Madrid's favorite guitarrero, and for a number of years became the chief provider of guitars to the growing number of professional flamenco guitarists. During that period he had a great deal of work, and took on several fine apprentices, including Julián Gómez Ramírez (no relation), who later set up shop in Paris, Enrique García, who did likewise in Barcelona, Antonio Viudes, likewise in Buenos Aires, Rafael Casana, likewise in Córdoba, and his son, José Ramírez II who, after learning the trade, moved to Buenos Aires and did not return to take over the shop until his father's death. José I's most brilliant apprentice, however, stayed in Madrid and eventually became his chief competitor: his younger brother, Manuel Ramírez.

As we have seen, José Ramírez I enjoyed a heyday of some years, but then progress, in the form of Antonio Torres' new ideas, caught up with him. Being a staunch traditionalist and highly stubborn to boot, José I refused to alter his style of guitar-building in any way. After all, he argued, if his "guitarras de tablao" were good enough for the famed guitarist Javier Molina, they were good enough for any of the modern young whippersnappers. The modern young whippersnappers, however, did not think so, and switched over nearly en masse to brother Manuel, who by then had set up his own shop and had embraced, and even begun improving upon, Torres' concepts. It was then that the young whippersnappers began referring to José I, Manuel's outdated maestro and brother, as "el malo" (the bad one), and to Manuel as "el bueno" (the good one). This, on top of numerous other violent squabbles that had taken place between the brothers, caused them to cease speaking to each other many years before their deaths.

José I never did alter his old-time style. He fought it out with the new generation to the bitter end.

Manuel Ramírez (c.1866-1916). Manuel Ramírez learned his craft from his older brother, José Ramírez I, but soon fell under the influence of Antonio Torres and was compelled to break with his brother, and the old school, and open his own shop. He then began experimenting with, and even improving upon, Torres' methods, and consequently started constructing guitars of such qualilty that Torres himself recognized Manuel as his most brilliant competitor. After Torres death, and until his own, Manuel was recognized as Spain's outstanding guitarrero. He left three excellent disciples: Santos Hernández, Domingo Esteso, and Modesto Borreguero.

José Ramírez III tells of a trick that Manuel played on the day's most influential critics and guitarists. It came to pass that even after his death Torres' prestige was so high that Manuel's excellent work did not receive the recognition he thought it deserved. So Manuel devised a plan. He built a number of guitars in Torres' style, firmly glued in his own labels, but then over them placed labels of Torres' that he had on hand, only lightly glued at the corners. He then called in the critics and guitarists to see and test these marvelous Torres guitars. They, of course, raved about them, and said things like what a shame no one would ever again make guitars as well as Torres. After really hooking them, Manuel tore off the Torres labels and beamed triumphantly.

After that there could be no reasonable doubt. Manuel Ramírez was proclaimed the king of guitarreros.

Santos Hernández (c.1870-1942). The most prodigious student of Manuel Ramírez, Santos went on after his maestro's death to make innovations of his own in guitar construction, resulting that his guitars today are the most highly-esteemed, and highly priced, of any in flamenco's history.

From the time he opened his own shop, in 1917, to his death twenty-five years later, Santos was as secretive about his art as many gypsy guitarists are about their own creations. He only permitted one young boy at a time on the premises, for sweeping and cleaning up, and when the boy arrived at the age when he might begin observing and copying Santos' secrets, Santos fired him. Thus, Santos had no apprentices, and it was not until after his death, when Marcelo Barbero went to work for Santos' widow in Santos' old shop, that someone was able to glean something of Santos' techniques (from the building forms, half-finished guitars, and other paraphernalia that still littered the shop).

Domingo Esteso (c.1884-1937). Another brilliant student of Manuel Ramírez, Domingo Esteso ranked in prestige second only to his good friend Santos Hernández in the Spanish guitar world. Like Santos, Esteso began constructing on his own in 1917. Unlike Santos, Esteso was not compelled to secrecy, and left behind three accomplished disciples: his nephews, known as the "Sobrinos de Esteso," who still carry on in Domingo's old shop in Madrid.

José Ramírez II (c.1885-1957). José (Simón) Ramírez II learned the art of guitar construction from his father, José I, but soon found he was little attracted to such a sedentary life. Thus, he travelled to Buenos Aires as a professional musician when still a young man, there remaining until his father's death, at which time he returned to run the family shop. He wisely decided to discontinue his father's traditional line of "guitarras de tablao," by now completely outdated, and leaned more towards the techniques of uncle Manuel Ramírez. He did not, however, attempt to compete with the maestros of the day, but rather contented himself with a good business based on making guitars for the casual amateur. Two fine guitarreros were formed in his shop: Marcelo Barbero, and José II's son, José Ramírez III.

Marcelo Barbero (c.1904-1956). Marcelo Barbero entered the world of guitar construction as a clean-up boy for José Ramírez I, apprenticed under José Ramírez II, and then later went to work for Santos Hernández widow after the old maestro's death. There Barbero became acquainted with many of the features of Santos' guitars, and was soon making outstanding guitars in Santos' style. Barbero's next step was to open his own shop, and take on one apprentice: Arcángel Fernández. Barbero's premature death prevented him from instructing his young son, Marcelo II, who is presently working with his maestro, Arcángel Fernández.

Modesto Borreguero. The youngest disciple of Manuel Ramírez, Borreguero took over Ramírez shop upon his maestro's death in 1916. Although a talented guitarrero, Borreguero soon passed from view due to what was described to me as "non-productivity due to bohemianism and irregular working habits."

5. FLAMENCO GUITAR CONSTRUCTORS TODAY.

A. *General Review.*

What with the guitar boom of the past twenty-five years, guitar makers have sprouted like mushrooms in a pine forest. What could be more pleasant than to create in the solitude of one's home or small shop, and to make a good living at it to boot? Yes, there are a multitude of fine luthiers throughout the world today, but Spain, in my opinion, still maintains that margin of consistent excellence at more or less reasonable prices. This is above all true in the realm of the flamenco guitar.

Within Spain there are dozens of guitar constructors of some renown. In his "Partial Directory of Spanish Guitar Builders," published in the January, 1979 issue of Guitar and Lute magazine, author Henry Adams lists over sixty. It is a good list, containing most of the better known, but still definitely only partial, for hidden away in the hinterlands and poorer neighborhoods of the cities are scores more of very talented craftsmen who will be up there tomorrow if the guitar fever continues.

We have seen in "Old Versus New Guitars" (Part 2 of this appendix) that the demand for new flamenco guitars has fallen off sharply, and that most guitar builders are working nearly full-time on filling their piles of orders for classical guitars. The top quality flamenco guitars that are being constructed presently are the works of a relatively small number of craftsmen, many of whom dedicate a large percentage of their time to classics but who will fill flamenco orders when they receive them. Ten of the most renowned are:

MADRID (in order of seniority) (1):

Conde Hermanos, Sobrinos de Esteso, Calle Gravina 7, Madrid-4. Faustino, Mariano and Julio Conde, nephews of the great Domingo Esteso and perpetuators of his style, have been making excellent guitars under their own label since their uncle, and maestro, died in 1937. Conde Hermanos are among the few constructors who still produce far more flamenco than classical guitars, many of the flamencos being of the concert rosewood variety.

Manuel Rodriguez (II), Calle Hortaleza 32, Madrid-4. Manuel came by his afición and knowledge in an ideally natural manner: his grandfather was a flamenco guitarist, his father (Manuel Rodríguez I) a guitar craftsman who worked both for José Ramírez I and II. In 1939, at age thirteen, Manuel II entered the shop of José Ramírez II as an apprentice, rising to chief master craftsman (foreman) before leaving in 1955 to open his own shop (in the same building where good friend Marcelo Barbero was then constructing). In 1959 America beckoned and Manuel spent the next fourteen years constructing quality guitars in the Los Angeles, California area, returning to Spain in 1973 to establish himself on the Calle Hortaleza. Son Manuel III is also immersed in the family tradition, presently constructing some accomplished guitars of his own.

José Ramírez III, Concepción Jerónima 2, Madrid-12. José Ramírez III, third generation in the same shop (José Ramírez I and II), today mainly plays the role of supervisor, coordinating the output of the various craftsmen he employs, selecting the woods used, and generally conducting the business. Initials on the inside of any particular guitar give a clue as to the identity of the actual constructor. Some of Ramírez' experiences as an active constructor are recounted in the following section (Experimentation).

Marcelino López, Fernán Núnez 17, Madrid-17. This constructor, a luthier in the strict sense of the word because lutes actually do make up part of his production, has an unusual history in the Madrid guitar-building annals in that he is largely self-taught. Born in 1931, Marcelino was a cabinet-maker when smitten with the guitar bug, although at first not in the form of building, but playing. He began serious guitar studies with the maestro Daniel Fortea, which lasted for six years, until Fortea's death in 1953. During that period Marcelino also began repairing, then constructing guitars, learning largely by trial and error although aided considerably by "extremely valuable tips afforded me by Santos Hernández widow and later by Marcelo Barbero." Marcelino maintains his classical guitar playing, and construction of classical and flamenco guitars, at a high level, and has become in addition renowned for his masterly replicas of renaissance and baroque stringed instruments. His home is like a museum, with his collection of stringed instruments, some his, some antique. His workshop, as can be seen in the photo, is any luthier's dream.

Paulino Bernabé, Calle Cuchilleros 8, Madrid-12. There are certain similarities between Paulino Bernabé and Marcelino López. Both were cabinet-makers, both studied the classical guitar under Daniel Fortea, and both make excellent guitars. There the similarities end, however, for Paulino did receive formal luthier training in the shop of José Ramírez II, entering in 1953 and rising to chief master craftsman (foreman) before leaving to open his own shop in 1969.

Arcángel Fernández, Calle Jesús y María 26, Madrid-12. Arcángel gave up a professional flamenco guitar career to apprentice under Marcelo Barbero, later moved to his own shop and began building his own outstanding guitars upon Barbero's death in 1956. Arcángel's only apprentice is *Marcelo Barbero, Jr.,* son of his late maestro, who today is making his own accomplished guitars in the shop of his friend and mentor, Arcángel Fernández.

Manuel Contreras, Calle Mayor 80, Madrid-13. Obviously, cabinet-making is excellent preliminary training for guitar-making, for Manuel Contreras is still another cabinet-maker turned luthier. Contreras received his guitar construction training in the shop of José Ramírez III, entering in 1959 and leaving in 1963 to set up his own shop. Working with two apprentices, he quickly established himself as one of today's most brilliant craftsmen.

(1) There is some confusion today regarding "The Madrid School of Guitar Construction." Until recently,

205

the term signified simply guitar-making in Madrid along the traditional lines of Francisco González, the Ramírez Family, Santos Hernández, Domingo Esteso, Marcelo Barbero, and so forth. The present confusion arises, however, in that recently a group of eight Madrid craftsmen have united, for purposes of marketing their produce more effectively and inexpensively, under the name "La Escuela de Madrid" ("The Madrid School"). These gentlemen are all accomplished craftsmen, but by no means include all of Madrid's excellent guitarreros; neither the Sobrinos de Esteso, nor José Ramírez III and his present craftsmen, nor Arcángel Fernández, for instance, are members.

Thus, for purposes of tradition, accuracy, and this book, I prefer the term "Madrid School" to encompass all of Madrid's guitar makers.

The eight constructors who presently form the School within the School are (in alphabetical order by first name); Félix Manzanero, Juan Alvarez, Luis Aróstegui Granados, Manuel Contreras, Manuel Rodríguez, Marcelino López, Paulino Bernabé, and Vicente Camacho.

CORDOBA

Manuel Reyes, Calle Armas 4, Córdoba. Manuel Reyes is another of the few guitarreros to make the big time in this difficult art who is self-taught. Due to the lack of apprentice opportunities in Córdoba, he had to learn by trial and error except for some pointers he received from an obscure Córdoban constructor, and one intensive day he spent with Marcelo Barbero. Despite these difficulties, in just a few years Reyes earned an excellent reputation in the Spanish guitar world. With the recent death of veteran Córdoban constructor *Miguel Rodríguez,* Reyes today is undisputed king of guitarreros in Western Andalusia.

GRANADA

Antonio Marín Montero, Cuesta de Caidero 1, Granada. Of the many guitarreros in Granada (I know of some eighteen, and there are no doubt more), Antonio Marín Montero is declared to be the best constructor of flamenco guitars by the knowledgeable guitarreros and guitarists I have consulted. Montero learned the guitar construction principles from *Eduardo Ferrer,* another Granada guitarrero of some fame, after which he began building on his own some years ago.

ALMERIA

Gerundino Fernández, Travesía de Buenavista 4, Almería. Gerundino Fernández is the first guitarrero of renown to come forth in Almería since the days of Antonio Torres, molder of the modern Spanish guitar. Now fifty years old, he started constructing at the age of seventeen, and has slowly built up an excellent reputation in the world of flamenco guitar construction, an accomplishment made far more difficult by the remoteness of Almería to flamenco action.

B. EXPERIMENTATION

There exists very little complacency among today's great guitar builders. Each seems to be striving to create the perfect instrument, an instrument that would have large volume without sacrificing tonal quality, the perfect, easily achieved pitch, the ideal balance between bass and treble strings, and strength, achieved by strong construction that in no way detracts from the desirable qualities above mentioned.

Generally speaking, the most common experimentation lies along the lines of trying out different woods of distinct thicknesses, as well as all types and designs of strong inner bracing that impede as little as possible the clear emergence of the sound. Some makers, however, have gone considerably further in their search for the perfect instrument, a few of whose innovations we shall consider in continuation.

José Ramírez III's experience clearly demonstrates the evasiveness of the problem. He early decided that guitar construction is largely a matter of physics and mathematics, and he rejected those traditional techniques that have always depended to some degree on luck (measuring the thickness of wood to the millimeter by touch alone, etc.), "which caused even the greatest of the past masters' output to be uneven in quality." José III felt that science must be called upon to correct such haphazard techniques. In addition, he rebelled against the usual course of merely following someone else's proven school of guitar construction. He did not just want to construct guitars, he wanted to know all about them. He wanted to discover, in scientific terms, *why* a great guitar is great, and what can be done to improve it even further. Encouraged and sustained by his father, José III launched into sixteen long years of experimentation in guitar construction. He poured over books on mathematics and physics, and devised mathematical formulas for the perfect guitar. However, on building these guitars, flawless on paper, some other factors were always lacking. "Many of those guitars," he says, "were absolute monsters, only good for firewood. But with each I learned a valuable lesson, and progressed a little further."

After sixteen years he finally arrived at a model that satisfied him, that which is produced in his shop today and which, ironically, is very similar to the model developed by his uncle, Manuel. One of José III's conclusions from his experimentation and study: "The man who invented the first guitar was a genius. The advanced mathematics and physics that he employed in it, almost certainly knowingly, are astonishing. It took me sixteen years of hard work to find that out, but it was worth it. Now I know *why* a guitar is constructed as it is, not merely how to construct it."

Is José Ramírez III through experimenting? "I am, yes, because I've reached the limits of my mathematical capabilities. But I have hopes that my son will carry on. He is already very interested in mathematics and physics, and may quite possibly innovate the superior guitar one day. I, in the meantime, satisfy my instinct for experimentation by tracking down exceptional woods. I am already using Canadian pine, which I find superior to the normally used German and Middle European, and am investigating an area which I think might give even better results: the vast forests of Siberia."

Manuel Contreras' experiments have led him to the double harmonic top (gluing one top onto another). This, as Contreras is the first to point out, is contrary to the accepted practice of making the top as thin as structurally practical so as not to hinder the free release of the sound. Nevertheless, Contreras reports that "over two years have been spent in this enterprise and without going into great technical detail, I must say that my theory of the 'dual sounding board' has proved positive. Once I had found the right position for the interior 'top' and the relative measurements, depending on the varying thickness of the guitar, I had to modify with each individual instrument the interior structure and supporting structures so that all would complement not only in the function of projecting sound but also in that of improving the actual quality of sound."

Contreras is not alone in believing positive the results of his experimentation, judging by the long list of guitarists who are waiting to be served their Contreras double-harmonic-top guitars.

Manuel Rodríguez' search for improvement led him to create a bridge on which each string can be adjusted slightly as to length, with the purpose of achieving more perfect tuning of the guitar. String stress is also slightly affected, just enough to cause a minuscule but perhaps important hardening or softening of the action. Those who have tried the Rodríguez "movable bridge" sing its blessings, above all in the classical field, in which such highly refined tuning is more necessary.

Gerundino Fernández has gone several steps further than the above in his experimentation in that he has not only altered considerably the inner structure of the guitar and the very shape of the guitar box itself (see photo), but in addition has added a twentieth fret to the usual nineteen-fret neck. Gerundino writes that his new flamenco model is "mathematically more complete, with a macho, stereophonic, profound sound without having lost the flamenco timbre and quality. It not only is still more feminine in looks than the traditional guitar, but has resulted in improved volume and tonal quality." As for his new classical model, Gerundino states that "presently I am completing two palo santo guitars. I cannot tell you how they will be as I have not as yet put on the strings."

I personally have not played nor heard play this new instrument, so cannot comment, but Gerundino, in his present enthusiasm, feels that his creation may well be a major breakthrough.

And so forth. Many guitarreros are looking for perfection, in whatever form it may come. Is José Ramírez correct in judging the present-day guitar, as developed by Antonio Torres and by his uncle, Manuel Ramírez, mathematically perfect? Or will Gerundino Fernández, or perhaps another luthier, succeed in altering the guitar in some successfully revolutionary manner? What will the guitar of tomorrow be like?

Antonio Torres
(c. 1817-1892)
creator and initiator
of the modern style
of flamenco guitar
construction.

This card was originally sent from Antonio Torres to one of his clients, the guitarist P. González Campos, in 1885. González Campos, in turn, converted it into his own post card, and sent it to his friend Manuel Ramírez, stating on the back that it «is generally agreed that *don* Antonio Torres is the only guitar maker who can substitute for you.»

THE MADRID SCHOOL

After the death of Antonio Torres, Madrid became the world's capital in construction of Spanish classical and flamenco guitars, an eminence it still maintains today.

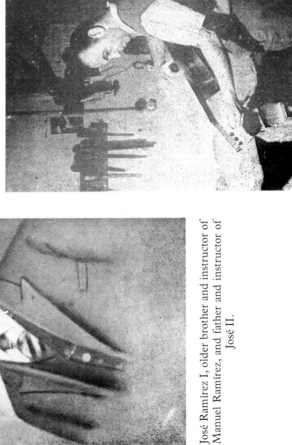

José (Simón) Ramírez II, inheritor of the José Ramírez shop from his father.

José Ramírez III, son of José II, third generation on Madrid's calle San Jerónimo.

José Ramírez I, older brother and instructor of Manuel Ramírez, and father and instructor of José II.

An Historic Photo in the Annals of Flamenco Guitar Construction.

The old shop of *maestro* Manuel Ramírez, in the street Arlabán, 11, Madrid, around 1904.

Two repairmen, the accountant, Manuel Ramírez, Santos Hernández, Modesto Borreguero, Domingo Esteso, and a helper.
Manuel Ramírez, Santos Hernández and Domingo Esteso, together with Antonio Torres, are the most revered figures in the history of Spanish guitar construction.

Above: another of the greats, Marcelo Barbero, was maestro of today's Arcángel Fernández (below right), who in turn apprenticed Barbero's son, Marcelo Jr. (below left).

THE MADRID SCHOOL

Above, L. to R.: *Julio*, *Faustino*, and *Mariano Conde*, nephews of Domingo Esteso and perpetuators of his style of guitar building.

Below: *Manuel Rodríguez*, from a family of guitarists and guitar-makers, worked with José Ramírez II and III before going on his own.

Paulino Bernabé

THE MADRID SCHOOL

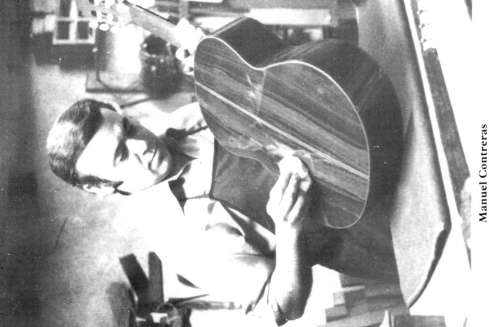

Manuel Contreras

Both of these luthiers were cabinet-makers before becoming guitar builders, and both constructed in the Ramirez workshop before

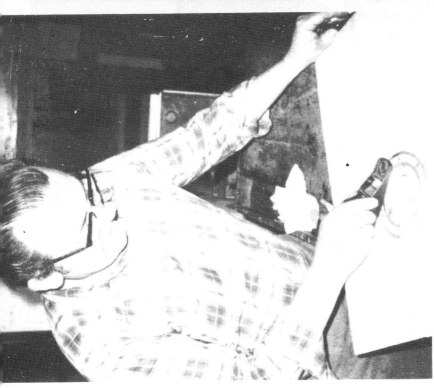

ANDALUSIA

With the death of fellow Córdoban *Miguel Rodríguez*, *Manuel Reyes* (photo) is undisputed king of guitar makers in western Andalusia.

THE MADRID SCHOOL

Marcelino López was also a cabinet-maker before becoming luthier. An accomplished classical guitarist, he is here shown in his workshop surrounded by instruments of his making.

ANDALUSIA

In eastern Andalusia we can single out as tops *Antonio Marín Montero,* (left) from Granada, and *Gerundino Fernández,* from Almería.

GLOSSARY

Many of these terms have several meanings. Only those pertinent to this book have been stated.

a palo seco — without guitar accompaniment. See section «The Song».

afición — a strong enthusiasm for something (in this case, for flamenco).

aficionados — enthusiasts.

afillá — refers to a type of singing voice. See section «The Song».

aguardiente — a strong Spanish alcoholic drink, also called «dry anís».

aire — literally «air»; in flamenco an approving reference to the general character
of, or manner of performing, a flamenco form. Examples: «he has
a lot of *aire* when he plays that form», or such and such a form
«has so much *aire* that it sets it apart.»

algo — something.

alivio — easing up, relief.

alto — up, high.

amigo — friend.

anda, primos — come on, cousins.

andaluces — Andalusians.

arpegio — a guitar-playing technique. See section «The Guitar».

bailaor — male flamenco dancer.

bailaora — female flamenco dancer.

Baile — the flamenco dance.

baile — a particular segment of the flamenco dance.

bajo — down, low.

banderillas — barbed sticks placed in the bull during a bullfight.

banderillero — placer of banderillas.

bandoleros — bandits.

bien — well, good.

bonito — pretty.

brazos — arms.

buenas tardes — good afternoon.

burro — donkey.

cabales — the faithful; a style of *siguiriyas.*

café — coffee, cafe.

caló — an impure form of *Romaní,* the gypsy languâge; a mixture of *Romaní*
and Spanish.

cambio — change; a change in a *cante.* See section «The Song».

cantaor — male flamenco singer.

cantaora — female flamenco singer.

Cante — flamenco singing.

cante — a particular segment of flamenco singing.

cantes camperos — country *cantes.*

caramba — an exclamation, such as «holy cow», or «holy smokes».

caray — the same as *caramba.*

caseta — a small dwelling; during provincial fairs *casetas* are constructed as
temporary party quarters for individual families or groups.

209

chico — little, light.
chiquillas — chicks, girls.
churros — a traditional Spanish pastry, consisting of deep fried flour, salt, and
        water; often eaten with sugar.
claro está — it is clear.
cola — tail, train of a dress.
compás — rhythm, beat.
con — with.
concurso — contest.
conquistadores — conquerers.
coño — an exclamation, not socially acceptable.
copitas — shots.
corto — short.
cuadro — group.

de — of, from.
desplante — a break in a dance.
Dios — God.
duende — soul of flamenco, feeling for flamenco.
eco gitano — literally «gypsy echo»; another term for «*voz afillá*».
en fin — in summation.
entrada — entrance, beginning.

falseta — a melody played on the flamenco guitar. See section «The Guitar».
feria — fair.
Fiesta — spectacle of bullfghting.
fiesta — party.
finca — ranch. ·
fino — a type of sherry (wine from Jerez de la Frontera).
flamenco de verdad — pure flamenco.

gitana (o) — gypsy female, male.
gitanerías — gypsy doings.
gracia — charm, wit.
grande — large, exceptional.
guitarra — guitar.
guitarrero — guitar-maker.
guitarrista — guitarist.
guardia — guard.
guardia civil — civil guard.
gusto — pleasure.

hombre — man.
hondo — same as *jondo*.

intermedio — intermediate.
jaleo — hell-raising; also a component of flamenco. See section «The *Jaleo*».
jondo — deep, profound.
Jota — a regional song-dance of northern Spain.
leche — milk; also an exclamation (not socially acceptable).
ligados — a guitar-playing technique. See section «The Guitar».
llanto — mourning, lament.

macho — (1) real man (2) an ending to a *cante*. See section «The Song».
maestro — master.
Manoletinas — a bullfight pass created by the bullfighter Manolete.
manzanilla — a type of dry white wine.
mañana — tomorrow, morning.
Montilla — a type of dry white wine.
mucho — much, a lot.

natural — the most pure bullfight pass.
niña — young girl; also a term of endearment.
no decir ná — not saying anything, not getting through.
no dice ná — he (she) says nothing, doesn't get through.
novillero — amateur bullfighter.
novio (a) — fiance, bride-to-be.

olé! — shout of approval.
oye — listen.
ozú! — an exclamation (mispronunciation of «Jesús»).

palmas — hand-clapping.
payo — non-gypsy.
peleón — fighter; the creative section of a *cante*. See section «The Song».
picado — a guitar-playing technique. See section «The Guitar».
piropos — flatteries, compliments.
pitos — finger-snapping.
planteo — the beginning section of a *cante*. See section «The Song».
por — by, for, through.
primo — cousin; a gypsy term expressing friendship.
pulgar — thumb.

que — what, how.
quitapenas — sorrow (pain) killer.

rajo — raucous, hoarse.
rasgueado — a guitar-playing technique. See section «The Guitar».
rematando — finishing.
remate — finish off, complete. See section «The Song».
Romaní — the gypsy language, a derivative of the Indian Sanskrit.

salero — wit, charm, full of life.
si — if.
si Dios quiere — if God wishes.
sí — yes.
sierra — mountain range.
simpático — winning, charming.

tablao — modern version of the «*café cantante*»; flamenco night club; literally
         means «platform».
temple — temperament.
tercio — section or passage of a *cante*.
tinto — red wine.
tocaor — flamenco guitarist; literally «toucher» or «vanity dresser».
Toque — flamenco guitar-playing. See section «The Guitar».
toque — a particular segment of the Toque.
traje — dress, suit.
trémolo — a guitar-playing technique. See section «The Guitar».
tumba — tomb.

utrero — two-year-old fighting bull.

valiente — valiant, brave.
venta — country inn.
verdad — true, truth.
veremos — we'll see.
viejo — old, old man, old one.
vino — wine.
voz — voice.
voz afillá — See section «The Song».
voz naturá — natural (unadorned) voice. See section «The Song».

zapateado — footwork in the dance.